D1596085

UNWINDING MADNESS

UNWINDING

What Went Wrong with College Sports—
and How to Fix It

MADNESS

GERALD GURNEY

DONNA LOPIANO

ANDREW ZIMBALIST

BROOKINGS INSTITUTION PRESS

Washington, D.C.

The Brookings Institution is a private nonprofit organization devoted to research, education, and publication on important issues of domestic and foreign policy. Its principal purpose is to bring the highest quality independent research and analysis to bear on current and emerging policy problems. Interpretations or conclusions in Brookings publications should be understood to be solely those of the authors.

Library of Congress Cataloging-in-Publication data

Names: Gurney, Gerald Sherman, author. | Lopiano, Donna A., author. | Zimbalist, Andrew S., author.
Title: Unwinding madness : what went wrong with college sports— and how to fix it / Gerald Gurney, Donna Lopiano, Andrew Zimbalist.
Description: Washington, D.C. : Brookings Institution, [2017] | Includes bibliographical references and index.
Identifiers: LCCN 2016030048 (print) | LCCN 2016049282 (ebook) | ISBN 9780815730026 (hardcover : alk. paper) | ISBN 9780815730033 (ebook)
Subjects: LCSH: College sports—United States. | National Collegiate Athletic Association.
Classification: LCC GV351.G87 2017 (print) | LCC GV351 (ebook) | DDC 796.04/3—dc23
LC record available at https://lccn.loc.gov/2016030048

9 8 7 6 5 4 3 2 1

Printed on acid-free paper

Typeset in Minion Pro

Composition by Westchester Publishing Services

Contents

Part III

A RETURN TO SANITY

Preface

College sports are in educational, ethical, and economic turmoil. During the last ten years, litigation after litigation have sprung up alleging that the NCAA violates antitrust laws, runs afoul of the Fair Labor Standards Act, and imposes arbitrary, morphing and unfair definitions of amateurism. The football players at Northwestern University attempted to unionize, and the National Labor Relations Board (NLRB) wrote in its 2015 decision not to certify the effort that "it would not promote stability in labor relations to assert jurisdiction in this case" and that "there have been calls for the NCAA to undertake further reforms that may result in additional changes to the circumstances of scholarship players." In other words, it concluded that college sports are changing too rapidly for it to be prudent to enter the fray. The NLRB noted a need for the U.S. Congress to take a close look at college sports and provide guidance.

The authors of this book have been involved in the movement to reform college sports for more than four decades. During the past two years, we have been part of a working group connected to the Drake Group to study college sports and formulate a vision of a new governing system for intercollegiate athletics.[1] The group has issued position papers on why reform is needed and what it should look like on the following topics: congressional initiatives, the treatment of college athletes, NCAA academic metrics, student fees and institutional subsidies, due process, the rights of college athletes, a limited antitrust exemption, the NCAA's dysfunctional enforcement system, freshman eligibility, _O'Bannon_ and amateurism, academic integrity, and NCAA Division I restructuring.[2]

The authors have also lent their support to H.R. 2731, which calls for the establishment of a presidential commission to study college sports and to consider public policy options for promoting its reform. Along the way, we have met with members of Congress, the White House senior staff for domestic policy, former secretary of education Arne Duncan, academic colleagues, college administrators, and executives of the American Association of University Presses, the Knight Commission on Intercollegiate Sports, and the American Council on Education, among others.

While we note that the NCAA's new public relations mantra insists that its priorities are "academics, student-athlete well-being, and fairness," we believe this statement is disingenuous. From the perspectives of college athletes, academics, sport fans, or even the most casual observers, this assertion seems merely to repeat broken promises.

The forces of commercialism are transforming college sports. The pace and substance of this change will likely deepen over the coming five years. The opportunity to influence the reform debate and the future trajectory of college sports is too alluring to pass up. That's why we wrote this book.

Our narrative proceeds in three parts. Part I sets the historical context and identifies key junctures along the way at which college sports deviated from the educational path. Understanding these junctures and the institutional environment is key to informing an intelligent discussion of our current options. Part II takes a closer look at what is wrong today in college sports and begins a consideration of what types of change would make sense. Part III concludes with a more targeted discussion of reform strategies, principles, and policies.

Throughout, we adhere to a consistent theme. We believe that intercollegiate athletics is at a tipping point. The status quo is not stable, and change is coming. This change can move college sports further toward commercialization and professionalism or it can endeavor to reinforce the historical vision of college sports as an amateur activity subordinated to and in harmony with the educational mission of U.S. colleges. The former path will lead to increasing academic scandals, widespread financial insolvency, and diminishing support for Olympic sports and Title IX. The latter path, while not without its own challenges, may succeed in restoring a proper balance between athletics and academics. We lay out a multifaceted proposal that links favorable fiscal and legal treatment for college athletics to the NCAA or another governing body providing robust and comprehensive educational reforms.

Our critique of college sports pertains mostly to Division I, its Football Bowl Subdivision, and the Power Five conferences. It is inevitable that within each of these groups there is behavioral variance among schools, college administrators, athletics directors, and coaches. While we note some of this variability, we focus on the central dynamics and common elements moving the system.

Numerous colleagues have helped us formulate the positions we articulate in the book. In particular, we would like to single out Ted Fay, Roger Noll, Amy Perko, Brian Porto, Dave Ridpath, Steve Ross, Allen Sack, and Mary Willingham. We are also indebted to Jayma Meyer for extensive comments on an early draft of the manuscript. Of course, any errors that remain are entirely our responsibility.

PART I

Lessons of History

ONE

How College Sports Lost Its Way I

The phrase "American exceptionalism" is frequently used to mean that the United States does things differently—and, by connotation, better—than the rest of the world. There is little question but that intercollegiate athletics in the United States is different from athletics in other countries. In England and elsewhere, college athletics is largely organized on an intramural or student club basis, offering students a recreational respite from the intellectual rigors of the classroom. Highly competitive elite-level sport resides in private clubs outside the institution. In the United States, from its earliest days, elite-level sport has been embedded within the educational institution. This structural distinction, the integration of elite sport with academia and the concomitant annual striving to win in head-to-head competition against other institutions, lies at the root of current challenges. However, this structural differentiation does not fully explain why National Collegiate Athletic Association (NCAA) Division I athletic programs have lost their way. To understand the growth of the most corrosive aspects of increased commercialism, the rejection of athletic program resource controls, the demands for plutocracy, the NCAA's selective enforcement of rules, and the turning of a blind eye to academic fraud, it is necessary to trace the history of how college sport has failed at critical decisionmaking junctures.

American Higher Education Embraces Commercialized Sport

Despite the pretenses of U.S. collegiate sports to be educationally oriented, strictly amateur activities, the commercial aspects of college sports programs have progressively encroached on the educational terrain and, at the upper reaches of Division I, have subverted it. It is important to understand how college presidents developed the convictions that successful sports teams afford prime promotion opportunities for the school and that winning elite-level sports contests results in significant marketplace advantages for the institution.

The first college sports contest, the rowing match between the Harvard and Yale boat clubs on Lake Winnipesaukee in 1852, was infused with commercial motives. The manager of the Boston, Concord and Montreal Railroad organized the event to advertise the line's rail service to wealthy clientele in New York and Boston. The railroad company lured the boat teams to the match with "unlimited alcohol" and "lavish prizes." The first known college sports eligibility abuse came three years later at another Harvard-Yale meet, when the Harvard team's coxswain was not a student.

In 1862 the first Morrill Land Grant College Act was passed to provide states with federal land on which to establish state schools to teach agriculture, engineering, and military tactics. Many states took advantage of the program to establish universities, even when they did not have a sufficient qualified population to enroll in postsecondary education. With land grant colleges added to the usually religiously affiliated liberal arts colleges, technical institutes, and preexisting state universities, there emerged an intense competition to fill the appreciable excess supply of available beds at U.S. colleges. In this context, schools sought whatever competitive advantage they could identify. Intercollegiate sports came to be seen as central to promoting a college to prospective applicants.

What began as a student-run activity to pass time and offer some relief from rigorous academic studies would rapidly be seized on by college presidents as a tool to promote their universities, raise funds, and attract students. The athletic branding of universities began as early as 1869, when Charles Eliot, one of America's best-known educators and then in his first year as president of Harvard University, proudly noted that Harvard excelled in the "manly sports."[1] In the same year, President Francis Amasa Walker of the Massachusetts Institute of Technology bemoaned the fact that intercollegiate athletics had lost its academic moorings and opined that "if the movement shall continue at the same rate, it will soon be fairly a question whether the letters B.A. stand more for Bachelor of Arts or Bachelor of Athletics."[2]

In 1874, the president of Columbia University, Frederick Barnard, was gushing about his school's victory over Harvard and Yale at a regatta in upstate New York and congratulating the team's oarsmen: "that in one day or in one summer, you have done more to make Columbia known than all your predecessors have done since the founding of the college."[3]

Two years later the Intercollegiate Football Association organized a championship game to be played on Thanksgiving Day in Hoboken, New Jersey. In 1880 the game was moved to New York City, and its popularity exploded:

> Within a decade it was the premier athletic event in the nation. Princeton and Yale played each other almost every year in this game, and by the 1890s they were drawing crowds of 40,000. Players, students, and fans wore their school colors, while banners flew from carriages, hotels, and the business establishments of New York City. Thanksgiving Day church services were ended early to accommodate the fans, and the game became the event that kicked off the season for New York's social elite.[4]

Affirming this view, Allen J. Sack and Ellen J. Staurowsky in 1998 wrote:

> In the late 1800s few campus activities could better meet that need than intercollegiate sport. Nothing could better attract the attention of mass media, and nothing had a greater appeal to the practical-minded business leaders who provided financial support and who increasingly came to dominate academe's governing boards.[5]

In 1890 Woodrow Wilson, then president of Princeton University, told alumni, "Princeton is noted in this wide world for three things: football, baseball, and collegiate instruction."[6] Wilson's comment was famously elaborated on by Clark Kerr, chancellor of the University of California, Berkeley, some sixty-seven years later when he responded to a question at a faculty meeting about on-campus parking by observing that his job had come to be defined as "providing parking for faculty, sex for the students, and athletics for the alumni."[7]

College Presidents Support Financial Excess and
Academic Misconduct

Rainey Harper, University of Chicago president in the early 1890s, hired former Yale football star Amos Alonzo Stagg to coach football. Harper told Stagg to "develop teams which we can send around the country and knock out all the colleges." Harper reportedly provided Stagg with a trust fund of $80,000, originally earmarked for low-income students, for recruiting and subsidizing athletes, and commented, "We will give them a palace car and a vacation too."[8]

Chicago, of course, was not the only school driven to excess in promoting its football team. The payment of athletes, many of whom had little pretense of being students, was widespread. A 1906 article by Charles Deming, a former Yale athlete, detailed the findings of a Yale faculty investigation into the school's athletic practices. It uncovered a $100,000 trust fund that had been used to tutor athletes, give expensive gifts to athletes, purchase entertainment for coaches, and pay for trips to the Caribbean.[9]

Since the first intercollegiate football game, in 1869, when Rutgers beat Princeton with the help of ten freshmen, three of whom were failing algebra, college presidents have been complicit through inaction or ineffective action with regard to maintaining academic standards. In 1889, Harvard president Charles Eliot undertook a study of the relationship between academic success and football participation among Harvard freshmen. Over a two-year period he found that freshman football players had nearly four times as many D's and F's as A's and B's. He reasoned that first-year students should be ineligible for intercollegiate sports while they sought their social bearings and established themselves academically. Further, allowing first-year students to play facilitated the use of ringers and "tramp" athletes, who could matriculate one day and play football the next. Eliot's appeal was too enlightened for Harvard alumni and students at the time. Like other college presidents of his day, Eliot backed down.

McClure's magazine ran a two-part series in 1905 on corruption in college athletics. Author Henry Beech Needham attacked the prestigious Ivy

League schools for the "prostitution of college athletics" and condemned the practices of hiring tramp athletes, squandering athletic income, cheating in the classroom, the collusion of faculty with athletes, the unethical practices of coaches, building costly stadiums, and the continuing brutality of football.[10] In a prophetic analysis of the dilemma college presidents faced in trying to reconcile the academic and the commercial aims of the university, William T. Foster, president of Reed College, wrote in 1915:

> If intercollegiate athletics can then be conducted as incidental and contributory to the main purposes of athletics, well and good. But first of all the question must be decisively settled, which aims are to dominate—those of business or those of education. And it will be difficult for a college already in the clutches of commercialism to retain the system and at the same time cultivate a spirit antagonistic to it.[11]

Schools began to lavish resources on athletic fields and stadiums to advance their teams. In 1903, Harvard was the first college to build a concrete stadium, designed explicitly for football. Yale followed with the Yale Bowl in 1914, the University of Pennsylvania's Franklin Field was expanded for football in 1922, the University of California at Berkeley built a stadium with a seating capacity of 76,000 in 1923, Baker Field at Columbia University was finished in 1928, and so it went, with one school after another readily raising their football budgets in an effort to stay competitive. By 1930 there were thirty concrete college football stadiums in the country.[12]

Having grandiose stadiums, however, was not sufficient to develop a winning team. It was also thought to be necessary to have strong coaching. In the early decades of intercollegiate football, it was deemed inappropriate to pay coaches. Coaches were expected to be members of the faculty who volunteered their time, just as they did to participate on administrative committees. They were supposed to be amateurs, just like the players. Soon the win-at-all-costs approach disrupted this fantasy, and schools began to compete fiercely over coaching services.

By the first decade of the twentieth century, football coaches were often paid more than full professors and sometimes as much as the college president. Columbia hired George Sanford for $5,000, more than double the salary of its full professors. Harvard paid its twenty-six-year-old Bill Reid $7,000. John Heisman signed a contract at Georgia Tech in 1903 for $2,250 plus 30 percent of net gate receipts, and concluded his career with a $12,000 salary at Rice. In 1924, Centenary College, in Shreveport, Louisiana, the nation's first liberal arts college west of the Mississippi, was denied accreditation by the Southern Association of Colleges and Schools because the school placed an "undue emphasis on athletics." The primary evidence of Centenary's misplaced priorities was that the school paid its football coach more than it paid its college president.

The most heralded coach of the epoch was Notre Dame's Knute Rockne. In 1924 Rockne signed a ten-year contract with Notre Dame for a total of $100,000. In 1926, with a career record of seventy-five wins and but six losses, Rockne received an offer for three years at $25,000 annually from Columbia. Ironically, Columbia's president at the time was Nicholas Butler, who years earlier had banned football at the school. Questioned about the Rockne offer, Butler responded that the coach's hiring matter "is out of my line. It is a matter for the students and alumni."[13]

The transition from volunteer member of the academic faculty to professional coach was both emblematic of the incipient full-throated commercialization of college sport and instrumental in transforming the underlying dynamic away from the educational enterprise. In other extracurricular areas of student life, such as music, dance, or theater, the teachers of these subjects come with academic credentials, generally either a master's degree or a doctorate in their field. These areas remain attached to the academic culture. In elite-level college sports, the pretense of looking for academic or health credentials in coaches was long ago jettisoned in favor of hiring coaches who had achieved competitive success in their sport. With this change, coaches' inclinations to nurture the educational commitment and progress of athletes diminished or vanished. And the absence of any requirement regarding health or physical education credentials for coaches denoted a general disregard or ignorance of the devastating physical consequences that can ensue from playing contact sports.

Why Faculty- and President-Led Reform Has Failed

The rapid commercialization of college sports, its subversion of educational goals, and the growing publicity about the brutality of football engendered a reform movement. The strongest push for reform came from faculty, but some college presidents joined the effort. The faculty at Harvard initiated one such campaign in 1886–87. During that academic year, Harvard participated in ninety-four intercollegiate athletic contests, including thirty-four away games. The faculty prevailed on the president and the board of overseers to curtail this involvement, which, they argued, was distracting students from academic pursuits, exposing them to dubious moral practices at away games, and turning college sports into a business rather than a gentlemanly contest. The board of overseers' Advisory Committee on Athletics agreed and recommended by a four-to-one margin banning all intercollegiate sports, while expanding intramural sports and athletic facilities.[14] But, following protests from students and the trustees, the recommendation was not adopted by the full board. Eventually, the solution at Harvard and other schools to the faculty calls for reforms was to form president-appointed friendly and powerless athletic "advisory" committees comprised of students, athletically sympathetic faculty, and administrators. The faculty lost control over athletics. Thus, in 1895, following a particularly brutal football game between Harvard and Yale, the Harvard faculty voted by a two-to-one margin to abolish football at the school. The athletic committee promptly voted unanimously not to do so and the board of overseers sided with the committee.

Although university presidents have always had it within their power to reform college sports, they have not found it in their interest to do so.[15] College presidents spend an average of six years in their jobs and are expected to accomplish a lot in that time. Taking on the establishment of intercollegiate athletics is not one of them. Those few college presidents who have denounced the excessive commercialization of college sports and their deleterious effects on the educational mission have found their wings clipped by their boards of trustees. Instead, presidents dedicate their efforts to raising money, renovating the physical plant, restructuring the curriculum, hiring faculty, recruiting students, and maintaining good relations with the host town or city. They allow the athletics department to do its thing—try to win. And they protect the athletics department from the faculty by handpicking athletics-friendly faculty to serve in relatively powerless positions, such as on advisory committees or as institutional representatives to athletic conferences or national governing organizations such as the NCAA. Today, nearly 80 percent of faculty athletics representatives in Division I sports are appointed by college presidents, while only 20 percent are nominated by the faculty and approved by the president.[16]

Though college presidents and trustees successfully blocked reform from within the institution, external national pressures were also repelled in a more artful way, inhibiting the NCAA from addressing the need for change. At the national level, football's brutality was taking its toll. In 1893 seven fatalities were reported in college football. Twelve more deaths occurred in 1894. In 1905 eighteen players were killed in college football games, bringing the total during 1890–1905 to more than 300. Observers attributed these deaths to the use of mass formations, such as the flying wedge; the loose rules regarding running starts; the lack of effective officiating; and the absence of protective equipment.

After President Teddy Roosevelt's son sustained a broken nose in a freshman football game at Harvard early in the 1905 season, Roosevelt called representatives from Harvard, Yale, and Princeton to the White House to discuss the future of the game and the need for reform. Two months later, in December 1905, the Intercollegiate Athletic Association of the United States (IAAUS) was formed to address football's rules, as well as the broader regulation of college sports.

The IAAUS (which changed its name to the National Collegiate Athletic Association, or NCAA, in 1910) had only thirty-eight founding members. Many of the dominant universities, including Harvard, Yale, and Princeton, did not join for several years. The more successful football programs did not want to surrender control of the game to smaller schools.

But the fledgling organization had few resources. At its first annual convention, in December 1906, the treasurer reported a balance in the IAAUS's bank account of $28.82. Both because of its meager financial endowment and because of the need to attract the larger programs into the organization, the IAAUS resolved to follow a policy of "home rule." That is, each school would be its own boss and could choose which IAAUS policies it wanted to implement. The first bylaws of the organization called for "each institution . . . to enact and enforce such measures as may be necessary to prevent violations of the principles of amateur sports."[17] And the 1907 constitution stipulated, "Legislation enacted at a conference of delegates shall not be binding upon any institution."[18] This clear policy of home rule led the college sports historian Ronald Smith to write, "For its first half century, the NCAA was principally a debating society for faculty representatives interested in intercollegiate athletics."[19]

The president of the NCAA from 1906 to 1913 and again from 1917 to 1929, Palmer Pierce, joined the debate, inveighing against the corrupt influences of college sports: "There can be no question but that a boy or young man, who is habituated to the endeavor to win games by means, some of which he knows to be unfair and against the rules, later will play the game of life with the same ethical standards."[20] Thus, from its inception in 1906 until 1952, the NCAA promulgated guidelines that its members were not required to follow. While the NCAA could advance increased safety by adopting and disseminating rules of play in each sport, it did not possess the legislative mechanisms to deal with the need for reform.

Amateurism: How NCAA Member Institutions Control the Cost of Their Athlete Assets

It is instructive to follow the evolution of the NCAA's definition of amateurism from its origins in a posture prohibiting all financial aid based on athletic ability to its current embrace of athletic scholarships and benefits with values far in excess of those afforded nonathletes. As long as the NCAA's policies were not implemented, it was inconsequential for the organization to adopt high-minded principles of amateurism to define its goals. According to Article VI of the association's 1906 bylaws, each member institution was to enforce measures to prevent violations of amateur principles. Included among these violations was "the offering of inducements to players to enter colleges or universities because of their athletic abilities or maintaining players while students on account of their athletic abilities, either by athletic organizations, individual alumni, or otherwise directly or indirectly."[21] Thus, athletic scholarships violated amateur rules. Need-based financial aid unrelated to sports did not.

The NCAA's first actual definition of amateurism appeared in 1916. According to Article VI (b) of the bylaws, an amateur is "one who participates in competitive physical sports only for the pleasure, and the physical, mental, moral and social benefits derived therefrom."[22] An amended version appeared in 1922. "An amateur sportsman is one who engages in sport solely for the physical, mental, or social benefits he derives therefrom, and to whom the sport is nothing more than an avocation."[23]

In truth, this initial definition of amateurism existed only as words of convenience. It enabled the NCAA to advance the public perception that college athletes were like other students rather than like paid professional athletes. Because the NCAA had no enforcement power at this point in history, its amateur rules were largely honored in the breach and violated with impunity. The abuses were cataloged in the 1929 Carnegie Foundation report on intercollegiate athletics, which found that three quarters of the 112 colleges investigated violated the NCAA's code and principles of amateurism. It concluded:

> A change of values is needed in a field that is sodden with the commercial and the material and the vested interests that these forces have created. Commercialism in college athletics must be diminished and college sport must rise to a point where it is esteemed primarily and sincerely for the opportunities it affords to mature youth.[24]

The report, so poignantly relevant today, concluded that college presidents could reclaim the integrity of sport and change the policies of professionalization previously sanctioned by their governing boards. That did not happen. Instead, as commercialism grew with the advent of television, powerful institutions opted to stratify and differentiate themselves from the collective educational model that had developed through faculty organization. Schools became separated into divisions based on their competitive success and ability to generate revenue.

A follow-up study by the *New York Times* in 1931 found that not a single college had changed its practices in response to the Carnegie Foundation report. An NCAA committee report in 1934 concluded that abuses in areas of recruitment and subsidization "have grown to such a universal extent that they constitute the major problem in American athletics today."[25]

Accordingly, voices of reform grew more outspoken during the 1930s. Hollywood movies, from the Marx Brothers' *Horse Feathers* to *Saturday Heroes* and *Hero for a Day*, mocked the duplicity of college sports. Robert Hutchins, president of the University of Chicago, wrote in 1931: "College is not a great athletic association and social club in which provision is made, merely incidentally, for intellectual activity on the part of the physically and socially unfit. College is an association of scholars in which provision is made for the development of traits and powers which must be cultivated, in addition to which are purely intellectual, if one is to become a well-balanced and useful member of any community."[26] The University of Chicago dropped football in 1939.

Although the commercialization of college sports slowed during the later years of the Great Depression and World War II, it accelerated as the war ended. At the end of 1946, the sports editor of the *New York Herald Tribune*, Stanley Woodward, wrote: "When it comes to chicanery, double-dealing, and undercover work behind the scenes, big-time college football is in a class by itself . . . . Should the Carnegie Foundation launch an investigation of college football right now, the mild breaches of etiquette uncovered [in the 1920s] . . . would assume a remote innocence which would only cause snickers among the post-war pirates of 1946."[27] The de facto payrolls of several college teams reached $100,000 and the coach at Oklahoma State estimated that its rival, the University of Oklahoma, annually spent more than $200,000 ($2.64 million in 2015 prices) on players.

The situation had gotten sufficiently out of control that the NCAA needed to become something more than a debating society. It began its attempt both to ratify the reality of financial aid to athletes and to actually enforce its code of amateurism.[28] In 1948 the NCAA passed what is referred to as the Sanity Code. For the first time ever, this legislation allowed schools to award athletically related financial aid as long as it was limited to tuition and incidental expenses and the athlete qualified for need. Aid exceeding tuition could be granted if based on superior academic scholarship. The Sanity Code, which stipulated that aid could not be withdrawn if a student ceased playing, was abandoned in 1950 when the NCAA membership voted not to expel schools that had violated the rule.[29]

In 1956, six years after the demise of the Sanity Code, the NCAA finally addressed allowable non-need-based compensation to athletes when it adopted athletic scholarships to cover commonly accepted educational expenses. In 1957, an "Official Interpretation" defined expenses as room, board, tuition, books, fees, and $15 a month for "laundry money."[30] (In 2015 dollars, this "laundry money" is equal to $127.35, or on an annual basis $1,528.20. This sum is roughly equivalent to a low-end "cost of attendance" stipend.)[31] Few of the people who attended the NCAA's first convention in 1906 could have conceived that by 1957, NCAA rules would have changed to allow a university to use these types of financial inducements to recruit high school athletes.[32]

The 1957 legislation contained provisions to counter the argument that athletic scholarships constituted "pay for play," which might expose its members to workers' compensation claims and social security contributions. Financial aid could not be "reduced (gradated) or canceled on the basis of an athlete's contribution to team success, injury, or decision not to participate." Indeed, the NCAA mandated the use of the term "student-athlete."[33]

In 1967 the NCAA moved even further from its original concept of amateurism when members began to complain that athletes were accepting four-year scholarships and deciding not to participate. One athletic director opined that this was "morally wrong." He then added that "regardless of what anyone says, this is a contract and it is a two way street."[34] To address this problem the NCAA passed rules that allow the immediate cancellation of a scholarship of an athlete who voluntarily withdraws from sports or does not follow a coach's directives.

The NCAA made a total break from the traditional model of amateurism in 1973 by requiring that athletic scholarships be considered for renewal on an annual basis.[35] This rule allowed a coach to cancel athletes' scholarships at the end of one year for just about any reason, including injury, contribution to team success, the need to make room for a more talented recruit, or failure to fit into a coach's style of play. The contingent contractual nature of this relationship and the control it gives to the coaches over the players' behavior have many of the trappings of an employment contract.[36]

In marked contrast to the British model of amateurism adopted by the NCAA in 1906, the 1973 version transformed athletes into highly specialized entertainers. In revenue sports, athletes' lives became routinized by coaches, leaving little time for other interests or extracurricular activities. Nonetheless, the drift away from earlier amateur practices has not detracted from college sports' popularity as commercial entertainment, and the NCAA's ability to arbitrarily define what constitutes amateurism has ensured that increasing subsidies to athletes did not pose a threat to the NCAA's brand of "amateur sport."

Another modification to its concept of amateurism is that the association has allowed explicit gifts to be given to student-athletes. For instance, the

NCAA permits players in football bowl games and the March basketball tournament to receive more than $3,000 in gifts. A March 2012 article in the *Sports Business Journal* provides some details: "For example, a senior on a team that runs the table and wins championships for the regular season, postseason conference tournament and NCAA tournament could secure gifts valued at up to $3,780. Last year's comparable total was $3,380. Up to 25 gift packages can be provided to a team by its school and by its conference for participating in this month's conference tournaments, according to NCAA bylaws."[37]

In response to cries of athlete exploitation, in recent years the NCAA has further tweaked its treatment of amateurism. In 2012 the NCAA approved legislation that gives Division I schools the option to award multiyear scholarships. In 2014 the association sanctioned expanded food service for athletes, beyond that available to other students. In 2015 the NCAA approved payments to parents to attend postseason bowl games and championships and allowed cost of attendance stipends (so-called laundry money, which had been ended in 1973, under a different name) to be paid to athletes in Division I.

The NCAA has modified its rules in ways that have little to do with the core notion of amateurism (that is, not being paid to play a sport) and are inconsistent with those of other amateur organizations. For instance, while the Amateur Athletic Union (AAU) allows broken-time payments (payments to athletes in training or in competition to compensate for lost income while away from their job), the NCAA does not. Nor does the NCAA allow student-athletes to receive sponsorship money even if it only covers basic expenses (a policy that prevented Olympic skier Jeremy Bloom from returning to the University of Colorado football team). The AAU not only allows broken-time payments, it permits athletes to receive income from endorsements.

The United States Golf Association's *Rules of Amateur Golf* for 2012 allows amateur members to compete in professional tournaments provided they do not receive prize money. Amateur members are also allowed to hire an agent and to receive compensation that is unrelated to winning a tournament. Neither practice is permitted by the NCAA.

Further, in some cases the NCAA has different rules for European student-athletes than for U.S. student-athletes. For example, professional tennis players from Europe are allowed to earn up to $10,000 while in high school and still play NCAA tennis, while U.S. student-athletes who have earned income playing tennis are not allowed to compete in college. The NCAA manuals are more than a thousand pages long, and the list of quixotic regulations that purport to uphold amateurism is extensive.

The NCAA also restricts student-athletes from contacting a lawyer or a player's agent to help them (1) arrange and prepare for appearances at player combines, which are essentially tryouts for the NFL and NBA prior to the leagues' amateur drafts, (2) receive information about the economic implications of their various options with respect to the amateur draft, or (3) enter into preliminary negotiations around signing a professional contract. Any of these activities would come before the athlete signing a contract, being paid, or becoming a professional.

It's All about the Money in Division I: The Structure and Functioning of the NCAA

The commercialized sport juggernaut that is Division I collegiate athletics has proceeded steadfastly forward, aided and abetted by an NCAA structure that methodically evolved into a smaller and smaller plutocracy as the financial stakes grew. Just as faculty- or college president–reform is an impossibility at the institutional level, NCAA reform at the national level is impossible because of the organization's nature as a plutocracy. At its most basic level, the true basic identity of the NCAA is as a trade association of athletics directors, conference commissioners, and coaches rather than a large association of institutions gathered to ensure an educational sport philosophy. The latter is little more than a branding vehicle designed to make the athletes' product unique and more valuable to alumni and fans seeking tax deductions for ticket purchases disguised as donations.

To understand the NCAA's resistance to reform, it is necessary to grasp the historical changes in the structure and functioning of the association, first as an aggregator of highly commercialized football and basketball programs and controller of the distribution of regular season televised games, and second as a producer of dramatic national championships. To exploit the economic value of these products, the NCAA had to "govern." Rather than recommend guidelines that were optional for adoption by members, which is how the NCAA functioned from 1906 to 1956, it had to legislate and enforce rules. The NCAA had to change dramatically from operating as a whole, with each member wielding one vote in a general assembly, to operating as a narrowing plutocracy, divided into smaller and smaller groupings of the members with an uneven distribution of power. To comprehend how the richest and most commercially successful athletic programs gained control of the NCAA and why they will never give up their control, one need only follow the money.

In 1956 the NCAA attempted to improve its regulatory efficiency by splitting its members into college and university divisions.[38] The popularity of football and men's basketball elevated the need to further separate competitive schools, and in 1973 the NCAA voted to establish Divisions I, II, and III. The rationale given by the institutions competing at the highest level was that they felt that rules related to recruiting and academics were impeding the development of revenue-generating sports and that the divisional separation would better protect their interests. As former Southeastern Conference commissioner Boyd McWhorter stated, "We must make certain that restrictions don't put any coach in an impossible position or create conditions where our game is unattractive to our patrons."[39] This divisional stratification increased autonomy for the most competitive schools and by doing so further isolated less competitive institutions, marginalizing their ability to contest unfavorable rules and slow the expansion of commercialism. As stratification increased, NCAA member institutions were forced to make commitment decisions that required far greater investments in athletics.[40]

This strategic stratification continued to intensify, further differentiating college athletic programs. At the 1976 NCAA Convention, Division I institutions would further divide by separating the institutions that participated in "true" major football conferences, including the Big Eight, Big Ten, Southeastern, Southwestern, Pacific-8, Western Athletic, and Atlantic Coast conferences. It was clear that these conferences aimed to invest more money in football, without restraint from less capable institutions in Division I. Divisions I-A, I-AA, and I-AAA were thereby born. In 2006, to ameliorate public and media confusion over the Division I-A and I-AA designations, the NCAA Board of Directors once more altered the subdivisional nomenclature by converting Division I-A into the Football Bowl Subdivision (FBS) and Division I-AA into the Football Championship Subdivision (FCS).[41]

The 1996 NCAA Convention brought yet another strategic attempt by the most powerful football playing schools to establish greater autonomy. Proposal 7 established an end to the one-member, one-vote system and relinquished power to the establishment of a new voting structure that included an NCAA Board of Directors and Executive Committee, a Board of Directors (in Division I) and a President's Council (in Divisions II and III). The sixteen-member executive committee was heavily weighted with eight representatives from major football institutions. Although the boards would be able to vote on the issues unique to their divisions, the move gave more power and control to Division I-A schools. The adoption of this restructuring kept the NCAA intact when the wealthiest schools threatened an exodus, but it also meant the abandonment of democratic membership-driven participation.[42] A tighter plutocracy resulted.

Indicative of the growing ability of the elite football and basketball programs to have their way, in an October 2011 precursor of what was to come, NCAA president Mark Emmert pushed for an increase in the maximum value of an athletic scholarship. A $2,000 stipend to athletes to cover the cost of college attendance was proposed as an addition to the funding of tuition, mandatory fees, room, board, and books. The NCAA Board of Directors adopted the legislation, but it was promptly voted down by the membership in December 2011. Not to be deterred, the wealthiest conferences continued to pressure the NCAA and Emmert, threatening once again to leave the association. In August 2014 the NCAA Board of Directors (now called Board of Governors) granted legislative autonomy to the five wealthiest conferences in the FBS, representing sixty-five institutions, and adopted a new governance structure to provide greater operational control to athletics directors and conference representatives.[43] College and university presidents emphasized the need to retain control on their campuses and within the NCAA for the new governance model to be successful.

This new model adds presidents, a student-athlete, a faculty athletic representative, and a female administrator to the Division I Board of Directors.[44] The new autonomy legislative privileges apply only to specific athlete welfare topics and include issues such as financial aid, health, recruiting restrictions, meals for athletes, and athletic time demands. Nonetheless, competition among all universities to keep pace with the escalation of athletic costs is expected to rise to unsustainable levels.[45] Bob Kustra, president of Boise State University, described the autonomy legislation as a "power grab" that facilitated the NCAA's attempt to perpetuate the dominance of a few dozen universities with the most resources to continue to pull strings. "It seems they are never satisfied with their bloated athletic budgets, especially when threatened in recent years by upstart, so-called mid-major programs that steal recruits, oftentimes beat the big boys, 'mess with' the national rankings and sometimes take postseason bowl games and revenue."[46] Faced with this additional stratification of football and basketball, the non–Power Five institutions with distressed budget constraints were left with no choice but to maintain competitiveness by offering similar benefits or to drop further behind in the race.[47] In January 2015 the NCAA formally adopted super-conference autonomy in governance. Presidents from the five wealthiest conferences, known as the Power Five (the Big Ten, Big Twelve, Pac-12, Southeastern, and Atlantic Coast conferences, along with Notre Dame), reasoned that modern big-time sport was its own ecosystem, and its issues and the ability to resolve them were unique to their institutions. They appeared to be saying that opposition to the autonomy vote might result in the destruction of the organization's primary funding source.

In the future, the cost to compete at the highest levels will likely be subsidized increasingly by student fees or institutional operating expenses. The advancement of the commercial interest of the wealthiest institutions reverberates, creating economic instability throughout college sports and contributing to serious challenges to the academic integrity and efficacy of higher education institutions.[48] This unabashed stratification of the economic interests of the NCAA's wealthiest athletic institutions and conferences may ultimately spell a need for government intervention.

Just as college presidents abdicated their responsibility for controlling athletics on their own campuses, they delegated their involvement in the NCAA to athletics directors or relatively powerless faculty athletics representatives,[49] who in turn generally followed the wishes of their institutions' athletic conferences and conference commissioners. Thus the NCAA has long functioned as a trade association for commercialized athletic programs, and as these businesses continued to grow and experience revenue growth, so did the salaries and careers of the coaches, athletics directors, and conference commissioners. Although the governance structure reform of 1997, which eliminated the principle of one school, one vote, was supposed to slow or reverse the pattern, it actually made it worse by concentrating the control over NCAA policy in the hands of a smaller and smaller minority of the most heavily commercialized programs. And although college presidents were nominally put in a position of power to affect NCAA decisions, presidents' participation at NCAA meetings actually fell, and those presidents who served on NCAA boards tended to be the ones who had no inclination to curtail commercialization. College presidents have always had the ability to redirect college sports, but they chose then, and choose now, to leave control in the hands of athletics directors, conference commissioners, and coaches.

The structural evolution of this plutocracy led to the segmentation of the largest national collegiate athletic organization in the United States, resulting in growing inequality in both competition and revenue. Among the members within each division and subdivision, there is some agreement on minimum standards for membership in the division and control of maximum scholarship expenditures. But the absence of sufficient expenditure limits has produced significant gaps between the haves and the have-nots, nowhere as extreme as in the top competitive division and subdivisions.

A basic understanding of the NCAA membership structure is required to understand the forces at play that constitute barriers to reform. In 2015–16, there were 1,092 four-year institutions that were active voting members and an additional 44 members categorized as provisional or candidate nonvoting members.[50] Ninety-nine of 143 conference members had voting rights, and there were 39 affiliated nonmember organizations.[51] Of the 1,092 active member institutions, 346 were members of Division I, the highest competitive division; 307 were members of Division II (D-II), which is mandated to offer fewer scholarships and impose other athletic program operations restrictions compared to Division I; and 439 were members of Division III (D-III), the nonscholarship division.[52] The philosophy of Division I is openly commercial in that these institutions seek to maximize athletic program–generated revenues in order to have their athletic programs pay for themselves.[53] In addition to serving the student-athlete, Division I programs seek to provide a larger institutional audience (faculty, staff, students), as well as the general public,[54] with an entertainment product that enhances the affinity of these audiences with the educational institution.

Only ninety-four Division I members do not sponsor football (for example, Marquette, St. John's, DePaul, Boston University, and Georgetown).[55] The remaining Division I members are divided into two subdivisions for the sport of football, the Football Championship Subdivision (including Grambling State, Missouri State, Illinois State, Cornell, and the University of Delaware), with 124 members, and the Football Bowl Subdivision (such as the University of Texas, Ohio State University, the University of Alabama, and the University of Southern California), with 128 members (up from 120 members three years earlier).[56] FBS institutions sponsor higher-budget athletic programs and are committed to competing in basketball and football "at the highest feasible level of intercollegiate competition."[57] All FBS members sponsor spectator-oriented, revenue-producing basketball programs, and more than 250 sponsor spectator-oriented, revenue-producing football programs.[58] FBS athletic programs must also meet minimum requirements in four areas: (1) sports sponsorship (they must sponsor at least sixteen NCAA championship sports, including football, with each sport also meeting participant and regular season contest criteria minimums in order to count against the sponsorship standard); (2) scheduling (they must play at least 60 percent of their football schedules and at least five home contests against other FBS members, all but four men's and women's basketball games against Division I opponents, and 50 percent of contests in other sports against Division I opponents); (3) attendance at football games (they must average 15,000 people in actual or paid attendance per home game over a rolling two-year period); and (4) scholarship allocations (they must award 90 percent of the maximum number of football scholarships allowed and 200 grants-in-aids, or $4 million in total scholarship expenditures).[59] Total operating expenses in 2012–13 at FBS institutions ranged from $11.4 to $146.8 million.[60]

Notably, in 2013–14, only twenty-four Division I programs—all FBS institutions, but representing only 2.2 percent of all NCAA active members and 19 percent of the FBS schools—actually produced more operating revenues than operating costs.[61] The median in 2013–14 operating losses of all FBS schools was $14.7 million,[62] representing a 26.7 percent increase in operating losses over the previous year.[63] The overt expression of a commercial and entertainment sport philosophy—commemorated in the NCAA rules manual—and the practice of excessive spending has fueled an FBS arms race and a system of student-athlete exploitation.

NCAA FCS institutions have somewhat lower competitive subdivision criteria than the FBS institutions and lack a football game attendance requirement. FCS institution athletic programs must meet minimum requirements in the areas of (1) sports sponsorship (they must sponsor at least fourteen NCAA championship sports, including football, with each sport also meeting participant and regular season contest criteria minimums in order to count against the sponsorship standard); (2) scheduling (they must play at least 50 percent of regular season football contests against FBS or FCS members, all but four men's and women's basketball games against Division I opponents, and 50 percent of contests in other sports against Division I opponents); and (3) scholarship allocations (they are allowed to give a lower number, sixty, of scholarships allowed in football).[64] The athletic program's annual budget for these institutions in 2013–14 ranged from $3.9 million to $43.8 million.[65] The financial status of the athletics departments at these institutions is significantly more precarious than that of FBS institutions. No FCS athletics department generates more revenues than it spends.[66] They are heavily subsidized by institutional allocations (71 percent of total operating budgets).[67] Median operating losses of $10.8 million represent an 83 percent increase since 2004,[68] with losses ranging from a high of $35.7 million to a low of $2.1 million.[69]

The ninety-four nonfootball-playing Division I institutions must meet minimum requirements in three areas as well: (1) sports sponsorship (they must sponsor at least fourteen NCAA championship sports, with each sport also meeting participant and regular season contest criteria minimums in order to count against the sponsorship standard); (2) scheduling (they must play all but four basketball contests against other Division I opponents and at least 50 percent of their schedules in other sports against Division I opponents); and (3) scholarship allocations (they must award a minimum of 50 percent of the maximum allowable grants in fourteen sports, or an equivalent number of full scholarships, or an equivalent amount in aggregated total scholarship expenditures).[70] The total operating budget of these schools in 2013–14 ranged from $3.9 to $37.4 million.[71] The financial status of these institutions is as precarious as that of FCS institutions, if not more so, despite having significantly smaller operating budgets. Like FCS institutions, none of these institutions operates at a profit either.[72] They are heavily subsidized by institutional allocations (77 percent of total operating budgets).[73] Median operating losses in 2013 were $10.7 million, ranging from a high of $31.2 million to a low of $2.8 million.[74]

Key to understanding the financial relationships among the three Division I subdivisions is that they are all engaged in recruiting the same elite-level athletes, except that the FCS has accepted its second-class position in football. Thus, the so-called arms race affects all member institutions. When FBS institutions provide lavish locker rooms, computer centers exclusively for athletes, and other special benefits, the rest of the subdivisions are then pressured to match these investments. Particularly important to all Division I members is access to the sixty-eight-team Division I national men's basketball championship, commonly referred to as "March Madness" or the "Final Four." The single elimination nature of this championship makes "Cinderella" teams possible, and, as detailed later, the significant largesse of the media rights associated with the tournament gets returned to all Division I member institutions. Within the FBS, there is segmentation between the sixty-five institutions composing the so-called Power Five conferences,[75] which consist of the richest athletic programs, and the remaining sixty institutions in the FBS (in 2013–14). Thus, recruiting, financial aid, and other rules that result in differing treatment of athletes within the subdivisions affect the financial integrity of the entire Division I system. To be sure, even among the sixty-five Power Five universities, there are the twenty or so schools that manage to have a yearly operating surplus and roughly forty-five schools with operating deficits.

In contrast to the Division I philosophy, Divisions II and III make no mention of maximizing athletic program revenues. Division II centers its philosophical statement on the role of athletics, athlete "growth opportunities through academic achievement, learning in high-level athletics competition and development of positive societal attitudes in service to community. The balance and integration of these different areas of learning provide Division II student-athletes a path to graduation while cultivating a variety of skills and knowledge for life ahead."[76] Division II institution athletic programs must meet minimum requirements in only two areas: (1) sports sponsorship (they must sponsor at least ten NCAA championship sports with one sport in each of three sport seasons, with each sport also meeting participant and regular season contest criteria minimums in order to count against the sponsorship standard); and (2) scholarship allocations (they have lower limits on the number of scholarships that can be awarded in each sport and, generally, must award the equivalent of 50 percent of these lower maximum limits).[77] Total operating expenses at Division II institutions with football in 2013–14 ranged from $1.3 to $15.4 million.[78] Division II institutions without football programs had operating budgets ranging from $519,615 to $19.9 million.[79] These programs are almost entirely supported by institutional allocations.[80] The median athletic program–generated revenue for institutions with football is $672,717;[81] it is $345,563 for programs without football.[82]

Division III athletic programs place highest priority on the overall quality of the educational experience and on the successful completion of all students' academic programs. They seek to establish and maintain an environment in which a student-athlete's athletic activities are conducted as an integral part of the student-athlete's educational experience, and in which coaches play a significant role as educators.[83]

The Division's central qualifying premise is not to provide any "award of financial aid to any student on the basis of athletics leadership, ability, participation or performance."[84] In addition to the prohibition of athletic-based financial aid, the only other membership criterion is sports sponsorship based on the size of the institution—institutions with enrollments of 1,000 or fewer must have ten NCAA championship sports, and institutions with more than 1,000 students must have at least twelve NCAA championship sports.[85] Total operating expenses at Division III institutions with football programs in 2013–14 ranged from $811,665 to $16.0 million. Athletic budgets at institutions without football programs ranged from $446,514 to $9.8 million.[86] As for Division II schools but even more so, the bulk of these programs are funded through institutional allocations.[87] The NCAA does not gather data on revenues produced in this division.

TWO

How College Sports Lost Its Way II

The institutionalization of Division I Football Bowl Subdivision (FBS) self-interest, and now particularly the sixty-five institutions of the Power Five conferences that have legislative autonomy, is all about keeping as much national championship and other regular season revenue as possible for sixty-five Power Five schools. Thus, it is important to understand the sources of this national championship revenue, how it is distributed, and who determines the distribution. The NCAA makes most of its money by owning and selling marketing rights to its national championships; most of the remainder is derived from national championship gate receipts (see table 2-1). The NCAA currently sponsors eighty-nine championships in twenty-three sports.[1] Some of these postseason tournaments are restricted to competitive division members and some are "open" to teams from any member institution.[2] The bulk of current NCAA revenues is derived from the sixty-eight-team, single-elimination, Division I national basketball championship, branded "March Madness," which culminates in a four-team championship playoff weekend, the "Final Four."[3] This property generates an average of $771 million annually in NCAA media rights fees over a fourteen-year period. Gate receipts and sponsorships from the tournament add over $100 million in additional revenue.[4] In 2012–13,

TABLE 2-1: NCAA Revenues for the Year Ending August 31, 2014

Championship television and marketing rights fees	$753,595,560
Championships and NIT tournaments gate receipts/ sponsorships	$114,846,763
Investment income	$82,271,821
Sales and services	$28,324,776
Contributions-facilities net	$9,990,592
Total	$989,029,512

Source: NCAA, *NCAA and Subsidiaries, Independent Auditors' Report* & *Consolidated Financial Statements* (Indianapolis: NCAA, 2014), p. 4.

84 percent of the NCAA's total revenues of $912 million were derived from March Madness.[5] (In April 2016, the NCAA extended their March Madness television contract to cover 2026–33. While the annual average rights fee increases to $1.1 billion, in present value terms the value is below that of the current deal at any reasonable discount rate.)

A small percentage of that revenue is used to operate the NCAA's national office, including putting on the championship events (see table 2-2). But in the end, more than 90 cents of every dollar the NCAA generates is returned to member institutions, either for specified purposes to support student-athletes or unrestricted, in the case of revenues distributed based on Division I basketball championship participation.[6]

The Division I revenue distribution to member institutions is for the following specified purposes: basketball fund ($205 million, 38 percent of total), student-athlete athletic grants in aid ($136 million, 25 percent), special student assistance ($80 million, 15 percent), sports sponsorship ($69 million, 13 percent), academic enhancement ($27 million, 5 percent), conference grants ($9 million, 2 percent), and supplemental support ($19 million, 3 percent).[7] The basketball fund is a payoff system to conferences based on the finish of their teams in March Madness over a six-year rolling period.[8] The conferences subsequently determine how to distribute this money among their member institutions.[9] To its credit, the NCAA has significantly reduced the amount of distribution that is based on winning postseason basketball games and has increased amounts dedicated to reimbursing institutions for their athletic program expenditures on important

TABLE 2-2: NCAA Expenses for the Year Ending August 31, 2014

Distribution to	Amount	Percent of total
Division I members	$547,070,000	60.2
Division I championships, programs, and NIT Tournament	$98,145,966	10.8
Division II championships and programs	$34,747,363	3.8
Division III championships and programs	$28,727,905	3.2
Association-wide programs	$151,148,811	16.6
Management and general	$41,740,861	4.6
Total expenses	$908,580,958*	

Source: NCAA, *NCAA and Subsidiaries, Independent Auditors' Report & Consolidated Financial Statements* (Indianapolis: NCAA, 2014), p. 4.

*The difference between total revenues and expenses equals the yearly surplus (and contribution to net assets) of $80,448,554.

student-athlete benefits, such as academic support programs, scholarships, and sports operating costs.[10] However, the $200-million-plus portion based on basketball tournament participation is still very substantial. The non-basketball fund distributions are fixed amounts in some cases, such as for academic enhancement (the same amount is provided to each Division I member), and based on program size in other cases, as for sports sponsorships and scholarships.[11]

The NCAA has established a revenue distribution system that is dominated by the philosophy of returning the most money to the members responsible for earning that money, a for-profit business mentality, rather than by expectations that it should act as a tax-exempt, nonprofit association with an educational mission. The NCAA owns its national championships. The revenues derived from these championships are not used to best advance the mission of the organization, benefiting *all* of its members and *all* student-athletes, but rather to disproportionately benefit the athletes in the most commercialized programs. The NCAA has not adopted a non-profit philosophical position—for instance, that all national association revenues should be used in a way that contributes to the education, health, and welfare of the greatest number of student-athletes. Institutions with commercialized athletic programs earn significant revenues from their own regular season contests and shares of conference championships. National championship revenues do not assist all NCAA member institutions equally. In contrast, most conferences divide their revenue equally among its members, after allocations for the costs of participating in postseason games.

For the March Madness men's tournament in 2016, the athletic conference of each participating school received approximately $260,000 for each round of the tournament in which it participated, up to the last round. Thus, a school going all the way to the finals could earn its conference $1.56 million in 2016. In addition, the $1.56 million would also be paid out in each of the next five years, so the total earnings from going to the finals would be $9.36 million—a handsome payout.[12] In sharp contrast, and inexplicably, the NCAA pays out nothing to the participants in the women's March Madness tournament.

Notably, the NCAA does not sponsor an FBS football championship. The College Football Playoff, a four-team playoff accepted by the public as the FBS national championship, began in 2014–15[13] and is the sequel to the Bowl Championship Series and its two-team championship, which existed from 1998 through 2013.[14] The value of the new four-team College Football Playoff is in excess of $600 million per year, and it is owned jointly by all FBS conferences plus Notre Dame, rather than by the NCAA.[15] These College Football Playoff proceeds are not equally shared among all FBS members. The sixty-five Power Five conference members take home 75 percent of the proceeds, and the remaining 25 percent is distributed to the sixty remaining institutions via other FBS conferences[16] except for the $2.34 million that is distributed to some Football Championship Subdivision (FCS) conferences.[17] The average revenue to each of the Power Five conferences in 2014–15 was approximately $70 million from the playoff system, compared to approximately $30 million in 2013–14, the final year of the Bowl Championship Series.[18] The NCAA FCS championship is a sixteen-team tournament. Thus, it is reasonable to assume that it is only a matter of time before the College Football Playoff is expanded to eight teams or more, which would most likely increase its approximate value to more than $1 billion per year.

The fact that almost half of all NCAA revenues and 75 percent of all College Football Playoff revenues go to the Power Five conferences (representing just sixty-five out of 350 schools in Division I or out of more than 1,000 schools association-wide) reveals the dominance of highly commercialized and educationally questionable Division I football and basketball programs. These conferences have intentionally acted to control NCAA distributions and keep most of the revenues from the College Football Playoffs for themselves. The goal of the sixty-five Power Five conference institutions is clear: they want to win, and most will spend whatever it takes in their effort to build winning teams, all while maintaining a resource advantage over 94 percent of all other NCAA member institutions.

Until 1997 the NCAA generally operated as a one-institution, one-vote association.[19] Members convened annually in a deliberative assembly requiring a two-thirds vote to adopt legislation that was constitutional in importance, and voting as a whole or by division (generally by majority vote) on legislation of lesser importance.[20] In 1997, Division I moved from a one-institution, one-vote assembly to a conference-based Legislative Council, subject to review by the Division I Board of Directors.[21] Concomitant with this separation from Division II and III in 1997, using the threat of FBS institutions leaving the NCAA, FBS schools were successful in accomplishing three goals key to perpetuating the competitive dominance of the Power Five conferences: (1) getting NCAA members to agree to a federated structure—which gave more autonomy to each division but gave FBS 50 percent of all voting positions on the NCAA Executive Committee (the governance structure that has final authority over the association's budget and the power to call for a two-thirds vote of the entire membership to overturn the action of any division or subdivision) and 61 percent control of the Division I Board of Directors;[22] (2) passage of a legislative provision, approved by the entire NCAA membership, that relegated Division II's and Division III's joint share of NCAA national championship and organization revenues to no more than 8–11 percent and gave Division I control of the remaining, lion's share of the NCAA's revenue distribution;[23] and (3) specifying that if any new NCAA subdivision championship was initiated (practically meaning an FBS national championship), all of its revenue belonged to and would be under the control of that subdivision.[24]

These actions fully protected the revenues from the then new football Bowl Championship Series (the predecessor to the current College Football Playoff National Championship), a new national championship property, not owned by the NCAA, that was about to launch.[25] The NCAA had never developed a Division I-A (FBS) football championship because the schools in this division had argued that the many postseason bowl opportunities were more desirable than a national championship because they placed less pressure on student-athletes.[26] Even if the NCAA started an NCAA FBS national championship in the future, the FBS institutions would not share these NCAA revenues with other NCAA members, and the FBS would determine any such distribution among FBS institutions.[27] However, given FBS control of the NCAA's primary legislative mechanisms, it is highly unlikely that the FBS would permit the development of a competing product to its College Football Playoffs. The institutionalization of this plutocracy—giving voting control to a minority of the wealthiest athletic programs—is without precedent in either amateur or professional sports worldwide.

The financial support of Division II and III legislation actually reads, "Members are guaranteed revenue through allocations made to each division from the Association's general operating revenue. Division II shall receive at least 4.37 percent of the Association's annual general operating revenue. Division III shall receive at least 3.18 percent of the Association's annual general operating revenue."[28] The use of "at least" was disingenuous. In most years, Division II and III together (68 percent of NCAA active members) receive 7.55–11 percent of NCAA distributions.[29] In contrast, members of Division I (32 percent of NCAA active members[30]) received 69 percent[31] of 2012–13 NCAA revenues, and members of the Power Five conferences (6 percent of NCAA members) received 31 percent of the Division I distributions.[32] These sums do not include the College Football Playoff, which is not organized or owned by the NCAA. The likely intent of the legislation was to make clear to the rest of the membership that revenues earned by Division I would stay with Division I, and Division II and III should not expect support beyond the payment of expenses for their teams to participate in NCAA national championships and the benefits of limited association-wide programs, such as providing catastrophic insurance for all NCAA athletes.

The Power Five conferences achieved greater legislative autonomy in 2015.[33] They claim that they will use revenues from the College Football Playoff to enhance athletes' welfare by providing athletic scholarships covering the full cost of college attendance and lifelong scholarship support for former athletes wishing to complete undergraduate degrees,[34] both of which were legislative provisions previously rejected by the NCAA.[35] However, that claim is misleading because it gives the impression that only Power Five conference institutions have the financial ability to provide such benefits. For instance, the Power Five conferences have not proposed that the NCAA, rather than the FBS, own the College Football Playoff in the same way the NCAA owns the Final Four basketball and all other national championships, thereby creating the funding source to provide such expanded scholarship support to *all* Division I athletes. Instead, the Power Five conference institutions seek to enhance their existing advantage by providing only their athletes with benefits that members of other FBS or Division I conferences cannot match because of more limited financial resources. It is clear that the overriding goal of the Power Five conferences is to keep as much revenue as they can so that they gain the greatest advantage in attracting prospective student-athletes, thereby increasing the likelihood that they will win football and basketball games. At the same time, they must pay lip service to concern about all student-athletes to preserve their "amateur" standing and hence their tax preferences and other economic benefits.

The Threat of FBS or Power Five Departure from the NCAA

Given the aforementioned restructuring of the NCAA to give the FBS full license to act in its own self-interest, educators and the public should ask why non-FBS NCAA members don't unite to oppose such a governance imbalance, or why the membership allowed this to happen in the first place. The answer is that the FBS, and now most recently the Power Five conference institutions, threatened to leave the NCAA if the other divisions or subdivisions didn't give them what they wanted.[36] The implication of this threat was, and is, that without these top revenue-producing FBS institutions, Division II and III institutions would not receive their current benefits, including fully paid travel, hotel, and meal costs for those athletes and coaches participating in NCAA championships, catastrophic injury insurance for all student-athletes, and the benefits of other NCAA association-wide programs. In addition, the non-FBS members of Division I fear that a pullout by the FBS institutions would undermine the

value of the Division I Basketball Final Four, which is their most significant revenue source.

But what would actually happen if the FBS or the Power Five conference institutions pulled out of the NCAA? Is this really a viable threat, or
is it an empty one? It seems reasonable to conclude that such a departure is
unlikely, for two reasons. First, because of the number of collegiate institutions that would be negatively affected by such a move, it is likely that those
institutions would pressure their congressional representatives to act to
stop such a possibility. In such a case, Congress could either withdraw its
substantial athletic program tax preferences or invoke institutional non-
qualification for Higher Education Act funding to dissuade such a move.
Such congressional actions might financially cripple the FBS athletic
programs and their larger institutional hosts, and the threat of such actions would probably be enough to deter their departure.

Second, the most commercialized athletic programs benefit from the
philosophical protection of the significantly larger number of Division II
and III athletic programs, which allows the NCAA to defend itself in court
and to public opinion, arguing that their members conduct educational
sport programs in which amateurism is a critical element. These notions
of Division I football and basketball programs being educational rather
than professional sports operations are currently being attacked by a number of antitrust lawsuits, discussed in chapter 8.[37] Although the 2014 ruling by the regional office of the National Labor Relations Board (NLRB)
classifying the Northwestern University football players as employees was
not upheld by the federal NLRB, the federal NLRB did not rule on the substance of the question and left open the possible future unionization of
student-athletes at private universities.[38] The federal NLRB specifically suggested that, with regard to the National Labor Relations Act, Congress
should make its wishes known on the question of whether college athletes
should be considered employees. The courts have, as of this writing, largely
supported the NCAA's position in most cases.[39] Even the 2014 ruling and
the 2015 Ninth Circuit appellate decision in the O'Bannon v. National Collegiate Athletic Association, while undermining the NCAA's definition of
amateurism, acknowledges the need to keep compensation of student-
athletes within the range of federal student financial aid maximum limits.[40] Because they control the bulk of media rights revenues, if the FBS or
the Power Five conferences were to depart, they would find themselves in

the crosshairs of these lawsuits and unionization efforts and, arguably, significantly more vulnerable with regard to an educational-sport defense.

It is clear that the NCAA in general and Division I in particular are incapable of major reform because of the previously described institutionalization of FBS legislative self-interest at both the NCAA organizational and the Division I governance levels. Depending on the FBS to navigate the return to a student-centered focus runs counter to a history deeply devoted to pursuing commercial, sport revenue outcomes. The current lack of appetite for non-FBS NCAA members to rise in opposition to recent FBS proposals for more legislative autonomy and power appears to reflect an environment of resignation. NCAA members will most likely go along with continued FBS efforts to solidify a plutocracy.[41] Thus, it is unrealistic to imagine that this wealthy, ruling class will voluntarily give up power.

The Sordid History of Clashes between the NCAA and Academics

Although there are differences among NCAA divisions, the one thing all have in common is that the participants are nominally full-time college students, with the academic responsibilities that accompany this role. Acknowledging this, one of the NCAA's stated basic principles for the conduct of intercollegiate athletics is "the principle of sound academic standards," which is described in section 2.5 of the NCAA's manual and reads as follows:

> Intercollegiate athletics programs shall be maintained as a vital component of the educational program, and student-athletes shall be an integral part of the student body.[42]

It is within this pursuit of balance that academic, ethical, and legal concerns exist, seemingly pitting institutional financial interests and college athlete educational opportunity against one another.

The colossal clashes between academic integrity and intercollegiate athletics are nearly as old as American college sports. As early as 1880, it was observed that students entered the university to participate in intercollegiate athletics rather than college academic studies. Academic officials questioned this diversion from the missions of the university, noting "the object of their college course is quite as much college sports as college studies."[43]

By 1915, just ten years after the inception of the NCAA, William T. Foster, president of Reed College, lamented the disconnect between the educational mission of higher education and college presidents' use of athletics conducted for business and advertisement:

> When athletics are conducted for business, the aims are (1) to win games—to defeat another person or group being the chief end; (2) to make money—as it is impossible otherwise to conduct athletics as business; (3) to attain individual or group fame and notoriety. These three—which are the controlling aims of intercollegiate athletics, are also the aims of horseracing, prize-fighting, and professional baseball.[44]

Academic standards for athletic eligibility have oscillated for six decades since the 1950s as the NCAA and college presidents struggle with pressures from rabid donors and high-profile coaches to relax admission standards with a critical, and sometimes outraged, faculty in opposition. Prior to the 1950s, the institutional policy, interinstitutional agreements, or conference policy largely determined admissions and eligibility.[45] The notion of a national standard for initial eligibility began with a bold plea before the NCAA Convention from Rixford Snyder, the faculty athletics representative and dean of admissions at Stanford University in 1959. With the advent of the Cold War and the space age era of Sputnik, Snyder told the delegates, "the age of rockets and satellites will not accept the free ride for an athlete of limited academic potential while the physicist with only modest physical prowess goes unaided financially."[46] Significant academic reform has come in four major movements since Snyder's plea at the NCAA's 1959 convention. By 1960 the Atlantic Coast Conference (ACC) had instituted standards for initial eligibility requiring a minimum joint score of 750 on the SAT. In 1962 the NCAA followed the ACC's lead by adopting a formula that combined high school rank and test scores to predict a 1.6 grade point average after the first year of college, known as the 1.6 Predictor Rule. This first phase of academic reform lasted until 1973.

The influences and impacts of the freshman eligibility rule on football and basketball, the Vietnam War, the civil rights movement, and open admissions in higher education led to the demise of the 1.6 Predictor Rule.

Citing the unfairness of the 1.6 Predictor Rule to inner-city blacks, the new NCAA 2.0 rule merely required prospective freshman athletes to achieve a high school GPA of 2.0 (C average) in all high school courses, without requiring minimum standardized test scores. The new rule met both opposition and support from faculty athletic representatives. The civil rights movement and the trend toward open college admissions swayed some institutions in favor of the less restrictive rule. The 2.0 rule passed in a close vote. Walter Byers, executive director of the NCAA, later recalled, "Losing the 1.6 rule was one of the most painful experiences in the 22 years I had then served as Executive Director."[47] The drive to admit elite athletes, irrespective of whether they had attained the academic credentials or possessed the skills to compete in college, won the day.

The predictable academic scandals resulting from this action would spawn another major phase in reform. The lax 2.0 standard led to public concern about the academic preparedness of college athletes and their ability to obtain a college education. In 1983 the NCAA passed what became known as Proposition 48, establishing a minimum standardized joint test score of 700 on the SAT or 15 on the ACT and a 2.0 GPA in eleven core academic courses. The legislation went into effect in 1986. The test score requirement came under opposition from the Black Coaches Association and historically black colleges and universities, which claimed it had a disparate impact on minorities and economically disadvantaged students. With several adjustments to the legislation, the basic tenets of Proposition 48 continue today—with two significant tweaks: greater weight is placed on core-unit high school GPA, and greater access to higher education is possible regardless of low test scores.

In 1996 the NCAA adjusted and strengthened the re-centered SAT and ACT score standard with a sliding scale by raising the core unit GPA of 2.0 to 2.5, to correspond to an SAT score of 820 or an ACT score of 17, and created a partial qualifier status for athletes achieving a minimum SAT score of 720 and a GPA of 2.75 or above. The partial qualifier could receive an athletics scholarship immediately and practice with the team, but could not compete, and would lose one year of eligibility. Successful minority basketball coaches John Thompson of Georgetown University and John Chaney of Temple University protested that the standardized test score cutoffs were culturally biased and precluded academic opportunities for first-generation, economically disadvantaged African American students who were capable of success in college with academic assistance. These arguments challenged higher academic standards and college presidents' desire for more academically skilled athletes able to compete among an increasingly capable student body.[48]

Soon after, in a 1997 class-action lawsuit, Cureton v. National Collegiate Athletic Association, brought by a group of minorities led by Tai Kwan Cureton, Leatrice Shaw, and others in federal district court, the NCAA was sued for denying access to higher education and creating a disparate impact on incoming African American student-athletes in violation of Title VI of the Civil Rights Act. The plaintiffs received an initial favorable ruling but lost to the NCAA on appeal to the U.S. Third Circuit Court of Appeals. The NCAA provided a vigorous defense of the use of standardized test cutoff scores, asserting that the test scores strongly predicted the graduation of college student-athletes.[49] Although the NCAA won the case on appeal, its board of directors launched an effort to consider alternative models of initial eligibility that did not have a disparate impact on minorities.

The legal battle in Cureton spurred the current and most recent phase of the NCAA's struggle to find the correct competitive formula of academic standards for its diverse university membership. The latest academic standard initiative emerged as the cornerstone of newly appointed NCAA president Myles Brand's 2003 Academic Performance Program. Brand's reform aimed to respond to claims that the use of minimum test scores had a disparate effect on minority access to higher education by altering initial eligibility standards and increasing levels of accountability for institutions and coaches for poor academic performance. In response to the Cureton case, the NCAA discarded the partial qualifier status and minimum standardized scores and created a complete sliding initial eligibility scale that enabled a student with a 3.55 GPA and a minimum score of 400 on the SAT to be eligible by signing his name, with zero correct answers on the standardized test. In describing his efforts, President Brand was quoted as saying, "The goal of the academic reform package is to reinforce good behavior. The new reforms are tough but fair."[50] Just a year later, Brand declared that the NCAA academic reform "is becoming one of our greatest success stories." We discuss the content of Brand's reforms below.

At each stage of these changes and additions to the NCAA's academic standards, the NCAA lost its way by failing to maintain an alignment with

Principle 2.5, Sound Academic Standards described earlier. First, the NCAA has yet to effectively address the issue of institutions waiving of regular admissions standards for a disproportionate number of athletes. Second, the NCAA has departed from the almost universal standard of a 2.0 cumulative GPA as representative of good academic standing for continuing eligibility progress toward degree standards. Third, the NCAA has failed to address the common practice of athletic departments running academic advising and support programs for athletes, a clear conflict of interest inviting fraud. Fourth, the NCAA has invented new academic performance standards such as the Graduation Success Rate (GSR) and the Academic Progress Rate (APR), which are fatally flawed because they depart from Principle 2.5, which holds that athletes' academic standards and performance should be compared to those of the general student body.

The APR was crafted under Brand's leadership as a metric purporting to be a real-time assessment of team academic performance. This metric, established in 2003, included a numerical threshold, falling below which would lead to punitive measures for athletic teams. The APR is a rate calculated using points earned by individual teams for the retention of team members and maintaining athletic eligibility. The APR metric came under immediate criticism from the media and professionals in athletic academic counseling, who speculated that the changes would be a catalyst for large-scale cheating.[51] (See pp. 64–69 for a more detailed discussion of the APR.) Cheating by athletes to gain admission and stay in college is nothing new. However, implementation of the APR and its penalty structure have raised the stakes to recruit and keep elite athletes in football and basketball. Coaches, institutional staff members, and even faculty have employed clever yet fraudulent schemes to get athletes admitted and to keep them academically eligible to play (see Appendix for a list of infractions related to athlete eligibility). Within the first two years of APR's implementation, Pete Thamel and Duff Wilson of the *New York Times* exposed a quick-fix $399 high school diploma mill for elite athletes at University High in Miami to obtain whatever grades were necessary in order to establish NCAA eligibility.[52] The NCAA expressed shock and outrage at the affront to the integrity of its standards and launched an investigation into the fraud. Twenty-eight elite high school athletes were able to establish eligibility through University High correspondence courses at eleven Division I institutions, including Auburn, Central Florida, Colorado State, Florida, Florida State, Florida International, Rutgers, South Carolina State, South Florida, Tennessee, and Temple. The following year, Wilson uncovered several more suspect prep schools. These prep schools identified athletic talent and operated freely under the not so watchful eyes of the NCAA staffers at their Eligibility Center, the unit of the NCAA created to review and monitor transcripts and records of athletes for certification of qualifications to compete. The NCAA eventually dropped the schools from their approved list of high schools only after Wilson exposed these fraudulent schemes.[53] Athletes graduating from these schools were admitted into academically competitive institutions, athletically eligible but with little or no hope of graduating or receiving a meaningful education.

In an effort to avoid APR penalties, schools have developed more elaborate cheating schemes, and significant academic fraud scandals have recently emerged. For example, at the University of Southern Mississippi, a head coach directed his assistant coaches to produce fraudulent papers for his athletes.[54] At the University of Louisiana–Lafayette, an assistant coach arranged for a prospective football player's ACT exam to be altered.[55] At Syracuse University, the NCAA identified multiple instances of academic misconduct in which athletics staff produced coursework for basketball players.[56] The largest and most publicly visible scandal occurred at the University of North Carolina at Chapel Hill (UNC), where eighteen years' worth of academic fraud was documented, including enrollment in fake classes or illegitimate independent study classes and tutors writing athletes' papers.[57] The scandal damaged the reputation of this institution.

In 2015 the media attention surrounding the UNC transgressions and the shocking results of North Carolina's own independent investigation prompted the NCAA to reopen its investigation after accepting what was eventually determined to be a false 2012 UNC explanation that these were academic rather than athletic matters that should be handled internally by the university. Based on the results of the independent investigation and the university's failure to be forthright in previous explanations of the scandal to UNC's accrediting agency, the Southern Association of Colleges and Schools Commission on Colleges (SACSCC) put UNC on probation, imposing its most severe sanction. They explained that UNC had violated seven accreditation standards: overall integrity; program content; control of intercollegiate athletics; academic support services; academic freedom;

faculty role in governance; and compliance with provisions of federal financial aid law.[58] The commission concluded: "There is also strong evidence that the reforms designed to open access to higher education to more athletes and punishing institutions failing at academics came at the expense of the integrity of the academy at large."[59]

In 2014, Brad Wolverton published a piece in the *Chronicle of Higher Education* describing a vast scheme of cheating among elite, revenue-generating football and basketball athletes and coaches. In this example, an aspiring basketball coach took online classes at Brigham Young University and Adams State University for hundreds of elite athletes needing to establish course credit hours and grades for initial and continuing eligibility. At the request of coaches needing elite players on the court or field, this aspiring coach, for a price, took online courses for their athletes. Although NCAA investigators say they knew of the deception, they failed to make a fraud case.[60] Wolverton later uncovered a similar scheme for basketball players at the University of Texas.[61]

The first priority of any university is the integrity of its educational mission. Yet it is abundantly clear that pressures placed on institutions of higher education, high schools, coaches, and athletes to cheat continue to grow unabated. New sophisticated schemes are attempted and often successfully open doors for underprepared athletes to access and continue participation in college sports. During 2015, the University of Louisiana–Lafayette and Syracuse University were found to have committed serious academic fraud violations. Rather than acceptance of the steady beat of academic fraud and misconduct scandals as the price of winning athletic programs, university faculty and administration must face this ethical crisis of misplaced priorities.

Failure to Address Gender, Race/Ethnicity, and Disability Discrimination

Few would deny that, historically, American higher education and athletic programs operating within this environment reflected gender, race/ethnicity, and disability discrimination as practiced in the larger American society. It wasn't until the 1960s that Congress acted to prohibit such discrimination, using its legal authority to set conditions for receipt of federal funding by public and private institutions of higher education.[62] The following civil rights laws were enacted to clearly state the law of the land:

Civil Rights Act of 1964: "No person in the United States shall, on the ground of race, color, or national origin, be excluded from participation in, be denied the benefits of, or be subjected to discrimination under any program or activity receiving federal financial assistance."[63] Title VII of the act specifically prohibits employment discrimination based on race, color, religion, sex and national origin.

Title IX of the Education Amendments of 1972: "No person in the United States shall, on the basis of sex, be excluded from participation in, be denied the benefits of, or be subjected to discrimination under any educational program or activity receiving federal financial assistance."[64]

Rehabilitation Act of 1973 and Americans with Disabilities Act of 1990: "Subject to the provisions of this title, no qualified individual with a disability shall, by reason of such disability, be excluded from participation in or be denied the benefits of the services, programs, or activities of a public entity, or be subjected to discrimination by any such entity."[65]

It was at this point that leaders of intercollegiate athletic programs should have been expected to (1) embrace their responsibilities for identifying and correcting discriminatory practices within NCAA operations and events and by its members; (2) exercise their governance authority to establish rules that required members to comply with federal laws and to monitor such compliance; and, (3) to assist members to achieve such compliance through the provision of educational materials and other types of assistance. While the NCAA belatedly made limited progress on the first and third expectations, the organization has not demonstrated its "governance" responsibility required to achieve the second.[66]

In fact, rather than embrace these civil rights obligations, the NCAA and its member institutions fought against the full application of Title IX gender equity requirements to athletics by supporting numerous Congressional amendments that would have killed the regulations in their entirety or excluded men's basketball and football programs from gender equity assessments.[67] Following the issuance of the Title IX athletics regulations in 1975, the NCAA challenged their validity by filing a lawsuit against the U.S. Department of Health, Education and Welfare (HEW).[68] With regard to gender and racial/ethnic legal requirements, the NCAA essentially paid these laws lip service by including their mention in the NCAA's "principles for the conduct of intercollegiate athletes," appointing committees, producing reports, and publishing education materials, but the organization never promulgated rules or required hiring or appointment practices that would advance their achievement.[69] Further, rather than calling out discriminatory hiring practices affecting women and racial or ethnic minorities as the cause of minority underrepresentation, the NCAA advanced the rationale that these minorities were not being hired because they were underqualified and undertrained. They supported this myth by funding women's coaching and administrative academies and mentoring programs to address the supposed "deficiencies" of these victims of discrimination—a classic response of the powerful white male majority designed to continue their dominance and control of intercollegiate athletics.

In addition, the NCAA virtually ignored the absence of collegiate athletic opportunities for students with disabilities, producing several videos and publications on this issue but offering no championship programs and refusing to govern sports for individuals with disabilities. The NCAA does support "reasonable accommodation" in the mainstreaming of individuals with disabilities on existing athletic teams for individuals without disabilities. However, it has never directly confronted the responsibility of educational institutions to create "separate but equal" programming specifically for students with disabilities, in addition to mainstreaming as required by 2013 Office of Civil Rights guidance, in the same manner as separate gender teams are provided to address gender inequities in intercollegiate athletics.[70]

The NCAA could have established a requirement that any member institution not in compliance with Title IX would be ineligible for postseason play. The NCAA could have acted to immediately establish national championships for athletes with disabilities. The NCAA could have required the collection and publication of data *by each institution* (NCAA demographic data are provided only in the aggregate) to expose the significant underrepresentation of racial/ethnic minorities in sports participation and employment within the NCAA and its member institutions and conferences. Such transparency could have been used to provide an incentive for institutional members to do better. Even though the NCAA began publishing aggregated demographic data in 2007–08, this information is not identifiable to member institution or conference.[71] The NCAA could have acted to adopt rules requiring member institutions to include a sufficient number of minorities in job applicant and finalist pools, similar to the NFL's "Rooney Rule." None of these "governance" responses occurred. Thus the NCAA lost its way by failing to exercise its governance responsibilities in these civil rights areas.

Granted, the NCAA did establish a standing committee on Minority Opportunities and Interests in 1991 to "review issues related to the interests of ethnic minority student-athletes, NCAA minority programs and NCAA policies that affect ethnic minorities"[72] In 2010 the NCAA established the Office of Inclusion with a charge to "provide or enable programming and education, which sustains foundations of a diverse and inclusive culture across dimensions of diversity, including, but not limited to age, race, sex, class, national origin, creed, educational background, disability, gender expression, geographical location, income, marital status, parental status, sexual orientation and work experience."[73] This office has collected an adequate selection of educational materials dealing with inclusion, with information on international students, pregnant and parenting student-athletes, and LGBTQ issues. But these are not legislative mandates that produce positive changes in institutional practices. This is not "governance."

Similarly, a Committee on Women's Athletics was established in 1989 with the following mission statement:

> The mission of the NCAA Committee on Women's Athletics is to provide leadership and assistance to the association in its efforts to provide equitable opportunities, fair treatment and respect for all women in all aspects of intercollegiate athletics. Toward these ends, the committee shall seek to expand and promote opportunities for female student-athletes, administrators, coaches, and officiating personnel. The committee shall promote governance, administration and conduct of intercollegiate athletics at the institutional, conference and national levels that are inclusive, fair and accessible to women. The

committee shall develop programs and resources, which can be of practical use to the association in its effort to achieve these ends.[74]

Again, the committee focuses on education and producing reports rather than on legislative solutions. In fact, the NCAA to this day regularly publishes gender equity reports that reiterate the lack of progress made in the employment and participation of women, but there is no NCAA legislation mandating compliance with the gender equity provisions of Title IX.

In addition to the Committee on Women's Athletics, the NCAA appointed a Gender Equity Task Force in 1993 and reconvened that group twenty years later to review progress. While the Gender Equity Task Force did successfully pursue two legislative initiatives—increasing the number of maximum financial aid awards for a small number of women's sports and establishing an emerging sports program for women—the latter effort failed to get NCAA member institutions to add more women's teams at the institutional level. The "emerging sports" strategy identified sports that institutions could add and reduced the minimum number of institutions required to establish an NCAA championship in those sports. This initiative was based on the assumption that NCAA members were looking for the opportunity to add new women's sports. In fact, its member institutions were trying to avoid adding sports for women. Many of these institutions maintained and continue to maintain that they qualify for an allowable Title IX "Prong Three" excuse—that there aren't enough institutions sponsoring a new women's sport that they could compete against in their normal competition areas. The legislative tactic that would have worked would have been for the NCAA to mandate that conferences with a majority of members using the Title IX Prong Three exception add the same new women's sport, which would have removed the "no competition within a reasonable geographic area" excuse.[75]

The most notable exception to this charge of lack of governance policies to advance the purposes of federal civil rights laws was the establishment of the NCAA Division I Certification program in 1993.[76] Modeled after the accreditation self-assessments of institutions of higher education, the NCAA self-assessment and external peer review program directly addressed NCAA member institutions obligations to identify and correct gender and racial/ethnic inequities, as well as departures from established standards of governance, and to uphold a commitment to rules compliance, academic integrity, and student-athlete well-being. Inexplicably, in January 2011 NCAA president Emmert announced that he had asked the NCAA staff to evaluate the program to reduce the burden on institutions, increase cost-effectiveness, and improve the overall value. Then in April 2011 the Division I Board of Directors voted to approve a two-year moratorium on the program.[77] The response of the gender and racial/ethnic minority rights community was immediate and highly critical. In an August 5, 2011, letter signed by twenty-one civil rights and athletics leaders, significant concerns were expressed, which can be summarized as follows:

> The Certification process is particularly important to women and minorities in athletics because it requires schools complete a self-study on gender and racial equity every ten years, led by the institution's president or chancellor and requiring campus-wide participation. The end product is required to include measurable goals, the steps the institution will take to achieve those goals, timelines and persons responsible.

> Without the NCAA certification process, it is unlikely that the campus will engage in such a meaningful review of women's athletics, and the task will fall to those without institutional power: coaches, the senior women athletic administrator, the Title IX coordinator or student-athletes in private litigation.[78]

The two-year moratorium expired, and the Division I Certification program was not reactivated. Rather, the NCAA launched a replacement Institutional Performance Program (IPP) in June 2015 that is intended to serve as a dashboard display of "vital and significant data to assist with planning, performance and oversight" of each member institution's intercollegiate athletics program.[79] The president or chancellor of the institution controls who on campus has access to the data. There is no transparency requirement. The data are inaccessible to the public and even the faculty of the institution. Unlike the certification program, which required campuswide review committees, external peer review, identification of deficiencies, and plans to remedy such deficiencies, with NCAA penalties for failure to do so, the IPP program has no compliance requirements. It is clear that the certification program is dead. Once again, the NCAA lost its way.

Alas—If the NCAA Only Adhered to Its Stated Principles for the Conduct of Intercollegiate Athletics!

Key to the ethical conduct of athletic programs is the development of anchor principles that guide subsequent more detailed rule-making. These anchor principles should serve as guideposts that clearly define the proper conduct of educational sport. Interestingly, there is nothing wrong with the NCAA's statement of basic principles in its constitution for the conduct of intercollegiate athletics in this regard. Many of the essential principles are there and well stated. For example, the NCAA's *Division I Manual* includes the following principles:

1.3.1 Basic Purpose. The competitive athletics programs of member institutions are designed to be a vital part of the educational system. A basic purpose of this Association is to maintain intercollegiate athletics as an integral part of the educational program and the athlete as an integral part of the student body and, by so doing, retain a clear line of demarcation between intercollegiate athletics and professional sports.

2.2 The Principle of Student-Athlete Well-Being.
Intercollegiate athletics programs shall be conducted in a manner designed to protect and enhance the physical and educational well-being of student-athletes.

2.5 The Principle of Sound Academic Standards.
Intercollegiate athletics programs shall be maintained as a vital component of the educational program, and student-athletes shall be an integral part of the student body. The admission, academic standing and academic progress of student-athletes shall be consistent with the policies and standards adopted by the institution for the student body in general.

2.9 The Principle of Amateurism.
Student-athletes shall be amateurs in an intercollegiate sport, and their participation should be motivated primarily by education and by the

physical, mental and social benefits to be derived. Student participation in intercollegiate athletics is an avocation, and student-athletes should be protected from exploitation by professional and commercial enterprises.

2.12 The Principle Governing Eligibility.
Eligibility requirements shall be designed to assure proper emphasis on educational objectives, to promote competitive equity among institutions and to prevent exploitation of student-athletes.[80]

The problem lies with the lack of connectivity between stated principles and the NCAA rules and enforcement system. Often, no rules exist to implement the principle, or if rules do exist, they are inconsistent with stated principles. For instance, the principle of "maintaining athletes as an integral part of the student body" appears to be inconsistent with allowing the construction of lavish "athletes-only" facilities and academic support programs conducted by athletics departments rather than by academic authorities, two common practices not addressed by NCAA rules. "The admission, academic standing and academic progress of student-athletes shall be consistent with the policies and standards adopted by the institution for the student body in general" is a principle, but there is no rule prohibiting the common practice of institutional waivers of normal admissions standards for athletes disproportionate to other groups benefiting from such treatment. "Student-athletes should be protected from exploitation by professional and commercial enterprises" is a principle that appears to have been disregarded when the athletics department itself is the professional and commercial enterprise. Thousands of football and men's basketball players, producers of the largest part of revenues, the majority of whom are racial minorities, have graduation rates significantly below those of the general student body and are those most likely to receive waivers of regular admission standards, a reality that flies in the face of any principle aimed at preventing the "exploitation of student-athletes."

In fact, this book is a critique covering the myriad ways in which the majority vote of a self-interested NCAA membership or subdivision thereof has failed to uphold its stated principles. If the system is ever to be fixed, correction must start with making sure that stated principles are reinforced with rules that mandate behaviors consistent with these beliefs.

Failure to Comply with the Obligations of
Not-for-Profit Organizations

The line of demarcation between college and professional sports is a critical issue and supposedly central to the mission of the governance of athletics in higher education. That line is created in large part by the legal and ethical differences between for-profit and not-for-profit organizations. A core difference between the for-profit and the not-for-profit "business" lies in the use of excess revenues over expenses. In the case of the former, profits accrue to owners, investors, or shareholders, while in nonprofits, excess revenues must be reinvested in the organization and used to accomplish its stated educational, charitable or public service purposes. Individuals and companies invest in for-profit businesses with an expectation of return on investment, while individuals donate to not-for-profit organizations because of a belief in their purpose, with no expectation or benefit regarding financial return on investment. Individuals who work for nonprofit agencies understand the reason why they have lower salaries than their counterparts in the for-profit marketplace.

One of the best collections of guiding principles for the conduct of not-for-profit organizations was developed by a panel convened by the Independent Sector, a nationally recognized network of nonprofits, foundations, and corporations committed to advancing the common good.[81] Notably, the following seven of thirty-three key principles identified by the Independent Sector are virtually ignored in the current governance of intercollegiate athletics by the NCAA and indicate how the NCAA has lost its way:[82]

1. **Compliance with legal obligations.** The not-for-profit organization must "comply with all applicable federal laws and regulations, as well as applicable laws and regulations of the states and the local jurisdictions in which it is based or operates."[83] While the NCAA adopts this principle with regard to gender equity laws, it has no rules or processes to ensure such compliance.
2. **Code of ethics.** The NCAA has adopted no code of ethics defining professional conduct and respect that coaches should afford college athletes, nonexploitive conduct by institutions, or improper benefits to donors or institutional staff members. Such codes should lie at the heart of the moral compass governing athletics.

3. **Conflict of interest.** Avoiding the appearance or reality of a conflict of interest is virtually impossible today when weighted representation and voting rights within the NCAA allow the richest and most commercialized athletic programs to effectively control NCAA policies and thereby to maximize the revenues they receive from NCAA national championships, and in other ways advance their best interests. Further, institutional and national governance association rule-enforcement processes are fraught with conflict of interest, from representatives of competitor institutions determining penalties against each other to athletics department personnel influencing financial aid appeals brought by their athletes and interfering with institutional and community athlete disciplinary processes.

4. **Whistleblower protection.** Neither the NCAA nor its institutional members have protections that enable students, coaches, or other employees to come forward with information on illegal or unethical practices in athletics without fear of retaliation.

5. **Transparency.** Not-for-profit organizations are expected to make information about operations, governance, finances, programs, and activities widely available to the public, particularly information on the "methods they use to evaluate the outcomes of their work and sharing the results of those evaluations."[84] There are significant differences between the information made available by public versus private member institutions, and the NCAA has not openly shared complete information on its methods or exceptions, thereby not permitting the public to judge the efficacy of its rules.

6. **Majority independent board.** In serving a not-for-profit organization, the members of the NCAA Board of Governors (or highest governance authority) have a "duty of loyalty" under the law, and members are required to put the interest and purpose of the organization above the interest of the institutions they represent in all of the decisions they make.[85] This is especially true of the body that determines the distribution of resources, controls enforcement processes, and adopts rules related to the primary purposes of the organization. No such independent entity exists. In contrast, the current NCAA management structure is primarily composed of current presidents, athletics conference commissioners, and athletics directors, who treat the NCAA as a trade association designed to protect the best interests of athletic

administrators and coaches. Sitting college presidents who may be fearful of tinkering with their donors' entertainment are hardly able to exercise the collective courage to correct the course of college sports. This governance model represents a dangerous and clear conflict of interest.

7. **Personal inurement and lavish expenditures.** Every not-for-profit organization has a fiduciary duty to ensure that the greatest part of the financial resources at its disposal is used to fulfill the purposes of the organization. Individuals should not draw lavish salaries or be permitted to have excessive expense accounts or otherwise expend funds in unnecessary ways that would result in lesser resource amounts available to achieve the organization's mission. Individual NCAA member institutions in particular are guilty of violating this principle with regard to coaching and administrators' salaries, and by building athletic facilities of a quality inconsistent with facilities afforded nonathlete students and faculty.

These are rightful expectations of not-for-profit organizations that benefit from government protection of revenues through the granting of tax preferences. The tax preferences enjoyed by athletic programs include the following: (1) donations to athletic programs are considered tax deductible, even including 80 percent of those donations that provide the donor with athletic event seating and activity access preferences; (2) revenues from commercial activities, such as ticket sales, sponsorships, licensing fees and royalties, and television rights fees, are not considered "unrelated business income" and therefore are not subject to income taxes via the fragmentation principle; (3) athletic programs are permitted to use tax-exempt bonds to build athletics facilities; (4) there is no requirement for the colleges to pay payroll taxes for the value of room and board or to make workmen's compensation insurance payment for athletes under full-ride scholarships; and (5) the IRS has not determined that multi-million-dollar compensation packages provided to college coaches constitute private inurement in violation of the programs' nonprofit, tax-exempt status.[86] These preferences are significant and justifiable only to the extent that the intercollegiate athletics establishment conforms to these not-for-for profit legal and ethical principles.

PART II

What Needs to Be Fixed

THREE

Academic Integrity

It is undeniable that intercollegiate athletics is experiencing an unusual era of widespread media attention, public criticism, and faculty unrest related to incidents of academic fraud and misconduct. While the NCAA is weathering cries for reform regarding its definitions of college athlete amateurism, health benefits and safety considerations for athletes, rules violations and excessive athletic program expenditures, none of these issues is more central than academic integrity. Are all college athletes being afforded the education promised to them, and is the educational experience for nonathletes also being compromised by the current system?

A recent trend in academic fraud has become a classic example of sports programs usurping the education of college athletes. In 2010, Georgia Southern University was penalized for an assistant basketball coach posing as multiple athletes in online courses and performing classwork for his players, including the writing and submission of papers, essays, and tests.[1] Just six years later in 2016, Georgia Southern was again penalized for athletic staff performing academic work for three football athletes with show cause orders levied on compliance and academic services staff members.[2]

Replicating Georgia Southern's fraudulent methods, Syracuse University's director of basketball operations also performed substantial online work for players by posing as the athletes. This chapter examines the current profound discontent of faculty with the relationship between Division I athletics and the academy, the impact of the money-driven athletics system on campus academic integrity, the flaws and motivations behind the NCAA weak academic eligibility standards, and the impact of institutional admissions practices and athletic participation on the academic life of college athletes.

Flawed Academic Metrics Enable Academic Fraud

Throughout the history of intercollegiate athletics, the NCAA has used flawed metrics to measure the academic success of college athletes. It has skewed the numbers to overstate performance. It then touts its academic reforms, even though the evidence suggests a different assessment. For instance, while graduation rates for athletes by the NCAA's measurement have been trending upward, the NCAA fails to mention that graduation rates and academic performance measures for Division I football and men's basketball are significantly below those of the general student body and other nonrevenue college athletes.

For purposes of the following analysis, only current Division I standards and results are examined. Revenue growth and perceived publicity benefits enjoyed by successful athletic programs in Division I have created huge pressures to keep athletes eligible, often resulting in abuses to "beat" the NCAA's academic metric.

Eligibility Standards

The NCAA differentiates two standards regarding athlete eligibility for practice, competition, and athletic-related financial aid. Initial eligibility refers to minimal standards of high school grades, courses and standardized achievement test scores. Continuing eligibility, also known as progress towards degree, refers to those standards of college coursework and grades necessary to maintain athletic eligibility for each year of athletic competition.

Initial Eligibility Standards—High School Students   According to the new 2016 NCAA standard for participation in intercollegiate athletics, a high school student is required to have completed sixteen core courses with a minimum GPA of 2.3, to earn a 900 combined minimum SAT score on a sliding scale, and to graduate from high school to be eligible immediately for athletically related financial aid, competition, and practice. Eligibility standards had been reformed in 2003. Under the new standards, which did away with an anchor minimum standardized test score, a student theoretically could fail every question on a standardized test and still qualify with a grade point average of 3.55. The stated purpose of this initial eligibility standard compared to the standards in place prior to 2003 was to increase the number of minority athletes who graduated from college. The actual results have been negligible gains in minority access to higher education through big-time college sports. Between 1999 and 2002, the African American participation rate in Division I men's basketball grew at 1.7 percent annually.[3] But between 2003 and 2009, after the relaxed standard was put in place, the participation rate grew by only 0.8 percent annually, less than half the previous rate. The same growth trend was evident in football: between 1999 and 2002, African American participation increased by 3.5 percent annually, but between 2003 and 2009, it increased by only 0.7 percent annually, or one-fifth of the prereform rate. According to the NCAA's reports on federal graduation rates of African American student-athletes in Division I, the most recent data for men's basketball revealed a one-point decline in the 2003 cohort, to 43 percent, and for football a one-point increase, to 48 percent, over the previous year.[4]

The current low-test-score standard, coupled with high school grade inflation, has resulted in more athletes who meet NCAA eligibility standards with very low test scores. These students generally possess inadequate skills to manage college academics, increasing the need for academic support services at institutions already struggling with tight budgets.[5] The absence of a minimum standardized test requirement has challenged the academic integrity of higher education by widening the gap between the average academic profiles of athletes and nonathletes. The result is a depreciation of a degree's worth, coupled with an invitation to institutions to maintain an athlete's eligibility by committing academic fraud.

The academic fraud commonly used to assist underprepared college athletes to maintain their athletics participation eligibility includes counseling underprepared athletes to (1) enroll in less demanding academic majors, (2) select the least demanding courses available, whether or not they are needed to earn a degree, (3) enroll in courses taught by faculty who are "easy" graders or who require little to no work to complete course requirements, or, alternatively, (4) participate in acts of academic dishonesty in conjunction with academic tutors, coaches, and staff members hired by the athletic department. As a result, member institutions fail to provide a strong majority of their football and basketball athletes with a meaningful education. The richest athletic programs have developed multi-million-dollar academic support programs, hiring academic support professionals and counselors who focus on keeping athletes eligible.

Academic fraud also exists at the high school level, where preparatory schools now offer higher GPAs at a price. The result is massive grade inflation, as individuals have learned the system and recognize that an artificially high GPA can offset a poor performance on a standardized test.

As of August 2016, the NCAA raised to 2.3 (from 2.0) the minimum high school GPA for eligibility to practice, compete, and receive financial aid, and now requires the completion of ten core units prior to the start of the college athlete's senior year. The NCAA has also created an "academic redshirt" year for college athletes who would otherwise qualify under the former GPA/test-score sliding scale. An academic redshirt athlete who fails to achieve the minimum 2.3 GPA may not compete during his or her first year but is eligible for financial aid and to participate in practices. Counterintuitively, there are no restrictions on practice time, and the athlete is not required to seek remediation or academic support.[6]

Restoration of the minimum standardized test for freshman athletics eligibility or a similar requirement to establish minimum reading and mathematics competencies for incoming students would ensure that college athletes have at least rudimentary academic skills. It also would make sense to require institutions to apply their own entrance requirements equally to both athletes and nonathletes. Absent minimum scores on standardized tests, institutions must address the admission of underprepared athletes in some other effective way, such as through remedial courses prior to matriculation. Failing this, they will continue to exploit predominantly minority football and men's basketball players, and academic fraud designed to keep athletes eligible to play will persist.

Revising NCAA initial eligibility standards would eliminate many of the pervasive problems and unrealistic expectations of athlete academic performance. Most important to the academic success of any college freshman athlete is finding the correct institutional match based on the academic skills of the athlete and the qualities of the university rather than on the recruiting rhetoric of a coach. The Drake Group, a national faculty-based organization promoting academic integrity in college sports, proposes requiring an institutional match of the academic profiles of high school recruits to within one standard deviation of the academic profile of the previous year's incoming class, recommending that any athlete falling below this benchmark should be ineligible for full athletic participation during the freshman year.[7] As the academic preparation of college athletes more resembles the academic profiles of the student body, athletes will be a better institutional fit and more likely to balance academic responsibilities with athletic time demands. Coaches may be more cautious about recruiting underprepared athletes if they anticipate a year of no competition and limited practice time.

It is clear that the initial eligibility NCAA metric is ineffective at best and, at worst, a strong incentive for academic fraud and the exploitation of largely minority athletes in football and basketball. If higher education is willing to continue to turn a blind eye to this reality, it may be too late to address the depth of moral corruption within commercialized Division I athletic programs. If sanity has the possibility of being restored, the pieces of the academic metrics puzzle needed for a solution are clear: (1) a standardized test score minimum that is less susceptible to grade inflation and outright high school GPAs for sale, (2) an effort to match the academic profile of incoming athletes with the institution's general student body academic capabilities, (3) a consideration of mandated basic reading, math, and academic skills testing and remediation for underprepared admits, (4) a reduction in time spent on athletic activities, possibly including freshmen athletics ineligibility and less than full-time course loads for athletes requiring intensive remediation, and (5) objective faculty oversight of decisions to grant waivers of admissions standards for recruited athletes.

Continuing Eligibility Standards—GPA and Satisfactory Progress The NCAA currently requires continuing academic eligibility standards, as depicted in table 3-1. These standards disregard the commonly accepted

TABLE 3-1: NCAA Progress toward Degree Eligibility Requirements

Academic requirements	Before 2nd year of enrollment	Before 3rd year of enrollment	Before 4th year of enrollment	Before 5th year of enrollment
Regular academic term	6 semester/6 quarter hours of credit	6 semester/6 quarter hours of credit	6 semester/6 quarter hours of credit	6 semester/6 quarter hours of credit
Regular academic year	18 semester/27 quarter hours of credit	18 semester/27 quarter hours of credit	18 semester/27 quarter hours of credit	18 semester/27 quarter hours of credit
Degree credit	Credits are accepted toward any degree offered at the institution.	Credits used must go toward the designated degree.	Credits used must go toward the designated degree.	Credits used must go toward the designated degree.
Annual/percentage-of-degree	24 semester/36 quarter hours of credit	40% of the designated degree must be completed.	60% of the designated degree must be completed.	80% of the designated degree must be completed.
Grade point average	90% of the minimum GPA required for graduation (1.8 if a 2.0 is the minimum)	95% of the minimum GPA required for graduation (1.9 if a 2.0 is the minimum)	100% of the minimum GPA required for graduation (2.0 if 2.0 is the minimum)	100% of the minimum GPA required for graduation (2.0 if 2.0 is the minimum)

measure of college academic performance for all students: a cumulative GPA of 2.0. When universities require students to remain in "good academic standing," they often use as a floor the minimum acceptable GPA required for graduation within a particular major. The NCAA allows sophomore athletes to participate in their sport with a 1.8 cumulative GPA and junior athletes with a 1.9 GPA. While a 2.0 standard by itself would not abate the temptations for academic misconduct, it would be a step toward expecting college athletes to perform in a manner similar to the student body.

Graduation Rate Measures

An important difference distinguishes the Federal Graduation Rate (FGR), a measure that originated in the Higher Education Act (HEA) of 1972, from the Graduation Success Rate (GSR), which the NCAA developed. The FGR applies to all students, whereas the GSR applies only to athletes, allowing no comparison with nonathlete peers. An institution's FGR is tabulated as the number of fall semester, full-time freshmen students in an entering cohort who eventually graduate from their original institutions within six years, divided by the number of students in the original entering cohort. The HEA requires all institutions that participate in federal student aid programs to use the FGR to disclose graduation rates for the student body and to disaggregate the data by gender, race, and ethnicity.[8]

The HEA disclosure requirements also apply to schools that offer athletically related student aid in any form. Thus the FGR for athletes, whether used to examine the FGR for an entire athletic program or a particular team, includes only athletes who receive athletically related aid. All students in the athlete FGR cohorts must be first-time, full-time freshmen entering in a given fall term while receiving athletically related financial aid.[9] College athletes who do not receive such aid at entry or who transfer into the institution are excluded from the cohort. Whether for athletes or nonathletes, the retention of all students who were admitted and who persisted to graduation is the most important measure of institutional success.

Admittedly, the FGR is limited because it includes only students who enter college in the fall as first-time, full-time undergraduates. Still, it is the only nationally available graduation measure that permits a comparison between the academic success of recruited athletes who receive athletic financial aid and that of their nonathlete counterparts. The NCAA does not use this measure, though. Instead, it developed and uses its own manufactured Graduation Success Rate, which it insists measures academic success more effectively.

The GSR ranking cohort includes only those athletes who receive athletic financial aid. But it removes from the calculation for an institution any athlete who transferred but was academically eligible to continue athletics participation at the original institution if the athlete had remained there. It includes in the calculation for an institution any athlete who transferred to that institution and received athletics-related aid. As a result, nearly 40 percent more student-athletes figure into the GSR than are part of the federal calculation, and the GSR is roughly twenty percentage points higher at most institutions than the FGR. Of note, the GSR lacks a comparison measure for the nonathlete portion of the student body.

The GSR is more flawed than the FGR. The GSR adjusts institutional rates for transfers out even though institutions have no means of verifying that athletes who transfer out actually graduate. Because it adjusts for transfers out, the GSR also encourages institutions to push out athletes who might not graduate or who are easily replaced. To further complicate matters, the GSR is inflated compared to the FGR because athletes are required to be full-time students progressing toward a degree, making them more likely than nonathletes to graduate in six years. The FGR, on the other hand, has a lower rate because it includes many entering full-time students who must work and who often drop down to part-time status and take longer to graduate. The GSR also includes 11,000 Ivy League and military academy student-athletes who (1) do not receive athletics-related aid, (2) are not admitted as athletes, and (3) are considered properly as regular students in the FGR. By including the military academies and the Ivy League schools in the GSR cohort, the NCAA graduation rates appear significantly higher as a result of adding students who do not receive aid, in large part are highly successful in college, and should not be included in the student-athlete cohort. Finally, the NCAA's common use of the aggregated GSR rate to represent the graduation success of all athletes is misleading because female athletes graduate at significantly higher rates than male athletes participating in the revenue-producing football and men's basketball programs.

The GSR for Division I college athletes climbed to 86 percent for the entering class of 2008—two percentage points above the previous year and the highest rate ever. "Student-athletes continue to make important gains in the classroom, and the NCAA and its member schools are thrilled with their success," said NCAA president Mark Emmert. "We also are proud of the role academic reforms have played in helping students earn their degrees. We will continue to support rules and policies that encourage students to progress toward graduation."[10] This use of the GSR masks the significant academic underperformance of male athletes and is a deliberately misleading statistic when there is no general student body comparator.

Thus the NCAA has created a graduation measure that misleads the public into thinking that athletes graduate at higher rates than the general student body. Table 3-2 compares FGR and GSR data using the 2015 NCAA Division I Final Four Basketball Championship as an example.

Despite this masking of low graduation rates at individual institutions, the NCAA regularly trumpets the results of aggregated GSR data to argue that overall, college athletes perform better than nonathletes in the classroom. For the most recently available six-year cohort (2007), the NCAA reports a 66 percent FGR for athletes nationwide, compared to a 65 percent FGR for all students and an 82 percent NCAA GSR.[11] The reported FGR of 66 percent is an aggregate figure for all athletes; the rate is much lower for men's basketball (47 percent) and football (57 percent) athletes. Many athletes benefit from financial awards that the vast majority of nonathletes do not receive and, hence, drop out for financial reasons. By not reporting the progression of all athletes who leave the institution, and by allowing numerous other adjustments to mitigate low graduation rates (such as not counting against an institution's total an undergraduate who leaves to join a professional team), the GSR fails to measure graduation rates accurately.

Beyond overstating college athletes' graduation rates, the GSR blinds the higher education community to critical issues. For instance, Albert Bimper notes that of the seventy colleges and universities that competed in football bowl games after the 2012 season, more than half had a twenty-percentage-point gap between the graduation rates of black and white athletes. One quarter of all teams had a thirty-percentage-point gap.[12]

Equally distressing is that athletic programs with the most financial resources can manipulate the GSR to their advantage. For instance, an institution can push out an unwanted (from a talent perspective) and

TABLE 3-2: Federal Graduation Rates Compared to NCAA Graduation Success Rates—2015 NCAA Final Four Field

School	Federal graduation rates (FGR) (percent)			NCAA graduation success rates (GSR) (percent)	
	4-year student body	4-year men's basketball	Difference from student body	GSR	Difference from men's basketball, FGR
Xavier	78	67	−11	89	22
Wyoming	54	25	−29	64	39
Wofford	82	62	−20	91	29
Wisconsin	83	33	−50	40	7
Wichita State	43	25	−18	64	39
West Virginia	57	62	5	89	27
Virginia	93	64	−29	82	18
Villanova	90	69	−21	100	31
Virginia Commonwealth	54	62	8	87	25
Valparaiso	71	67	−4	90	23
Utah	58	42	−16	88	46
Cincinnati	60	8	−52	43	35
Northern Iowa	67	42	−25	60	18
North Carolina	89	54	−35	88	34
California, Los Angeles	90	43	−47	60	17
California, Irvine	85	30	−55	82	52
Alabama, Birmingham	47	50	3	53	3
Texas Southern	12	50	38	52	2
Texas	80	41	−39	100	59
St. John's	57	60	3	83	23
Stephen. F. Austin	44	56	12	53	−3
Southern Methodist	77	69	−8	75	6
South Dakota State	66	55	−11	63	8
Robert Morris	58	33	−25	54	21
Purdue	70	46	−24	73	27
Providence	86	47	−39	67	20
Oklahoma	66	60	6	77	17
Oregon	67	56	−11	73	17
Oklahoma State	69	9	−60	30	21
Ohio State	81	36	−45	53	17
Northwestern	94	75	−19	82	7
Notre Dame	95	85	−10	100	15
New Mexico	46	46	0	64	18
North Carolina State	73	54	−19	80	26
North Dakota State	53	92	39	85	7
Mississippi	58	36	−22	75	39

School	Federal graduation rates (FGR) (percent)			NCAA graduation success rates (GSR) (percent)	
	4-year student body	4-year men's basketball	Difference from student body	GSR	Difference from men's basketball, FGR
Michigan State	78	62	−16	73	11
Maryland	82	82	0	100	18
Louisiana State	67	36	−31	50	14
Louisville	51	38	−13	58	20
Lafayette	89	64	−25	90	26
Kentucky	59	40	−19	89	49
Kansas	62	43	−19	100	57
Iowa	70	64	−6	100	36
Indiana	74	8	−66	42	34
Iowa State	69	13	−56	64	51
Hampton	58	54	−4	67	13
Gonzaga	82	73	−9	91	18
Georgia State	50	70	20	77	7
Georgia	83	33	−50	71	38
Georgetown	93	38	−55	70	32
Eastern Washington	46	13	−33	72	59
Duke	94	67	−27	100	33
Dayton	76	62	−14	100	38
Davidson	92	85	−7	100	15
Coastal Carolina	46	50	4	80	30
Butler	74	75	1	100	25
Buffalo	69	64	−5	64	0
Belmont	68	100	32	100	0
Baylor	73	73	0	92	19
Arkansas	59	25	−34	55	30
Arizona	61	50	−11	82	32
Albany	65	54	−11	80	26
Avg. difference					24
Harvard[b]	97				

Source: "NCAA 2013–2014 Graduation Success Rates and Federal Graduation Rates" (http://web1.ncaa.org/GSRSearch/exec/homePage).

a. Data based on the most recent six-year 2007 cohort; the four-year student body and men's basketball percentages represent an average of the last four years.
b. Does not award athletic scholarships.

academically weak basketball or football athlete by combining a threat with an incentive. The institution informs the player that it will not renew his or her financial aid, but it dangles the offer of a full transfer release without athletic participation restrictions or penalties to enable the athlete to transfer to another institution if the athlete attends summer school and raises a deficient GPA enough that the current institution will not suffer a GSR (or APR) loss. This ploy is most prevalent in football and men's basketball, sports in which recruiting underprepared athletes is common because of the financial payoff to the school from winning. Even without such summer school and transfer shenanigans, richer athletic programs can afford a cadre of academic support staff devoted to keeping athletes eligible to play.

Thus, it is clear that not only should the NCAA discard the GSR as a metric based on its poor statistical reliability, the NCAA should follow its own statement of sound academic principles by using *"consistent standards adopted by the institution"* for the student body in general. The FGR is the only standard that meets this criterion. Higher education should commit to measuring the academic success of athletes and nonathletes by means of the same instrument. The GSR has no comparable nonathlete measure; therefore, it prohibits a comparison to college athlete peers.

Academic Progress Rate

Established in 2003 and enforced beginning in 2005, the APR is a direct measure of retention and an indirect measure of scholarship athletes' academic eligibility, including both minimum GPA and satisfactory progress toward a degree. It is also a real-time predictor of GSR, the NCAA's inflated graduation metric. According to the NCAA, "Each student-athlete receiving athletically related financial aid earns one retention point for staying in school and one eligibility point for being academically eligible. A team's total points are divided by points possible and then multiplied by one thousand to equal the team's Academic Progress Rate score."[13] Teams failing to achieve the minimum APR requirement, which was increased from an initial standard of 900 to 930 in 2014–15, are declared ineligible for postseason championship play,[14] and a three-level penalty system corresponding to each consecutive year in which the benchmark is unmet is imposed:

Level One: The team is limited to sixteen hours of practice a week over five days, with the lost four hours to be replaced by academic activities, representing a reduction of four hours and one day per week of practice time.

Level Two: Regular season reductions in the number of competitions are imposed, added to the first-level penalties.

Level Three: Penalty options are applied as determined by the NCAA Committee on Academic Performance. Options include coaching suspensions, financial aid reductions, and restricted NCAA membership.

The APR suffers from a similar defect as the GSR in that athletic programs with significant financial resources are better able than less affluent institutions to keep athletes eligible by manipulating the existing rules. Larger, wealthier institutions also provide additional course offerings, which may allow an easier path to a degree at such institutions. For large-roster teams such as are found in football, affluent institutions can increase their APR scores by recruiting some academically gifted players to compensate for those who are not. The NCAA has received heavy criticism about the lack of affluent, high-profile Football Bowl Subdivision (FBS) teams among those penalized for failing to meet the APR benchmark. Besides directing athletes to easy courses and majors and providing excessive tutoring help, these institutions manipulate the APR by means of the following:

- Liberal use of summer school financial aid to boost athlete GPAs and ensure that transfers leave with GPAs that do not cause APR point losses is commonplace among the highly resourced FBS institutions, but less of an option for the Historically Black Colleges and Universities (HBCUs) and smaller Football Championship Subdivision and Division I nonfootball institutions.

- Athletes who fail to meet initial eligibility standards and can demonstrate a learning disability will often be exempt from meeting standard initial eligibility requirements through an initial eligibility waiver. The NCAA may also waive the requirement to maintain a "full-time" academic load of twelve credit hours. A successfully written progress-toward-degree waiver can often allow athletes with certified learning disabilities who fail to meet NCAA standards to be granted continuing eligibility by passing enough degree-applicable credit hours. It takes highly skilled staff to maximize these opportunities. As Gerald S. Gurney and Richard M. Southall write:

> Navigating this educational landscape is a bureaucratic challenge for many NCAA institutions. However, the disparity between compliance staffing at FBS schools and "limited-resource" HBCU institutions is enormous. For example, the University of Oklahoma staff consists of 11 professionals, including several lawyers. The University of Southern California is similarly staffed with 11 compliance officers. The University of Alabama maintains a staff of eight. The University of Texas' Risk Management and Compliance Services staff has seven full-time professionals. Conversely, limited-resource universities must make due with almost nonexistent staffs. For example: Arkansas–Pine Bluff has a total of two compliance staff, Hampton University has a single compliance staff "coordinator" and a total of three full-time academic support staff and Mississippi Valley State University has only one compliance officer.
>
> As a result of their personnel largess, "un-limited-resource" institutions have staff whose primary duties involve writing admissions waivers and exceptions, as well as monitoring athletes' satisfactory progress toward degree. At one Big Twelve institution, a typical year's waiver writing assignments for a compliance attorney included one initial eligibility waiver and up to seven reduced-hour or other progress-toward-degree waivers and exceptions. Having someone specifically assigned to these tasks is necessary in order to make certain the institution does not suffer embarrassing penalties or fail to compete in postseason competition. Overworked and understaffed, HBCU athletic departments simply lack the human resources to address these issues. Being overwhelmed by the minutia of NCAA eligibility paperwork, they find it impossible to even address waivers.[15]

• Two common exceptions for satisfactory progress primarily used to manipulate APR scores are the medical exception and the missed term exception. Gurney and Southall:

> Athletes or members of their families who become ill with incapacitating injuries or illnesses may also escape APR eligibility penalties through being granted an exception. Athletes who experience de-

pression or suffer other mental illness may avoid progress-toward-degree consequences by withdrawing from classes or dropping down to a part-time academic load. Alcoholism, depression or substance abuse, for example, may be considered an incapacitating illness. The missed term exception permits an athlete to miss one or more semesters one time during their career if they leave eligible. The missed term exception may be used even if the athlete's absence is due to a suspension for academic dishonesty if they were eligible prior to the absence.[16]

Again, processing such appeals takes considerable staff time.

• Affluent schools also manipulate APR scores by providing financial aid to nongraduates who have exhausted their athletics eligibility so that they can return to the institution and earn their degrees. Such degree-completion programs may not be feasible for underfunded athletic programs. An example of the benefits of institutional affluence is the University of California at Berkeley, which recently implemented a degree-completion program for athletes who had exhausted their eligibility without obtaining a degree.[17] For many institutions, degree-completion programs are not economically feasible because of the escalating costs associated with running athletics departments.

The continued use of the APR and GSR metrics is a "bait and switch" of the worse kind. Arguments that the GSR takes into consideration athletes leaving in good academic standing and athletes who transfer into an institution, and that it encompasses a larger percentage of athletes (because of the inclusion of the inclusion of transfers, Ivy League, and U.S. military academy athletes), cannot and should not hold any weight because comparisons to the general student body are impossible.

As a result, since the introduction of the GSR, NCAA athletes' reported graduation success has dramatically increased. What has been lost amid the NCAA's public relations campaign is the continued existence of large (30–40 percent) negative graduation gaps between NCAA Division I football and men's basketball players and the general student population. In some cases teams report graduation rates of zero. Simply put, the athletes on whose skill the entire commercial enterprise depends, college football and men's basketball players, are dramatically less likely than other students to obtain a degree. This is to say nothing about the quality of the education to which they have access.

By repeatedly and simply asserting the GSR is a better measure than the FGR because it "more accurately assesses the academic success" of college athletes and by steadfastly referring to GSR rates, NCAA members have convinced the media to use, almost exclusively, the new, more favorable metric. Intentionally or not, the NCAA's APR and GSR metrics confuse the media, fans, and the general public. Using the GSR and APR to tout graduation success and increased academic standards is undoubtedly savvy marketing and public relations, but these metrics are fundamentally nothing more than measures of how successful athletics departments are at keeping athletes eligible, and they have increasingly fostered acts of academic dishonesty and devalued higher education in the frantic search for eligibility and retention points.[18] Another important annual graduation rate, offered by the College Sports Research Institute (CSRI), is the Adjusted Graduation Gap (AGG). The AGG statistically estimates and adjusts institutional graduation rates through regression analysis for students who drop down to part-time status. The adjustments then become the basis for analysis and have shown that football and men's basketball graduation rates are actually significantly lower than one might believe from the NCAA reported rates.[19] In its 2016 report, CSRI found the adjusted gap for part-time bias between the FGR and the NCAA's reported GSR graduation rates for Division I men's basketball players in major conferences to be significantly larger (by 36.4 percentage points) and getting worse. Their adjusted AGG graduation rate has also demonstrated a steady downward trend since the initial 2011 report, with results that contrast sharply with the NCAA's contention that graduation rates are improving.[20]

Even when the FGR is used, several factors still distort an accurate comparison between athletes and nonathletes. For example, the FGR makes no adjustments for members of the general student body who experience family issues, medical issues, and learning disabilities. Athletes have a huge retention advantage compared to the general student body because they are required to be full-time students and they receive financial aid, so they do not have to work. Furthermore, athletes benefit from sophisticated academic support programs. The FGR does not reflect such general student advantages; indeed, it is artificially low as a comparable standard because many initially full-time students drop down to part-time and are unable to graduate in six years but must still be counted. Some commentators argue that the FGR should be adjusted if the athlete returns to school after six years and graduates. But many nonathlete students do the same, yet the FGR is not adjusted. The FGR is useful because institutions cannot easily tamper with it; that is precisely why the NCAA should adopt it. It will thwart athletic department gamesmanship. Last, because the APR is pegged to retention and current eligibility to compete, any penalty imposed on a current team (such as banning the team from postseason play) for failures of previous members of the team penalizes students who are not responsible for the benchmark failure. The institution, not the athletes, should suffer the penalty.

Thus the APR, along with the GSR, should be discarded because its original purpose was to be a real-time predictor of GSR, which is a flawed metric. Besides being easily manipulated by affluent institutions, the APR, in potentially eliminating teams from postseason play, unfairly penalizes less affluent institutions and current athletes who are not responsible for their institutions' failure to recruit academically prepared athletes. It would be a step in the right direction if the NCAA enforced a uniform 2.0 cumulative GPA standard for continuing athletic eligibility. The FGR can hold institutions and coaches accountable for fulfilling the promise of an education to the athletes they recruit. While not a contemporaneous metric in that the rates represent six-year graduation rates, use of the FGR to punish institutions and coaches that habitually fail to graduate their athletes would be a more appropriate and meaningful use of a graduation metric.

Key to having a desired effect on graduation is to replace the current one-year athletic scholarship agreement and "option" of guaranteeing athletic scholarships for five years with a "requirement" that athletic scholarships be guaranteed for four or five years depending on (1) the length of the college athlete's degree program and (2) continuing progress being made toward this degree consistent with a student passing a full-time course load each semester. (With new legislation in 2015, some schools in the FBS have already begun to grant four-year scholarships.) Institutions must be encouraged to recruit athletes who are capable of graduating and to invest in athletes' academic success for the duration of their college careers.

Coaches' Academic Progress Rate

In 2010 the NCAA established the Coaches' Academic Progress Rate, a database of APRs that are assigned to head coaches. Created by the

Committee on Academic Performance at the request of the Division I Board of Directors, the database aims "to create more transparency in the Academic Performance Program and strengthen the accountability of coaches for the academic performance of their student-athletes."[21] The Head Coach APR Portfolio includes the single-year team APR for a head coach at each institution where he or she has held that post, along with the average single-year APR in the coach's specific sport for comparison purposes. Interim head coaches are not included in the database. The current NCAA coaches' metric is fundamentally flawed because it is pegged to the NCAA APR. The NCAA should abandon the Coaches' APR as currently constructed and replace it with a new metric that simply shows the actual percentage of athletes recruited by an individual coach who have graduated within six years of initial enrollment.

The Need for Transparency in Academic Metrics

Academic integrity in intercollegiate athletics requires a system of checks and balances and transparent academic metrics. These safeguards should ensure that learning occurs, not just that athletic eligibility is maintained. The Federal Education Rights Protection Act (FERPA) is a privacy protection act. Institutions often use FERPA to hide evidence of academic corruption and exploitation of football and men's basketball athletes from public scrutiny while releasing only good news. They will release information about the excellent student but will not discuss the number of athletes clustered in an eligibility-friendly major. FERPA has also enabled institutions to deny knowledge of academic misconduct committed by athletics department staff, coaches, and even faculty members. The public cannot evaluate claims of academic improvement without knowing the classes players take, the names of the instructors, and the overall course and team GPAs. True academic reform cannot occur without public accountability.[22]

There is no reason why aggregate, anonymous data describing athletes' educational records cannot be released. Because disclosure would not reveal athletes' names, no harm would occur to any individual student, nor would anyone's privacy be invaded. Such use would be in keeping with the letter and the spirit of FERPA. Yet the aggregated use of individual data would expose institutional misbehavior by identifying athletes' course selections, their choices of professors and academic majors, their advisers, and the team GPAs. Without identifying any student by name, this information would expose academic clustering, suspect courses, and issues like those that occurred at Auburn and the University of North Carolina.

Majoring in Football and Basketball

Academic integrity issues are ensnarled in the systemic impingement of athletics-related activities on Division I college athletes' academic time commitments and their ability to pursue a quality education. The NCAA's collegiate model is justifiable as long as athletes, especially those in the sports of football and basketball, receive an educational opportunity that permits quality academic engagement on campus toward the end of achieving a baccalaureate degree as a fair and meaningful exchange for their efforts on the fields and courts.

In a 2008 *USA Today* study of college athlete majors and the institutional practice of "major clustering," Steven Cline, a defensive lineman football player from Kansas State University, claimed he followed the advice of his academic counselor to settle for a less demanding sociology major to allow more time to concentrate on the demands of his sport rather than on his ambition to become a veterinarian. He stated, "The whole time I was at Kansas State I felt stuck—stuck in football, stuck in my major. Now I look back and say, 'Well, what did I really go to college for? Crap classes you won't use the rest of your life?' . . . I was majoring in football." Although Cline managed to graduate, at the time of the interview he held a manual labor position while attempting to get back to college to complete pre–veterinary medicine requirements.[23]

Although some may argue the fact that Mr. Cline and scores of others do not pursue their desired majors is a matter of personal choice and personal responsibility, college athletes are faced with the reality of overbearing athletic schedules, the prospect of serious injury, travel that frequently removes them from regular class attendance, and a year-round workout schedule that leaves them physically exhausted. The NCAA's own study acknowledges an average workload of 43.3 hours per week in-season in the sport of Division 1 football, demonstrating the time commitment college athletes are expected to make to maintain their sport participation and, most importantly, their athletic scholarships.[24] A 2015 Pac-12 Conference study in all men's and women's sports on athlete time commitments found that their athletes averaged fifty hours per week on athletics-related activities. Other key findings were that the lack of free time and uncertainty about the ability to succeed academically were the two biggest concerns of college athletes.[25] Evidence presented at a National Labor Relations Board (NLRB) hearing between Northwestern University and its football players requesting the right to unionize found similar time demands. The NLRB's regional director's report found that Northwestern football players spent fifty to sixty hours a week on football-related activities.[26] Long, overscheduled days paired with the NCAA's academic standards, which limit a student's ability to select or choose majors, are only a few of the many obstacles college athletes must overcome when attempting to take advantage of the NCAA's promise for a meaningful education.[27]

The Realities of Illiteracy

Academic preparation historically has not been an important consideration when recruiting and admitting elite athletes to a university. In the sport of basketball, Creighton University student Kevin Ross claimed he was unable to read when he graduated from high school and that his college coaches, those responsible for heavily recruiting Mr. Ross, knew of his deficiency. Nonetheless, they aggressively lobbied for this student, with an ACT score of 9 out of 36, to be admitted to the university. Kevin's ACT score was fourteen points below the average Creighton student. He was admitted to the university through the sidestepping process of special admissions. It is difficult to imagine being in a collegiate academic environment while illiterate. Kevin Ross's educational experience unfolded like that of so many in his position. He was kept eligible to participate for more than three years through a series of clever academic advisement and friendly professors until his athletic eligibility expired. Still functionally illiterate, in 1982 Kevin dropped out of college to return to elementary school to learn to read. Amid public outrage, Creighton paid for him to attend Westside Preparatory School to acquire basic learning skills. In 1989 Kevin Ross sued Creighton University for breach of contract, emotional distress, and educational malpractice. Eventually he settled out of court.[28]

Similarly, a popular professional football player in the 1980s, Dexter Manley, admitted in court that he was functionally illiterate after attending Oklahoma State University and being kept academically eligible for four years. Having a diagnosed learning disability placed him in special education classes, and he grew up without being taught basic literacy skills. As happens with many athletes, his teachers passed him through primary and secondary schools. Dexter would routinely sit in the front row and attend classes. His personal charm would be sufficient for his instructors to issue passing grades, a pattern that extended through college.[29]

These stories are neither those of disgruntled former athletes nor those of a few outliers. These examples are increasingly commonplace at selective universities with hopes of financial gain from successful athletic teams. While the NCAA may argue that the percentage of students who fit these descriptions is very small, at universities with top athletic programs, the concentration of these underprepared and unprepared students in the revenue-producing sports of football and men's basketball is unequivocally high.[30] College presidents are typically made aware of highly marginal athletes and concede admission in response to the heavy lobbying of his or her celebrity coaches. A denial of admission for a potential star is regarded as a failure to support the coach.

A striking example of presidential timidity occurred in a 2014 moment of unusual candor. Mark Schlissel, president of the University of Michigan, speaking before a faculty senate governance group, said, "We admit students who aren't as qualified, and it's probably the kids that we admit that can't honestly, even with lots of help, do the amount of work and the quality of work it takes to make progression from year to year." He also noted an individual's academic deficiencies were often overlooked to fill competitive rosters.[31] Two days later, President Schlissel crafted a hastily worded apology to the football coach for his comments on the academic shortcomings of football players.[32]

The practice of admitting underprepared college athletes into selective institutions, only to retain them for exploitation of their talent, has led some scholars to characterize this arrangement as a shameful type of plantation system.[33] Despite the NCAA's own proclamations of significant academic reform and success in graduation rates, well-publicized allegations of academically unprepared football and men's basketball athletes admitted to universities without the skills to be successful in the classroom persist. In a 2012 *Chronicle of Higher Education* story, "The Education of Dasmine Cathey," a University of Memphis football player maintained his eligibility for participation in college without being able to read. He ultimately graduated, despite having failed twelve classes.[34] Cathey and other highly marginal elite athletes are expected to compete in college classrooms despite being hopelessly outmatched by the academic potential of their classmates. Concurrently, they navigate the obstacles set in place by the very nature of their sport participation through a cadre of academic support personnel. In an attempt to help them, these students are heavily managed by a growing athletics department academic support network of advisers, tutors, and learning specialists. College athletes are frequently limited in their selection of courses, thus of academic major, and are kept eligible seemingly at all costs. The draw of big-money potential and the lure of athletic glory places tremendous pressure on students, athletic staff, and faculty, creating an academic environment that fosters "gray area" decisionmaking, with frequent exceptions to rules, one-time-only deals, and expectations of looking the other way. This culture is evidenced by the epidemic of cheating and academic fraud scandals that has emerged as a predictable by-product of these eligibility expectations.[35]

"I Was an Athlete Masquerading as a Student"

The well-publicized appeal of the O'Bannon case, demanding that athletes be allowed financial gain for the corporate use of their names, images, and likenesses, and several new major lawsuits are steadily making their way through state and federal court systems.[36] The lead plaintiff Ed O'Bannon's gripping opening testimony in his federal class-action lawsuit described a disconnected relationship between the NCAA's professed philosophy of the amateur and the college athletes' reality. "I was an athlete masquerading as a student. I did basically the minimum to make sure I kept my eligibility academically so I could continue to play."[37]

Finding itself more frequently under attack, the NCAA went into legal defense mode. Its attorneys' expenses increased by 37 percent in 2013–14 from the previous year. In response to the negative attention brought on by these legal challenges, the NCAA has escalated its lobbying of Congress, attempting to garner governmental protection for its newly exposed vulnerabilities. The NCAA's desire for congressional support is evidenced by the dramatic increase in lobbying expense to $580,000 in 2014—more than what it had spent in the previous three years in total.[38] Maintaining the ideal that participants on NCAA athletic teams are allowed a realistic opportunity to engage in a serious course of study, the idea of providing remuneration to these students for athletic purposes is consistently rejected by the organization. Vehemently against making payments to athletes, the NCAA adamantly insists that college athletes are students first, and NCAA president Mark Emmert characterizes the college experience as a fair exchange for the receipt of a "world-class education." Emmert states, "As long as I'm president of the NCAA, we will not pay student-athletes to play sports. Compensation for students is just something I'm adamantly opposed to."[39] Meanwhile, Emmert pulls down a salary of $1.8 million for defending "amateurism."

Academic Fraud

There cannot be a more serious allegation for an institution of higher education than "academic fraud." Yet, both the NCAA and the institution must be held accountable for its occurrence in the case of college athletics.

The NCAA's Role in Protecting College Athletes from Academic Misconduct

Spurred by the recent cases at the University of North Carolina and Syracuse University, among others, there is a current debate concerning the responsibility of the NCAA to afford college athletes protections against academic fraud and misconduct. The NCAA reported that it had twenty academic misconduct cases under investigation in 2015, compared to just one in 2014.[40] Further, a group of twenty college presidents led by Ohio University president Rod McDavis, the chairman of the NCAA's Committee on Academics, submitted a proposal in June 2015 "to better define when the NCAA should investigate cases of academic cheating by student-athletes."[41] Kansas State University president Kirk Schulz defended the institution's role in policing academics and said there was no need for NCAA involvement.[42]

Among the many legal challenges facing the NCAA is the case of McCants v. National Collegiate Athletic Association, a federal class-action lawsuit brought by former University of North Carolina athletes. The basis of the lawsuit was a systematic widespread cheating scandal lasting more than two decades at UNC that was exposed by former UNC learning specialist Mary Willingham in national and local media. A book co-authored by Willingham and UNC history professor Jay Smith exposed the educational failings of big-time college sports.[43] The plaintiffs, former members of the football and women's basketball teams, are alleging that the NCAA and UNC failed to "safeguard and provide a meaningful education to scholarship student-athletes."[44]

In response to this accusation, the NCAA asserts that, under the law, the organization has no liability for academic fraud perpetrated by its members or for athletes' failures to take advantage of meaningful educational opportunities. This assertion was issued even though an entire chapter on NCAA rules exists in the NCAA's *Division I Manual* not as mere suggestions but as enforceable academic eligibility standards and regulations, along with a long history of past enforced violations of academic fraud.[45] The NCAA's dedication to the academic achievement of its revenue-producing athletes seems to be more an apparition than a reality. As reported earlier, a basic principle of the NCAA as stated in Regulation 2.5 is: "Intercollegiate athletics programs shall be maintained as a vital component of the educational program, and student-athletes shall be an integral part of the student body. The admission, academic standing and academic progress of student-athletes shall be consistent with the policies and standards adopted by the institution for the student body in general."[46] Further, Bylaw 2.8.1 specifies the responsibility of the institution with the following:

> Each institution shall comply with all applicable rules and regulations of the Association in the conduct of its intercollegiate athletics programs. It shall monitor its programs to assure compliance and to identify and report to the Association instances in which compliance has not been achieved. In any such instance, the institution shall cooperate fully with the Association and shall take appropriate corrective actions. Members of an institution's staff, student-athletes, and other individuals and groups representing the institution's athletics interests shall comply with the applicable Association rules, and the member institution shall be responsible for such compliance.[47]

In addition, Bylaw 14 specifies rules on academic eligibility and frames them in the context of institutional responsibility to comply with such rules.[48] Bylaw 19 defines the NCAA enforcement responsibilities.[49] Insofar as the mission of the NCAA Infractions Program in Bylaw 19.01.1 is "to uphold integrity and fair play among the NCAA membership, and to prescribe appropriate and fair penalties if violations occur," it is peculiar that the NCAA asserts that it has no direct responsibility for ensuring academic integrity.

The NCAA's central role in maintaining academic quality and standards for college athletes is derived from its responsibility to establish initial and continuing eligibility rules for individual athlete sports participation and academic progress standards that affect the access of teams to postseason championship play. These academic performance-related rules create academic integrity pressures on the institution and set quality standards for the educational experience of college athletes that are not applied to general students. Once these rules are adopted, the NCAA is obligated to enforce them to ensure that member institutions do not academically exploit college athletes, just as they are required to enforce all other NCAA rules. The NCAA is composed of the institutions it regulates, and the NCAA and its member institutions share this responsibility.

Why the Institution Alone Cannot Be Held Accountable

There are six good reasons why the shared responsibility system (institutional faculty and nonfaculty employees, the institution as represented by its leadership, the national governance association, and the accreditation agency) should be held accountable rather than any individual faculty member delivering course content or the institution alone:

1. *Conflict of interest in protecting the institution's brand.* First and foremost, it is important to recognize that the institution has competing responsibilities that may interfere with its primary function of delivering an education to students that is above reproach with regard to academic integrity. Institutional admissions standards are routinely waived for academically underprepared athletes whose performances can deliver millions in gate and television revenues. As protector of the institutional brand, administrative leaders have commonly been

complicit in hiding professor misconduct, from inappropriate relationships with students to sexual assault and criminal behavior, fearful
that public exposure would damage student recruitment and alumni
donations. Similarly, administrative leaders may look the other way and
refrain from instituting oversight systems that could detect changing
grades, "ghost courses," awarding unearned grades, and the dispropor-
tional enrollment of athletes in independent studies, online courses, or
less demanding courses and majors.

2. *Involvement of athletics in academic support and advising.* Commonly,
many institutions allow the athletics department to conduct academic
support programs or advising for athletes, again looking the other way
with respect to practices that advance the athletic program's self-interest
in eligibility rather than the academic well-being of athletes. Administrative leaders may also fail to discipline or may delay disciplinary
proceedings for athlete misconduct when such discipline involves the
probability of ineligibility to play, dismissal from the institution, or
media embarrassment. Even when institutions have appointed faculty
members to participate in oversight responsibilities, the selection of
such faculty is often a presidential or institutional administrative appointment rather than that of the faculty senate, with such appointments resulting in the selection of faculty "friendly" or acceptable to
the athletics department. Thus there is a need for internal and external watchdog mechanisms that are designed to protect academic
integrity.

3. *Lack of depth in institutional evaluation of teaching.* The traditional
focus of the institution on the periodic evaluation of teaching pedagogy and the competence of individual faculty members does not typically reveal differences in the faculty member's treatment of college
athletes versus nonathlete students. A competent teacher of content
can engage in misconduct with regard to expecting less from or giving
higher grades to athletes. Revealing such misconduct does not require
"policing the classroom" or interference with the academic freedom of
professors. However, it does require institutional oversight committees, the national governance organization and the regional accreditation agency to exercise regularized auditing functions and to examine
comparative athlete versus nonathlete data over time for indicators of
differences in treatment.

4. *Absence of whistleblower protection and independent investigations.* Classes without academic rigor, with few if any assignments, and with no testing to assess learning are the most vivid examples of academic fraud. Such undemanding independent study arrangements are sought after by athletics academic advisers seeking less rigorous classes. These cases may be uncovered by "whistleblower" reports from individual students or employees. However, they are unlikely to be reported because sufficient protections do not exist for whistleblowers. When fraud is detected, the credibility of the whistleblower is attacked, a limited number of lower-level offending faculty or other employees are found guilty and alleged to be outliers and administrators, head coaches or other higher-paid employees are protected. Blame must be placed on the institution for not having a whistleblower protection policy and on national governance organizations and regional accreditation agencies for not requiring such policies. Further, the governance agencies must accept their responsibilities to fully investigate allegations and reports, as opposed to the institution that has a conflict of interest.

5. *Lack of oversight of the athlete academic advising process.* The most common form of academic exploitation is the practice of advising and course registration that direct athletes to enroll in courses or majors that historically have not been as challenging as other courses and majors. Many institutions also allow the athletics department to run its own orientation program for athletes, rather than requiring athletes to attend orientation programs conducted for new students. Academic advisers paid for by the athletics department or institutional academic advisers pressured by the athletic department often use knowledge of less strenuous courses and majors to give college athletes a better statistical chance to meet athletic eligibility standards, without regard to the college athlete exercising freedom of choice. This practice may occur with no misconduct by faculty teaching these courses or the inappropriate construction of special majors of study. Again, discovery of such practices requires examination of comparative athlete versus nonathlete data over time. Prevention of such practices requires close supervision of the athlete academic advising process.

6. *NCAA conflict of interest in investigating its own members.* The NCAA is not an independent nonprofit organization run by an independent board of directors. The NCAA is run by its member institutions and

staff members beholden to the wishes of those members. Institutional representatives are involved in judging peer institutions and may choose to penalize competitors to gain advantage on the playing field for themselves, or may "go easy," wishing for the same treatment if they are caught in similar circumstances. Institutional members may act as a collective to protect their public reputations or to advance revenue and winning self-interests by engaging in the following:

- Keeping initial and progress-toward-degree eligibility standards low to allow underperforming athletes to continue to participate;

- Hiding the low academic graduation rates and academic performance of college football and men's basketball players by displaying only the aggregated data for the entire athlete population or creating new, noncomparable standards like the NCAA's GSR to suggest that athletes perform better in the classroom than nonathletes, a posture that protects both the brand of the institutions themselves and the NCAA;

- Failing to require academic audits or oversight at the institutional level conducted by tenured faculty independent of the athletics department or higher administration;

- Failing to give tenured faculty and faculty senates (the higher education entity ultimately responsible for maintaining academic integrity) control over rules related to academic matters in order to avoid conflict with athletics departments' interests;

- Failing to appoint independent investigators or adjudicators to enforce academic or other alleged violations of rules and regulations in order to prevent the conflict of interest present when representatives from competing institutions are involved in enforcement proceedings; and

- Failing to investigate reports of academic transgressions by hiding behind an ill-disguised excuse of protection of the academic freedom of professors in the classroom and the supposed autonomy of institutions to police themselves on academic matters.

- Failing to provide adequate oversight over academic misconduct in athletics. The regional accreditation process with its three- to ten-year peer review system is inadequate alone to effectively police academic misconduct in athletics. Oversight systems must be annual and ongoing. Further, the standards established by regional accreditation agencies to review the operation of athletic programs need to be strengthened.

In summary, institutions facing the political reality that demands winning teams and maximization of revenue generation cannot be expected to police or govern themselves. In all cases of NCAA rules violations, institutions are required first to investigate themselves and impose their own sanctions and solutions before being reviewed or investigated by the NCAA. Suggesting that the NCAA has no role in enforcing academic or other rules that improperly keep athletes eligible to compete is irrational. Institutional faculty senates, expert external agencies such as the national athletic governance association, and the higher education regional accreditation agency must all share responsibility for acting as the checks-and-balances system that protects athletes from academic exploitation.

With regard to protecting college athletes from academic fraud or misconduct related to maintaining a college student's eligibility to compete for athletics, there are multiple individual (faculty, tutors, advisors, and administrators), institutional, and governance organization responsibilities that together produce a climate of academic integrity in the operation of intercollegiate athletic programs. It is this checks-and-balance system that is responsible for protecting the student from academic exploitation.

Faculty members teaching classes are responsible for actually conducting the class, transmitting appropriate educational content and experiences and ensuring regular class meetings, fairly grading assignments, and providing appropriate testing to produce a quality educational experience for all students. Essential is treating athletes like any other student. Faculty, professionals, and peer advisers are responsible for guiding college athletes in the selection of courses and majors congruent with their individual interests and abilities as opposed to ensuring convenience in athletic participation. The registrar or other comparably titled (chief certifying officer) administrator and the NCAA faculty athletics representative are responsible for certifying that continuing NCAA academic eligibility rules are met. Academic support personnel such as tutors or learning specialists are responsible for providing learning assistance but not for writing papers or preparing other work that is the responsibility of the student.

Faculty are responsible for making efforts to detect and enforce rules that prohibit student cheating or plagiarism. Coaches should not make extraordinary demands on the time of athletes that interfere with their academic responsibilities.

Similarly, the institution has responsibilities, such as periodically evaluating the performance of faculty members as teachers delivering the promised educational product to students and educating all college athletes and employees about their respective responsibilities related to academic fraud and misconduct and applicable NCAA academic rules. Institutions should have policies that afford whistleblower protection to college athletes and employees who become aware of possible academic integrity violations and enhance the ability of athletes to complete their academic responsibilities, such as restricting the maximum numbers of classes that may be missed for athletics participation and prohibiting athletic competition during the final examinations period. Institutional decisions such as determination of conference affiliations have significant implications with regard to reasonable team travel schedules. The institution should provide sufficient release time to its respective NCAA faculty athletic representatives and faculty athletics committees so that they exercise their oversight and certification responsibilities. In addition, the institution is accountable for determining whether a transcript is valid for purposes of applying appropriate NCAA legislation to the eligibility of a student-athlete when the institution receives notification, or otherwise has cause to believe, that a student-athlete's high school, preparatory school, or two-year college transcript is not valid.

The national athletic governance organization is responsible for administering the NCAA Eligibility Center for certifying that initial NCAA academic eligibility rules are met. In addition, fulfilling its national governance responsibilities, the NCAA promulgates academic eligibility and rules related to time spent on athletics-related activities (by setting limitations on the number of scheduled contests, the length of the season, and the like), should promulgate rules (but does not) that require auditing and transparency of the data that make it possible to discover institutionalized academic fraud or misconduct, should require institutions to afford whistleblower protection to college athletes and institutional employees, and should prohibit conflict of interest (involving the athletics department) in academic affairs (academic support programs, academic advising, determination of eligibility, and so forth). The NCAA does have rules that require external third-party review of rules compliance practices but has reneged on its responsibility to require peer and third-party review of athletic programs (certification programs, annual academic audits, and so forth). Unarguably, its most important responsibility is the execution of an enforcement process that promptly investigates and adjudicates credible reports of academic impropriety, thereby protecting the academic integrity of institutional members. Last, higher education regional accreditation agencies are responsible for conducting a regular comprehensive review of the operation of the athletic program as part of the Council of Higher Education accreditation process.

Without a recognition of shared responsibility, there will be no effective transformation of the academic culture surrounding athletics. Without a change in the culture, academic integrity will continue to be lacking.

FOUR

Governance

College presidents have always had oversight and potential control over athletics. They have chosen repeatedly to take a back seat and allow athletics directors and conference commissioners run the show. Meanwhile, the meteoric growth of big time college sports has led the NCAA and its leadership to behave like a protective trade association for coaches and athletics personnel rather than advocates for college athletes and students.

The Failure of College Presidents

In a prophetic analysis of the conflict posed to college presidents between the academic and commercial aims of the university, William T. Foster, president of Reed College, wrote in 1915:

> If intercollegiate athletics can then be conducted as incidental and contributory to the main purposes of athletics, well and good. But first of all the question must be decisively settled, which aims are to dominate— those of business or those of education. And it will be difficult for a college already in the clutches of commercialism to retain the system and at the same time cultivate a spirit antagonistic to it.[1]

For more than a century, college presidents have struggled over the control and restraint of the colossal conflict of interest between expansive commercialization and the core academic goals of higher education. This chapter examines several notions of presidential control of intercollegiate athletics through the NCAA's current governance model. Is it feasible for this model to coexist with good stewardship of higher education? Can college presidents control athletics on their own campuses, within their conferences, or nationally? Should the media, powerful athletic conferences, and athletics directors continue to shape the future of intercollegiate athletics in higher education? Is the momentum of college spectator sports irrepressible? Who should control college sports?

Chasing Flutie: An Expensive Gamble

College leaders maintain big-time revenue-generating sports as a means to market the university and to improve the general quality of campus life. An often cited example of the purported contributions of athletics to the success of the institution is the "Flutie effect," the miraculous Hail Mary pass by Boston College quarterback Doug Flutie to Gerard Phelan in the final seconds of the 1984 Cotton Bowl against the University of Miami. In the legend of the Flutie effect (the empirical reality of this effect is that the increase in applications merely continued a preexisting trend at Boston College), the publicity of this incredible feat brought an increase in applications to Boston College, enabling an increase in selectivity of students and tuition income. Presidents are hungry for such an example of transforming a regional university to national prominence through athletics on their campuses. Unfortunately, such hunger is based on a need to justify the compromises and exceptions often made to admit and maintain the eligibility of academically underprepared athletes. When these integrity gambles pay off, presidents are quick to grasp the lifeline, as was the case when Ohio State University won the 2014 football national championship. The university boasted of sizable increases in traditional academic quality. Measures of ACT scores and high school rank in the general student body increased. After the victory, Ohio State University reported that donations increased and its endowment soared.[2] However, no mention was made of the integrity gamble. And, contrary to presidential boasting, research indicates that gains from successful football and men's basketball programs may drive up the quality of student enrollees and student body graduation rates only temporarily, if at all, and the Flutie effect may be a myth. The perpetual quest for championships may be attractive entertainment for boosters and sports enthusiasts but requires an escalating expenditure of resources and a sacrifice of academic values.

Interested in this phenomenon, the Knight Commission on Intercollegiate Athletics set out to review the potential relationships between and among college athletic success, student quality, and public donations. The conclusion of the study was that alumni donations and applications for admission experienced an increase in a small percentage of institutions following a successful athletic season. The report noted that these increases were diminutive in magnitude and temporary in nature. Additionally, in a review of relevant research conducted by the *Economist,* scholars were divided over the long-term benefits provided by the Flutie effect. An NCAA-commissioned study by Robert Litan, Jonathan Orzag, and Peter Orzag found no relationship between spending on athletics and student quality.[3] In a further demonstration of the lack of substance to the Flutie effect, in another study Irvin Tucker found no positive relationship between athletic success and the quality of faculty.[4] To the extent that statistical studies show a significant positive correlation between athletic success and the number of applicants, the quality of the student body, or the amount of alumni donations (and there are no consistent or robust such findings), the correlation also implies that when athletic performance deteriorates, these variables will respond negatively. Further, in addition to the expense of pursuing athletic success, there is the risk that a school will be caught cheating and then suffer the consequences of the academic scandal that ensues.

But what of the gamble? Those institutions that pursue big-time college sports fame must also be willing to risk challenges to integrity. No universities are immune to these pressures, as was recently demonstrated by the University of North Carolina's public five-year athletic and academic scandal involving a massive 1,500 athletes who took fraudulent courses for the sake of maintaining athletic eligibility. When reflecting on these events that occurred during his term, the outgoing chancellor, Holden Thorp, came to the conclusion that college presidents were ill-equipped to run the exploding business of intercollegiate athletics. His suggestion was to hand over control of and oversight for athletics to athletics directors (which, in practice, is what college presidents have always done) and let them be responsible for failures of oversight. Thorp stated that the "presidential-control idea has sort of gotten away from us," and added that the model hadn't prevented corruption or the growth of a money-driven culture of college sports. Thorp concluded that an honest assessment of the role of college presidents in Football Bowl Subdivision (FBS) schools would be to admit that athletics is the most important part of their job.[5]

The Enticement of Football and Men's Basketball

In the sport of football, a modern stadium filled with more than 100,000 adoring fans affords college presidents at many of America's finest private and public research institutions a platform to showcase their campuses to the public, prospective students, and potential boosters. For example, before Nebraska football games a segment of scoreboard video highlights many of the extraordinary accomplishments of faculty research and teaching. Before one game each season the University of Oklahoma parades its National Merit Scholars onto the field to be recognized. Factoring in the television broadcast coverage of regional or national significance multiplies the effect of notoriety like no other advertisement could. The American public remains fascinated by the spectacle of institutions participating at the highest level of athletic competition. In today's media culture, the public perceptions of many of America's top research institutions tend to be shaped by the outcomes of the games and the opinions of sport commentators. Each week, college football and men's basketball rankings in the sport polls appear to become the source of the public's uninformed opinion of the quality of educational institutions. College presidents yearn for the 30-second spot in a nationally televised prime-time game to tout the virtues of their schools. It is an opportunity for presidents not only to showcase their university but also to shape the accomplishments of the president. ESPN, which continues to expand its broadcasting opportunities to almost daily college competitions, provides extra media focus for the top twenty-five football or men's basketball teams.

University governing boards, often appointed to their positions by virtue of their potential for large donations, are also enamored of the potential glory and pride of having winning basketball and football programs. As such, college presidents at major institutions eagerly join the chase for athletic fame and glory, praying to catch their own Hail Mary pass. George Lynn Cross served as president of the University of Oklahoma from 1943 to 1968, a period during which OU experienced unprecedented success in its football program under Coach Bud Wilkinson. Upon addressing the state legislature in a request for funding, Cross was asked by a member, "Why do you need so much money?" He replied, "I would like to build a University of which the football team could be proud."[6]

A Brief but Extinguished Spark of Hope

There was a decade in which college and university presidents imposed their will on the NCAA. In 1984 a group of forty-four presidents, with heavy representation of the major football powers, formed a Presidents Commission with the intent to exert greater influence over NCAA legislation. The commission wielded the authority to offer legislation and call special conventions. The 1984 Presidents Commission was formed out of frustration with academic scandal, spiraling athletic costs, and the lack of serious athletic reform.

The commission's initial exercise of power occurred at a 1985 NCAA special convention, characterized as the "integrity convention."[7] Eight proposals were advanced by the commission and all were adopted, including instructing the NCAA to develop a Division I Certification Self-Study assessment program to be undertaken by each institution every five years (this program would not be approved and implemented until 1993), mandating institutions to annually conduct outside financial audits, requiring athletic programs to follow normal institutional budgeting procedures, and strengthening the NCAA enforcement and penalty system.[8] Shortly thereafter the 1989 proposal of the Knight Commission showed promise to effect additional presidential control of intercollegiate athletics. Led by two former college presidents and renowned educators, Father Theodore Hesburgh of Notre Dame and William Friday of the University of North Carolina, the group offered a "one-plus-three" model for athletic governance. This model focused presidential control of athletics on academic integrity, financial integrity, and independent certification.[9]

The Presidents Commission and the Knight Commission (with many Knight Commission members having formerly served on the Presidents Commission) teamed up for a series of presidential reform successes adopted by four successive NCAA conventions. Proposals approved at the 1990 convention included (1) shortening the Division I spring football practice period, (2) reducing of the maximum number of Division I regular season basketball games, (3) decreasing the number of Division II football scholarships, (4) requiring Division I and II institutions to provide graduation rate information to prospective athletes, parents, coaches, and the general public, and (5) reducing time demands on college athletes during practice and playing seasons.[10] Although the changes were incremental, presidents finally appeared to be exercising their collective muscle.

Additional presidential wins were registered at the 1991 NCAA convention with a cost-cutting theme, including a 10 percent reduction in Division I maximum allowable athletic scholarships, lowering the allowable number of coaches in all sports, phasing out athletic dormitories or dormitory floors occupied solely by athletes, reducing the number of training table meals, and more restrictive criteria for Division I membership.[11]

The 1992 convention continued the presidents' reform winning streak, focusing on academic standards. Proposals approved included raising the number of high school core courses required for initial collegiate athletics eligibility, setting minimum degree completion and grade point average (GPA) requirements to advance to each year of athletic eligibility, and adopting an initial eligibility index based on high school GPA and SAT/ACT test scores.[12]

The centerpiece of the Presidents Commission reform agenda was adopted at the 1993 convention—an athletics certification program for Division I institutions. Accreditation through a comprehensive self-study process characterized by total campus involvement and transparency, followed by external peer review and a scheduled plan to remedy deficiencies, has always been the gold standard of higher education governance. The program followed this commonly accepted accreditation model. The commission's proposal was for the certification activities to occur every five years, but the interval was later changed by the NCAA to once every ten years. The Certification Self-Study program was the only mechanism whereby the entire campus community could examine the internal operations of its athletic program. More important, if deficiencies were discovered, measurable goals, timetables, and persons responsible for accomplishing remedies were to be identified. The certification program not only required plans to remediate but also carried penalties of membership expulsion, suspension (which would make the institution ineligible for postseason play), and public disclosure of certification status. Thus, at a minimum, failure to pass certification would cause public and faculty embarrassment.

In 2011, NCAA president Mark Emmert suspended the certification program. Citing staff time and expense as the reason for this suspension was simply a weak way to hide athletics directors' desire to eliminate a process that dampened their ability to conceal data and questionable practices. In particular, the self-evaluations had revealed that institutions were not in compliance with Title IX gender equity requirements and had turned up comparative academic performance and admissions data that were troubling with respect to the treatment of minority athletes, especially those participating in football and basketball. For instance, the self-study required the production of data on special admissions (normal admissions standards waived), test scores, Federal Graduation Rates (FGRs), academic progress rates (APRs), graduation success rates, and retention rates by sport, gender, and racial/ethnic group.[13] Student-athlete and staff composition were examined by race or ethnicity and by gender, and the institution's sports programs were scrutinized for rules compliance and internal governance systems.[14] The certification program, about to complete its third cycle of operation, was developing into a program that created a force for campus change.[15]

The ending of the NCAA Certification program eliminated the most significant achievement of college presidents during the Presidents Commission–led reform period—1984 to 1996. The commission would cease to exist as a result of a major restructuring of NCAA governance adopted at the 1996 convention, and the certification program was replaced by an Institutional Performance Program (IPP) in 2015. The IPP program would be nothing more than a data dashboard for institutional leaders, unavailable to campus faculty or the public and with no accountability mechanisms.

Asleep at the Wheel: College Presidents Accept a Plutocracy

In an effort led by the FBS conference commissioners, the 1996 NCAA convention brought an end to the one-member, one-vote NCAA governance system, and the Presidents Commission relinquished its existence and power to a new federated voting structure controlled by representation heavily skewed to favor the FBS. An NCAA executive committee was established as the most powerful governance unit, with members from all NCAA divisions. However, this sixteen-member group was heavily weighted with eight representatives from major football institutions. Similarly, the Division I Board of Directors was majority-weighted to give controlling power to FBS representatives. Although these boards, including the Division II and III Presidents Councils, were presidential bodies, in reality, the executive committee and the Division I Board of Directors were controlled by the FBS conference commissioners, who exercised their influence with president members.

As with previous restructurings of the NCAA governance system, this new and tighter plutocracy of the most commercialized athletic programs was accepted because the wealthiest schools threatened an exodus from the organization. The Presidents Commission and the Knight Commission were asleep at the wheel. Both groups supported the restructure, while Division II and III presidents went along out of fear. Joseph Crowley, former president of the University of Nevada–Reno, an NCAA officer and author of *In the Arena: The NCAA's First Century*, aptly described the Presidents Commission's role in mediating issues between the restructuring task forces and making possible the FBS (then Division I-A) takeover:

> Not surprisingly, conflicts between the task forces flared as the restructuring efforts went forward. The oversight committee was one of the venues for resolving these conflicts and securing agreement on an overall proposal to bring to the 1996 Convention. The Commission also became a key vehicle for achieving compromise. There was initial anger over the Division I demands for virtually complete control of the Association's future, but once that dissipated, civil discourse ensued and consensus formed around key issues. Paramount for Divisions II and III were the financial entitlements they would have in the new structure. A broader constituency worried about what this structure would do to the concept of shared values and commitments that had from the beginning fundamentally bonded Association members. In other words, what would hold this new NCAA together?[16]

The Façade of Presidential Power over Athletics

Following the recommendations of the now defunct Presidents Commission and the still operating Knight Commission's model of presidential control, the NCAA hired two consecutive former college presidents for the role of chief executive officer. Neither leader was successful in slowing the Division I football and basketball arms race. In addition, there has been a continuation of lip service regarding presidential responsibility in ensuring the integrity of the athletic program. In an effort to restructure the NCAA's governance in 2004 with an emphasis on presidential leadership, the executive committee recognized its "absolute obligation to make certain that intercollegiate athletics is successfully woven into the fabric of higher education."[17] These ideas were carried over in a 2014 summary of the rationale for the NCAA's new restructuring and included the intent to:

- Integrate intercollegiate athletics into higher education so that the educational experience of the student-athlete is paramount;

- Sustain the collegiate model of athletics, in which students participate as an avocation, balancing their academic, social, and athletics experiences; and

- Manage intercollegiate athletics so that it is understood as a valued enhancement to a quality higher education experience.[18]

The NCAA Division I Board of Directors, which has existed since 1997 and was restructured in 2014, currently consists of twenty-four members, including twenty college presidents or chancellors, one director of athletics, one senior woman administrator, one faculty athletics representative, and one student-athlete.[19] This new president-dominated voting structure represents a considerable change from the one-institution, one-vote general assembly action on all legislation that was typically performed by faculty athletics representatives and athletics directors as institutional proxies. One might logically expect a flurry of dynamic change emanating from presidents to fix college sports, similar to the 1984–96 reform activity of the Presidents Commission. However, in the twenty years since the formulation of the federated structure in 1996, the opposite has been the case. Little has been accomplished to fix the issues of runaway commercialism, athlete welfare, and academic integrity that continue to plague big time intercollegiate athletics. Indeed, the 2014–15 reforms that cut loose the Power Five conferences to legislate as they please on financial matters is a giant step away from academic control. The presidents serving on the NCAA boards appear to be those most infatuated with the bright lights of and media attention to intercollegiate athletics. These presidents appear to be little more than shills advancing the interests of commercialized sports.

Many college presidents have expressed exasperation over the pressures placed upon them on their own campuses from boosters, donors, and celebrity coaches. Presidents have allowed NCAA president Mark Emmert to eliminate the Division I Certification program with barely a whimper, citing the burden placed upon member institutions.[20] In 2015, Jon Duncan, the NCAA's vice president for enforcement, disclosed that the NCAA was currently investigating an unprecedented twenty cases of serious academic fraud, a number that suggested an epidemic level. The recent rash of academic fraud cases has not been initiated by institutional or NCAA investigations but rather through whistleblowers and local media. The fact that twenty cases were under investigation in 2015, of course, does not mean that academic fraud suddenly exploded in that year. It does mean that the growth of social media and a culture of openness have brought more cases to the public's attention.

College presidents privately reflect a spectrum of attitudes toward athletics, ranging from cheerleading to exasperation to ambivalence. It is, quite simply, not in a president's interest to get involved. Presidents have an average tenure of around six years on the job, have a plate full of duties and responsibilities other than athletics, risk alienating trustees, donors, and boosters if they speak out too loudly about reform, and have a history to ponder of outspoken presidents who have brought no enduring substantial change but have been released from or not renewed in their job.

Correspondingly, what was made clear from a 2009 presidential survey of NCAA FBS institutions was that college presidents feel a sense of powerlessness at the prospect of trying to control and reform college athletics. This report, commissioned by the Knight Commission, made equally clear that there was a lack of ideas for how best to create necessary change to address critical issues regarding sustainability. Regardless of how fervent college presidents may be to effect college sports reform, they tend to be acutely aware of the web of conflicts of interest and political pressures spun by their donors and governing boards. They face the very real potential that athletic scandals may affect their institutions and personal futures, and are pressured not to act in athletic matters that may not be in the best interests of higher education.[21]

The inflated importance of athletics in higher education and the enormous pressures exerted on college presidents were brought to the attention of one of the authors in 1989 while serving as the associate athletics director of academic affairs and compliance at the University of Maryland, during his investigation into an infractions case related to the men's basketball program. President John Slaughter had recently resigned from Maryland to become president of Occidental College and had been replaced by William (Brit) Kirwan. Kirwan, the former provost, was a popular choice. Shortly after Dr. Kirwin became chancellor, he made a memorable observation to one of the authors. He said, "Gerry, I observed from job postings in the *Chronicle of Higher Education* that nine of the last eleven college president resignations were related to athletic problems and I don't intend on being one."

Despite Kirwan's desire to avoid athletics-related scandal, he would be confronted with major infractions cases involving football and basketball at both Maryland and later as president of Ohio State University. In 2000 Kirwan became chancellor of the entire University System of Maryland. Kirwin has also served as cochair of the Knight Commission on Intercollegiate Athletics. Under NCAA Bylaw 2.1.1, college presidents are assumed to be responsible for the administration of all aspects of the athletics program.[22] Yet in a 2015 interview prior to his retirement from his chancellorship of the Maryland System, Kirwan reflected on the failure of college presidents to exercise control over intercollegiate athletics, saying, "It is the one area of a university where presidents are not really in control." Kirwan added that the hands-off policy of most institutions has contributed to what he described as a culture of excess among athletics departments: "There's sort of the façade of their being in control, but can you imagine a president of a big-time football power announcing they were going to de-emphasize intercollegiate athletics and concentrate more resources on academics?" he inquired. "The board would get upset. The legislature would get upset. Alumni would get upset. They couldn't handle it."[23]

Years earlier, Clark Kerr had concluded that "once started, university spectator sports could not be killed even by the worst of teams or the best of de-emphasis; and few universities have seriously sought after either."[24]

An example of this pressure on presidents occurred in December 2014, when the University of Alabama–Birmingham announced it was dropping football and two other team sports after a commissioned report revealed the athletics department expenses would grow to $49 million annually over the next five years, with $22 million needed for football upgrades. The university was already subsidizing roughly two-thirds of the athletics department's expenses. After considerable pressure was placed on President Watts, a new analysis was commissioned, and a $26 million fundraising campaign was undertaken, all three dropped sports were reinstated.[25] Of course, some schools announce downgrades and actually follow through on them; the most recent example is the University of Idaho, which announced in April 2016 that it would drop from FBS to FCS in 2018.

This fear of negative trustee and alumni reaction to the exertion of controls over athletics leads most Division I institutions to leave athletics departments without oversight at the campus level. The athletics director, and often the superstar football or basketball coach, insist on direct access to the president, and the athletics director often is invited to sit at the president's side in his or her senior cabinet. When the athletics director is supposed to report directly to the president, the president generally lacks the time or the expertise to exert appreciable influence. Even if the athletics director is placed under a vice president for administration or student affairs, the oversight responsibility is minimal, with the athletics director still having direct access to the president. Presidents have even developed a smoke-and-mirrors illusion of oversight by appointing a member of the faculty as the official conference and NCAA faculty athletics representative and an Athletics Advisory Council, which is supposed to recommend policy to the president. However, as a practical matter, extreme caution is taken with these appointments to make sure that faculty or individuals unfriendly to athletics do not fulfill these roles. The Athletics Advisory Council is further diluted by the appointment of student-athletes, wealthy alumni, or others with no institutional obligation or power to ensure the athletics department's accountability. These representatives receive free athletics event preferred tickets, special parking privileges, travel with the team or an administrative contingent to postseason championship events, invitations to eat at the training table with the athletes, and an array of other perquisites. The notion of having these roles played by tenured faculty elected by the faculty senate or another independent faculty governing body is an anathema because of the risk that commonly accepted athletics department practices may be criticized or exposed. Yet mandating such independent faculty involvement may be the only realistic recourse if presidents wish to prevent academic fraud.

Power Five Autonomy Initiative Further Diminishes NCAA General Presidential Power

In an October 2011 precursor of what was to come, NCAA president Mark Emmert pushed for an increase in the maximum value of an athletic scholarship. A $2,000 stipend to athletes to cover the cost of college attendance was proposed as an addition to the funding of tuition, required fees, room, board, and books. The NCAA Board of Directors adopted the legislation, but it was promptly voted down by the membership in December 2011. Not to be deterred, the wealthiest conferences continued putting pressure on the NCAA and Emmert, threatening to leave the organization. In August 2014 the NCAA granted legislative autonomy for the five wealthiest conferences in the FBS, representing sixty-five institutions, and a new governance structure to provide greater operational control to athletics directors and conference representatives.[26] Presidents emphasized the need to retain control on their campuses and within the NCAA for the new governance model to be successful.

The legislative autonomy privileges applied only to specific athlete welfare topics and included issues such as financial aid, health, recruiting restrictions, meals for athletes, and athletics time demands. Nonetheless, competition among all universities to keep pace with the escalation of FBS athlete support is expected to rise to unsustainable costs.[27] Bob Kustra, president of Boise State University, described the "power grab" by the Power Five as the NCAA's attempt to perpetuate the dominance of a few dozen universities with the most resources. "It seems they are never satisfied with their bloated athletic budgets, especially when threatened in recent years by upstart, so-called mid-major programs that steal recruits, oftentimes beat the big boys, 'mess with' the national rankings and sometimes take postseason bowl games and revenue."[28] Faced with this additional stratification of football and basketball, the non–Power Five institutions with distressed budget constraints were left with an unappealing choice either to attempt to maintain competitiveness by offering similar benefits and suffering growing financial losses or to opt out of the athletic arms race.[29]

NCAA Enforcement—or the Lack Thereof

An important part of the NCAA governance structure and a fundamental tenet of governance is its membership-approved enforcement process, which assesses penalties for violations of the association's bylaws. The temptation to violate NCAA rules so as to gain a competitive advantage has grown exponentially along with the financial rewards associated with success in big-time college sports. As a result, recruiting scandals, academic fraud, and impermissible eligibility certifications have occurred more frequently in recent decades. Criticisms of the NCAA enforcement process include that it is underresourced, inconsistent, selective with regard to which institutions get investigated, fails to provide due process for individuals and institutions accused of rules violations, and has been implemented in an arbitrary and capricious matter.[30] An example of ineffective and inconsistent enforcement of employment rules observed by one of the authors occurred when it was reported that a star football player had the use of a luxury automobile, a Lexus, for six weeks. The university's compliance staff explained to the NCAA that the athlete's prolonged test drive was a normal business practice offered to the public, according to the dealership. The NCAA accepted the justification, even though few would disagree that most prospective buyers would not be allowed a six-week test drive.

Before the television era began in the 1950s, NCAA member institutions and affiliated athletic conferences enjoyed complete autonomy. The NCAA promulgated only guidelines and principles, as opposed to rules and regulations, which required enforcement. In other words, institutions and conferences could do whatever they wished. There was no enforcement function exercised by the association.

In 1951 the NCAA Council approved a set of regulations dealing with the primary concerns of the membership that for the first time imposed limits on practice seasons, the number of competitions, postseason competition, academic eligibility, and financial assistance, and provided an enforcement system. These rules were approved at the 1952 convention meeting of the membership. A subcommittee on infractions together with a membership committee were designated to receive complaints and conduct investigations, with findings presented to the NCAA Council for Adjudication. Council penalty powers included probation, suspension, and termination from membership.[31]

From its inception, the NCAA enforcement system did not provide due process, and the courts supported this policy. Notably, the 1988 United States Supreme Court's decision in Tarkanian v. NCAA established the NCAA as a private entity that was authorized to conduct investigations without providing due process. Nevertheless, the NCAA examined its internal enforcement practices soon after the court's decision. Former solicitor general Rex Lee chaired the Special Committee to Review the NCAA Enforcement and Infractions Process. The Lee Committee recommended improving the process by providing greater protections for involved institutions and individuals. The Lee Committee advised the NCAA to:

1. Provide initial notice of allegations. The NCAA membership agreed to enhance the notice-of-inquiry process to ensure all parties are notified prior to an investigation.
2. Establish a summary disposition process. This was suggested as a method for accelerating the infractions process by adjudicating major violations at a reasonably early stage in the investigation.
3. Allow tape recordings and shared documentation of interviews.
4. Use former judges or other eminent legal authorities as hearing officers in cases involving major violations not resolved at the summary disposition process. Although the NCAA adopted the hearing officer recommendation, the hearing officer positions no longer exist. More important, the NCAA never adopted the recommendation of a truly independent trier of fact.
5. Create an appellate process. An NCAA Infractions Appeals Committee was developed in 1993.[32]

Even though the NCAA agreed to allow tape recording of interviews and to add outside individuals to the Committee on Infractions and the Infractions Appeals Committee, it rejected both an independent trier of fact and open hearings. The NCAA believed that open hearings would inhibit investigations and dissuade people with allegations and knowledge of misconduct from cooperating. The NCAA also worried that an independent trier of fact would be expensive and that the persons performing that function would not understand the complexities of college sports. However, the existing system is flawed because members of the Committee on Infractions and the Infractions Appeals Committee are employees of peer member institutions who have an inherent conflict of interest in adjudicating infractions cases. Their judgment can bar a rival institution from competition, revenue distributions, and recruiting or reduce its scholarships, rendering its teams less competitive over the longer term.[33]

Although the Lee Committee's recommendations have arguably made the NCAA enforcement process fairer during the past two decades, numerous flaws continue to plague NCAA jurisprudence. Besides the glaring omissions of an independent trier of fact and open hearings, the rights of confrontation and cross examination are notably absent from this quasi-judicial process. The NCAA's current "cooperative principle" requires member institutions to self-report violations of the association's rules, investigate themselves, and assist the NCAA in such investigations or face enhanced penalties for not cooperating or for failing to correct faulty procedures. Still, there is no right of subpoena (which would have to be granted by Congress), so institutions cannot force external third parties to cooperate with or supply information to NCAA investigations.

The need for strong processes designed to protect the rights of individuals and institutions cannot be overvalued. NCAA penalties can have numerous consequences. They can damage the reputations of institutions of higher education and cause coaches and athletic administrators to lose their jobs. They can also cause college athletes to lose participation and scholarship benefits. Given the persistent criticism and widespread agreement regarding the NCAA's flawed enforcement system, most would think it necessary to restore public confidence in this NCAA governance function. Key among important changes for all cases with the potential of significant consequences should be the installation of discovery mechanisms and enhanced procedural protections for individuals and institutions. It is also necessary to replace NCAA staff investigators and peer determination of guilt and penalties with independent third-party investigators and former judges hired by the NCAA as independent contractors. Congress would need to be engaged to grant necessary discovery powers. Both discovery and the use of experienced judges would promote due process for all and consistency of punishment.

It is also critical to address the significant imbalance of power between the NCAA and member institutions, on the one hand, and college athletes at the institutional and national governance level on the other.

Open amateur sport athletes in the United States have had such protections since 1978 when the Ted Stevens Olympic and Amateur Sports Act mandated the provision of an athlete ombudsman and binding arbitration as mechanisms to protect the rights of athletes to compete. There is a need for similar advocacy and procedural policies to protect college athletes. At the institutional level, athletics department personnel should not be involved in the adjudication of appeal processes related to termination of college athletes' scholarships. Due process protections at the campus and national governance association levels should be extended before athletes are declared ineligible for competition by their respective institutions or the NCAA for reasons other than an insufficient GPA, failure to make satisfactory progress toward a degree, or similar academic failure.

Another important provision that should be required of any national governance organization and its member institutions is whistleblower protection. College athletes, faculty, and other employees of NCAA member institutions who disclose unethical behavior or violations of NCAA or institutional rules related to the conduct of athletic programs should be protected from retaliation by their member institutions or institutional employees.

The Involvement of Athletes in Governance

The NCAA and member institutions at the campus level have historically limited athletes to advisory roles in their national legislative and governance structures. Under significant pressure during the 2014 NCAA convention by student-athletes voicing opposition to a governance restructuring proposal that did not include athlete voting privileges, the NCAA Board of Directors approved a revision that offered minimal athlete voting rights.[34] Out of twenty-four board members, it added one athlete. For its thirty-two-member NCAA Council, the NCAA adopted a membership makeup that would include two voting athlete representatives. A mere 8 percent representation on the NCAA Board of Directors and 6 percent representation on the NCAA Council offers athletes little ability to affect the direction of the enterprise to which they are the principal contributors (see figure 4-1).

FIGURE 4-1: Comparisons between Old and New
NCAA Division I Board of Directors and Management Councils

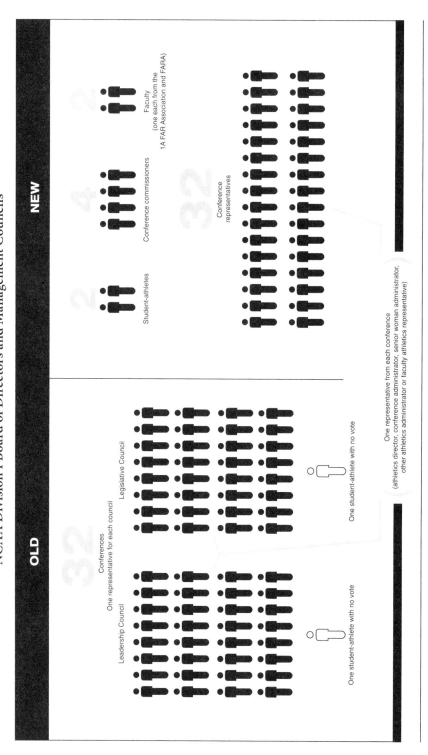

Source: Michelle Brutlag Hosick, "Board Adopts New Division I Structure," NCAA.org, August 7, 2014 (www.ncaa.org/about/resources/media-center/news /board-adopts-new-division-i-structure).

While this governance restructuring offers athletes a token of voting representation, it pales in comparison with the 20 percent athlete representation in the United States Olympic Committee (USOC) governance model. The USOC is required by the Ted Stevens Olympic and Amateur Sports Act to ensure at least 20 percent athlete representation with voting power on its board of directors and all committees. [35]

A significantly larger athlete participation governance model might better ensure that rules of athletics participation do not restrict the college athlete's access to full academic and educational choices. A stronger athlete representative model might also build up necessary athlete health and well-being protections and open avenues for athletes' rights to earn stipends in the same manner as other students or to obtain career advice.

The national athletic governance association and its member institutions should also be expected to promulgate and enforce rules that protect student-athletes from any of the following:

1. Discrimination based on color, disability, gender, national origin, race, religion, creed, or sexual orientation, in accordance with federal legislation;
2. Disrespectful pedagogical practices or other potentially injurious treatment;
3. Injury or other harm consequent on unsafe conditions, training, or competition practices; inadequate medical supervision; or unethical professional conduct;
4. Financial loss resulting from inadequate insurance benefits;
5. Exploitative or unfair decisionmaking that results in the removal of participation privileges or scholarship benefits;
6. Admissions, academic advising, or tutoring practices that place athletic eligibility above academic integrity;
7. Unfair limitations affecting access to professional athletics following collegiate eligibility or the college athlete's ability to obtain career advice;
8. Unfair restrictions that affect a collegiate athlete's right to earn money in the same manner as other students.

Current and recent former athletes are the best advocates for expanding these rights.

Role of the Faculty in Governance

Currently the NCAA recognizes a faculty athletics representative (FAR) as the representative of the institution and its faculty.[36] Eighty percent of FARs are presidential appointees, with no nomination from or consultation with the institutional body of faculty governance, often the faculty senate. The FAR must be a member of the faculty or an administrator outside the athletics department who holds faculty rank. Most are tenured. In theory, the FAR serves as the guardian of institutional academic integrity, maintaining and monitoring the academic welfare of the athlete.[37] FARs typically have a role in the review and approval of specially admitted athletes and ensuring that each athlete can succeed at the institution. The average FAR serves for seven years.[38]

In light of the overwhelming number of instances of presidential appointment without the consent of faculty governing bodies, it is questionable whether FARs represent the faculty or the commercial interests of college presidents and athletics departments. The lengthy appointment, absence of oversight, gifts of athletic apparel, team trips, paid salary in some cases, and numerous benefits bestowed on FARs make it difficult to maintain objectivity and independence and represent an inherent conflict of interest.

In today's environment of epidemic-level academic fraud cases, many FARs have repeatedly failed in their primary responsibility of safeguarding academic integrity at their respective institutions. Instead, FARs frequently take the position of chief athletics department advocate. Proper transparent data analysis requires serious review of grades, courses, major selection, tutorial systems, and athlete academic advising. Too often, the FAR merely signs a form attesting to certification of eligibility as the extent of ensuring integrity. The length of service FARs enjoy may encourage a sense of privilege or entitlement in their role as chief integrity inspectors.

A reconstruction of the FAR role should establish a nonrepeatable term of service and no monetary benefits, special seating, trips, or athletic apparel. The faculty senates should be the representative body to nominate and select the FAR for the academic perspective to be heard. Faculty must play a more central role in examining and ensuring academic integrity in athletics. One organization, the Coalition on Intercollegiate Athletics

(COIA), represents this perspective in a college sports reform alliance of sixty-four faculty senates in FBS institutions. COIA serves as a voice of college sports reform in the areas of academic integrity and quality, student-athlete welfare, campus governance of intercollegiate athletics, commercialization, and fiscal responsibility. COIA is committed to the development of effective strategies and proposals for significant, long-term reform in college athletics.[39] COIA represents a national movement to establish an objective academic perspective on athletics in higher education and should serve as an avenue for increased faculty dialogue.

FIVE

Athlete Health and Welfare

This chapter examines the many facets of the institution's relationship to the student-athlete to determine whether the currently operable quid pro quo between athletic programs and student participants is educationally and ethically defensible and balanced with regard to benefits. National collegiate athletic governance organizations and their member institutions have created a pact of rules and regulations governing the eligibility of undergraduate students to compete in intercollegiate athletic programs. If students want to participate in competitive athletics in college, they have no choice but to adhere to these rules. Further, as long as the institution adheres to additional governance association rules limiting the treatment and benefits athletes may receive, the institution is permitted to bestow special treatment and benefits that, in many instances, far exceed the benefits and privileges afforded nonathlete students.

On the other side of the benefits ledger the institution can go beyond governance association rules by formally and informally exercising excessive control over college athletes. Athletics time commitments may not allow the athlete to meet academic demands, access full academic choices, or take advantage of other experiences available to his or her nonathlete counterparts. Schools may inadequately protect athletes from injury or abuse, provide insufficient medical treatment or insurance coverage, or act in other ways to endanger athletes' physical or psychological health.

Restriction of Academic and Educational Choices

The previous chapter on academic integrity explained how the following academically related eligibility requirements or institutional practices permitted by NCAA rules negatively affect the educational success of college athletes. They bear emphasis and further explanation of how they restrict athletes' educational opportunities.

Low Eligibility Standards Invite Academic Failure of the Most Vulnerable Athletes

In recent years, one of the authors examined the credentials of athletes who qualified under NCAA eligibility standards with reading skills below a fourth-grade level. One in particular scored in the first percentile (lowest) range in reading skills. It is difficult to imagine how any student without the skills to understand college-level textbooks could successfully navigate or appreciate a college education.

Low academic standards for athletics eligibility invite academic failure of the most vulnerable athletes, those who enter college underprepared to compete in the classroom. The NCAA's rules governing the initial eligibility of incoming freshmen and transfer students and minimum grade point average (GPA) and normal academic progress standards that determine continuing eligibility are more lax than those required for a student to be eligible to play sports in high school. And they are lower than commonly accepted definitions of "good academic standing" based on GPA and other requirements for graduation.[1] For instance, when a 2.0 overall GPA is required of the general student body for graduation, it does athletes a disservice to allow a continuing eligibility standard below 2.0 (or one that gradually escalates to 2.0 by the start of their senior year.) Yet this is exactly what NCAA rules dictate. Athletes who are the worst-performing students are those most affected because they are allowed to devote extensive time to athletics practice, travel, and competitions when they most need this time to bring up their grades.

Further, it appears counterintuitive to require athletes to be "full-time" students, registering for no fewer than twelve credit hours per semester, then to require that they only pass courses worth in total six credit hours in their first semester as freshmen, and then eighteen hours during their regular academic years as freshmen and thereafter. In addition, NCAA athletes are required to achieve only 40 percent of their degree requirements by the start of their junior year and 60 percent by the start of their senior year as full-time students. These performance expectations of college athletes required to be full-time students should be unacceptable. More distressing, these minimal standards permit the institution to exploit the athletic ability of poorly prepared athletes who are struggling in the classroom for up to five years from initial enrollment. Setting academic standards based on keeping the most athletically talented but academically underprepared students eligible to play sports is clearly exploitive because the mechanisms used to help the underperforming college athlete recover from deficiencies are increasingly narrow course and major choices, often aptly described as "majoring in athletic eligibility."

These low academic expectations and standards contribute to an athletics culture in which academic achievement is devalued. The messages to Division I athletes in particular are abundantly clear:

- Concentrate on playing sports.
- Don't worry about passing all your classes or getting a high GPA. You can go to summer school on a scholarship to make up for any classes you fail or to bring up your GPA, and it will be advantageous since you can train in great facilities while you are here.
- You don't need a 2.0 GPA until you are a senior.
- It's okay to take easier courses and to take your time completing the more demanding courses required for your degree program because you only need to finish 60 percent of these courses by the time you are a senior, and don't forget that we can keep you on scholarship if you do not finish your degree by the time you complete your athletic eligibility.
- Just make sure you will be eligible to participate by the beginning of the next academic year so you don't lose your athletic scholarship.

Research demonstrates the institutionalization of this dysfunctional nonacademic culture within athletic programs. Compared to nonathletes,

Division I athletes in the aggregate (in both revenue and nonrevenue sports) have lower cumulative GPAs and experience less academic growth throughout their college careers.[2] We also know that the Division I pressure-filled athletics culture depresses the academic aspirations of athletes. Athletes' attitudes toward academics reinforce each other and become more homogeneous over time, resulting in what Peter Adler and Patricia A. Adler have called "collective academic detachment and diminished academic performance."[3]

Waivers of Normal Admission Requirements Produce a Large Cohort of Basketball and Football Players at Academic Risk

It is common practice for NCAA member institutions to waive normal admissions standards for a disproportionate number of students who have exceptional athletic ability and for these students to be overrepresented in the revenue-producing sports of men's football and basketball. Upper-level administration officials and athletics directors often argue that such practices contribute to the diversity of the student body and are used for nonathlete students with special abilities, such as outstanding musicians or individuals who excel in other performing arts. The NCAA does not and should not interfere with the right of an institution of higher education to determine the composition and abilities of its student body. However, such freedom should not result in student-athlete exploitation, and there is no obligation on the part of the NCAA to allow underprepared students to be eligible to participate in athletics. Indeed, to ensure the responsible use of such admissions standards freedom, the NCAA could easily adopt rules that limit freshmen or transfer eligibility or reduce hours permitted for athletics-related activity of specially admitted athletes if the results of required testing for learning disabilities or math, reading, or other skill deficiencies indicate a need for remediation. The NCAA has no rules of this type. A rule that ensured remediation and restricted first-year competition for specially admitted athletes who entered the institution needing academic skills improvement would afford the athletes a better chance of success or of changing the recruiting dynamics of elite athletes. Coaches might pay more careful consideration to the athlete's institutional fit in addition to athletic talent.

These admissions waiver practices begin a cycle of academic restrictions not experienced by nonathlete students. Athletes' choices of classes and majors generally are limited to a small fraction of the educational offerings of the institutions. The underprepared athlete is forced by academic counselors to register for classes and choose majors in which his or her limited capabilities will enable grades or completion of degree requirements sufficient to meet low NCAA eligibility standards. The result often is a degree that doesn't translate into a viable career skill set.

Even adequately prepared college athletes suffer from campus knowledge of special admissions exceptions awarded disproportionately to athletes. Faculty resent such special treatment and may rightly or wrongly assume lack of academic ability on the part of the athlete. Other students may have similar reactions. These practices support athlete stereotyping as being less capable and more privileged compared to nonathlete students.

The Impact of Excessive Athletics-Related Time Demands

Excessive time demands limit the ability of athletes to meet academic demands, make choices of academic majors and courses, and access other varied experiences of being a college student. As described in recent studies on athletic time demands for revenue-producing sports, powerful coaches demand the availability of athletes for practice sessions and team meetings. Typically, a combination of coach and athletic academic counselor pressure regularly encourages or requires athletes to avoid scheduling classes in conflict with practice hours, limiting their access to a full range of academic opportunities. Further, travel, athletic competition, or practice obligations often do not permit athletes to take advantage of enhanced educational opportunities available to other students, such as study abroad, intensive courses available between regular semesters, field trips, guest lectures, and similar opportunities. The pressure of excessive travel time shows no signs of abating as athletic conferences continue to restructure into megaleagues with national footprints in order to achieve the largest possible television viewership and garner the highest media rights revenues. In turn, efforts to command the highest media revenues encourage schools to schedule events during prime evening weekday times, in conflict with scheduled classes.

The NCAA rules requiring no more than twenty hours per week and four hours per day devoted to athletics-related activity are a myth, aptly described as such by the Northwestern University football players who petitioned the Region 13 office of the National Labor Relations Board (NLRB) to be recognized as employees eligible to unionize.[4] Travel time to competitions and "voluntary" workouts or film review sessions don't count in the twenty-hour limit. Even more disguised common practices result in continued excessive time demands being placed on athletes, particularly during the regular playing season. Rigid weekly restrictions also apply during the off-season. Athletes are required to have one day off per week during the regular season and at least two days off per week during the nonchampionship season. A 2015 Pacific-12 Conference study (409 athletes, all Pac-12 sports, 50–50 male-female ratio) revealed that typical full-time employees had more days off and more time off than athletes. Athletes reported the following:

- On average, athlete participants spent fifty hours per week on athletics during the regular playing season—twenty-one hours on required athletic activities, four hours on voluntary athletics, four hours receiving training room treatment, and twenty-two hours traveling to competitions.
- Fifty-four percent said they did not have enough time to study for tests.
- Eighty percent reported missing classes because of athletic competitions.
- Practices forced athletes to miss classes when practices ran late.
- Some athletes reported they were unable to attend critical academic review sessions that occurred outside scheduled classes because of practice and competition demands.
- Sixty percent of athletes reported overall lack of free time as their biggest concern.
- Seventy-two percent reported lack of time to sleep as the number one hindrance to academic and athletic success.
- Seventy-three percent reported they felt that sports activities designated "not required" or "voluntary" were actually mandatory if they wanted to play in the games.[5]

Similarly, a 2010 NCAA study of athlete self-reported experiences in all three competitive divisions supported a picture of seventy- to eighty-hour workweeks with unrealistic athletics time expectations and insufficient time left for academics and rest (see table 5-1). These data underscore the reality that NCAA college athletes do not have the time to participate in

TABLE 5-1: 2010 NCAA GOALS Study: Average Hours per Week
In-Season Spent on Athletic and Academic Activities

Sport	Athletic activities			Academic activities		
	D-I	D-II	D-III	D-I	D-II	D-III
Baseball	42.1	39.0	34.8	31.7	32.8	35.6
Men's basketball	39.2	37.7	30.8	37.3	35.8	34.8
Football (FBS/FCS)	43.3/41.8	37.5	33.1	38.0/38.2	36.8	37.9
All other men's sports	32.0	31.3	29.2	36.0	36.3	39.7
Women's basketball	37.6	34.2	29.8	38.9	37.3	41.3
All other women's sports	33.3	31.7	28.9	40.1	41.4	43.0

Source: NCAA, "Division I Results from the NCAA GOALS Study on the Student-Athlete Experience, 2010," presentation at the FARA Annual Meeting and Symposium, November https://www.google.com/#q=Division+I+Results+from+the+NCAA+GOALS+Study+on+the+Student-Athlete+Experience%2C+2010.

the full college experience and are dealing with fatigue and other pressures that diminish their ability to meet academic demands.

Unreasonable Rules Limiting College Athletes Ability to Transfer to Other Institutions

Murphy Holloway played basketball on full scholarship at the University of Mississippi for two years, after which his life changed and he found himself the primary caregiver for his infant daughter. He needed to return to his home in South Carolina, where he would be able to continue to go to school, play basketball, and fulfill his family responsibilities. However, NCAA transfer rules prohibited athletics participation eligibility and the receipt of athletics-related financial aid for one year.[6] College students who are nonathletes are more than three times more likely to transfer, and may do so without penalty.[7]

The NCAA imposes rules on college athletes that limit their ability to transfer to other institutions or limit their choice of institution on transfer. NCAA rules levy athletic participation penalties, such as the loss of a year of eligibility, ineligibility to participate for one year, or, when the current Division I or II institution refuses to give permission for the athlete to transfer to another Division I or II institution, ineligibility to receive an athletic scholarship. With the exception of a Division III to Division III transfer, all athletes must get permission from the institution they are attending in order to take advantage of the one-time transfer provision, and this exception is not permitted in selected sports such as football and basketball. This permission may be selective in that an institution may limit permission to transfer to a school not in its current conference. Non-athlete students face no such restrictions.

Transfer restrictions are imposed on college athletes for several reasons: (1) out of concern that the institution's considerable investment in the recruitment and financial aid offered or awarded will be lost; (2) out of fear that loss of the athlete will render an institution's sports program less competitive, thereby affecting its revenue potential; and (3) out of a desire to protect college athletes from "poaching" by representatives of competing institutions who seek to entice the athlete away from his or her original institution. The first two reasons treat athletes as a part of the labor force instead of as students seeking an education while also playing sports. These reasons stem from institutional self-interest and are exploitative in that the institution's well-being is placed above the freedom and well-being of the student-athlete. The third reason, protection from poaching, is valid but can be more fairly addressed through penalties applied to "poacher" coaches and their institutions rather than to the athletes being so victimized.

Supporters of transfer rules that require one year of residency argue that a year of adjustment benefits the athlete. However, this justification becomes indefensible when athletes are permitted immediate eligibility if they play in certain nonrevenue sports but not if they play football, basketball, or selected other sports. The irrationality continues because the athlete is allowed to spend the same time on athletics as he or she did at the previous institution, being permitted to attend practices and games but not to compete. In other words, if the institution doesn't need or want the athlete (as is the case for the nonrevenue sports), the year of residency isn't necessary.

Close to 25 percent of first-time four-year college students transfer to other four-year institutions during their six-year enrollment periods.[8]

Nonathlete college students, who may be gifted academically or talented in other areas, are not penalized when they leave their institutions. These students transfer for various reasons. For instance, students who connect with faculty mentors or engage in an artistic apprenticeship or research might feel compelled to follow a professor who has moved to another college. Students may elect to transfer so as to advance their educations or hone their talents in settings that better meet their needs. College athletes may consider transferring for any number of reasons related to personal choices or related to their athletic experiences. Whatever the details of the restriction, any barrier to a college athlete freely transferring for any reason is a questionable restraint of the freedoms commonly afforded nonathlete students. This unfairness is particularly distasteful in football and basketball because these sports have the highest-paid coaches, who generally can move to the highest-bidding institution without restriction. The only reason for the college football or basketball player's one-year residency penalty before becoming eligible to play is to protect the institutions' and coaches' investments in their athletic talents. College athletes should share in the freedom coaches and all other college students have to explore other institutional options, as opposed to being treated as commodities owned by the institution.[9]

Lack of Adequate Health Protection

Colleges and universities are not adequately addressing the physical and psychological health of athletes. Stanley Doughty lost a contract with the Kansas City Chiefs because of an undiagnosed spinal injury he'd suffered while playing for the University of South Carolina. The university did not pay for the surgery he needed—it simply didn't have to. NCAA member institutions are not required to provide long-term care for athletes who have exhausted their eligibility, graduated, or are no longer enrolled, as was the case for Doughty, who left the university twelve credits shy of graduating to play professionally.

Other student-athletes have lost their scholarships while they were still enrolled in college but unable to play because of injuries. Patrick Courtney played football at North Carolina A&T State University. Courtney suffered a hernia injury during training camp that required surgery. He was injured again when he rejoined his team on the field, and was forced to transfer when his scholarship was not renewed the following year.[10]

Athletic injury insurance is insufficient, national rules restricting contact practices in collision sports do not exist, preventive and predictive medical tools and practices are not required, and there are no common standards for the professional conduct of coaches, resulting in abusive and disrespectful instructional environments being unaddressed. There is a compelling need to recognize these protection deficiencies, especially since the public is increasingly aware of the lifelong debilitating impact of athletic injuries and the federal government is pressuring higher education to increase efforts to guarantee safe educational environments free from harassment and abuse. We must address these critical issues.

Inadequate Athlete Injury Insurance and Provision for Medical Expenses

While NCAA rules require member institutions to "certify insurance coverage for medical expenses resulting from athletically related injuries" that must be of "equal or greater value than the deductible of the NCAA catastrophic injury insurance program," the institution itself is not required to provide such insurance.[11] The rule specifies that the coverage may be provided by parents' or guardians' insurance, the participant's personal insurance, or the institution's insurance program. Thus, it is not uncommon for schools to adopt policies like the following:

- The Yale Athletics Department *does not* provide medical insurance coverage for athletic injuries.
- All medical expenses incurred (including deductibles, copayments, and other charges) for treatment of athletics-related injuries are the responsibility of the student-athlete. These expenses include all payments related to x-rays, MRIs, bone scans, lab tests, hospitalization, physical therapy, surgery, emergency room services, emergency transport service, and the professional fees associated with those services.
- There is no medical coverage even for injuries sustained in formal practice or competition while the student-athlete was representing Yale.[12]

The most common practices are for institutions to require the college athlete or his or her parents to provide proof of insurance coverage and for the institution to provide secondary or no additional coverage. While some colleges do cover full medical expenses and insurance policy deductibles even if they are not covered by their institutional secondary policies or the policies of the parent or student, the gaps most commonly encountered are significant and include the following:

- Parents' insurance plans often exclude varsity sports injuries, contain limits affecting out-of-state treatment, or do not provide full coverage of all expenses.
- While players' medical expenses that exceed the floor of the NCAA catastrophic injury coverage ($90,000, or $70,000 if the institution is participating in the NCAA's Group Basic Accident Medical Insurance program) are fully accommodated, treating injuries when expenses are below this floor are not covered.
- Most insurance policies, whether provided by the athlete or parents or the institution, do not cover medical treatment that occurs more than two years after the injury. However, some Football Bowl Subdivision (FBS) conferences have announced they will cover sport-incurred injuries for four years after graduation.
- Disagreements are common over whether the athlete is experiencing an uncovered illness or an athletics-related injury, and whether an athletics-related injury is the result of a preexisting condition.
- Institutional insurance or medical reimbursement policies may not cover high deductibles, common to many parent insurance plans.
- Injuries resulting in temporary or permanent disabilities that restrict future employment and earnings are not covered.[13]

Generally, NCAA rules regarding the institutional provision of medical expenses "permit" rather than "require coverage," with rules manuals in all competitive divisions containing the following statement:

16.4 Medical Expenses

An institution, conference or the NCAA may provide medical and related expenses and services to a student-athlete.[14]

Thus, for example, if an institution wishes to cover the medical expenses for an athlete to receive a flu shot, see a doctor, or receive a prescription to aid in recovering from the flu, or for a myriad of other expenses that would allow an athlete to return to play more quickly or participate more safely, it can do so or not, as it chooses. The line dividing illness or injury from the provision of corrective expenses is simply not clear. Therefore, while institutions may provide for the following expenses, they are not required to do so:

1. Medical insurance.
2. Death and dismemberment insurance for travel connected to intercollegiate athletics competition and practice.
3. Drug rehabilitation expenses.
4. Counseling expenses related to the treatment of eating disorders.
5. Special individual expenses resulting from a permanent disability that precludes further athletics participation. The illness or injury producing the disability must involve a former student-athlete or have occurred while the student-athlete was enrolled at the institution, or while the prospective student-athlete was on an official paid visit to the institution's campus. An institution or outside agency, or both, may raise money through donations, benefits, or like activities to assist the student-athlete or a prospective student-athlete. All funds secured shall be controlled by the institution, and the money shall be used exclusively to meet these expenses.
6. Glasses, contact lenses, or protective eye wear (such as goggles) for student-athletes who require visual correction in order to participate in intercollegiate athletics.
7. Medical examinations at any time.
8. Expenses for medical treatment (including transportation and other related costs). Such expenses may include the cost of traveling to the location of medical treatment or the provision of actual and necessary living expenses for the student-athlete to be treated at a site on- or off-campus during the summer months while the student-athlete is not actually attending classes. Medical documentation shall be available to support the necessity of the treatment at the location in question.
9. Medical expenses (including surgical expenses, medication, rehabilitation, and physical therapy expenses).
10. Dental expenses.[15]

These types of expenses related to the health and safety of athletes simply have not risen to the level of importance at which the NCAA would require member institutions to pay for them. Thus, institutions may choose to use media products, student fees, institutional general fund subsidies, donations, gate receipts, and other earned revenues to pay millions to coaches rather than placing the highest priority on caring for the health and safety of student-athletes and using such revenues to benefit the health of athletes.

Further, there are elite athletes who decide to remain in school to complete their degrees rather than participate in the National Basketball Association, the National Football League, Major League Baseball, the Women's National Basketball Association, Major League Soccer, the National Women's Soccer League or other professional drafts, which would make them ineligible for intercollegiate competition. Currently, the NCAA Exceptional Athlete Disability Program guarantees for players expected to be drafted in rounds one or two that these individuals could obtain a permanent disability policy (PTD) by borrowing against their future earnings at a yearly cost of $8,000 to $10,000 for every $1 million of coverage up to a $5 million limit, if the athlete sustains an injury in college that makes it impossible to participate as a professional.[16] Of course, if the athlete does suffer a disabling injury, then he or she is still responsible for paying the accumulated yearly premiums. The NCAA does not offer Loss of Value (LOV) insurance coverage, but it can be obtained as a rider on a PTD policy for an additional sum if the athlete wishes to purchase this additional LOV coverage.[17] Because of the amount of revenues generated by these athletes and the small number of athletes who qualify for first- or second-round professional drafts, it seems reasonable for the NCAA and its member institutions to be required to pay for such coverage.

It does not seem unreasonable, in light of the $1.4 billion in revenues currently generated by the Final Four and the College Football Playoff, that such revenues should first be directed toward providing for the cost of a national athletic injury umbrella insurance policy covering all NCAA athletes in all divisions.[18]

Failure to Mandate Health Protections

NCAA rules do not (1) prohibit harmful instructional practices by coaches, (2) require preventive, predictive or baseline medical testing, or (3) require members to adhere to model practices and policies recommended by medical authorities. For example, the NCAA annually publishes the *NCAA*

Sports Medicine Handbook, which contains guidelines for institutions conducting athletic programs.[19] All material in the *Handbook,* which is intended to provide the most up-to-date medical and safety policies and procedures, is only guidelines:

> The health and safety principle of the National Collegiate Athletic Association's constitution provides that it is the responsibility of each member institution to protect the health of, and provide a safe environment for, each of its participating student-athletes. To provide guidance in accomplishing this objective and to assist member schools in developing a safe intercollegiate athletics program, the NCAA Committee on Competitive Safeguards and Medical Aspects of Sports, in conjunction with the NCAA Sport Science Institute, creates a Sports Medicine Handbook.[20]

Such a position is counterintuitive at best and irresponsible at worst for an athletics governance organization established in 1905 to address deaths and other safety concerns in intercollegiate football. This posture seeks to protect the NCAA from legal liability by transferring legal responsibility to each member institution:

> This handbook consists of guidelines for each institution for developing sports medicine policies appropriate for its intercollegiate athletics program. In some instances, accompanying best practices, and references to sports medicine or legal resource materials are provided for further guidance. These recommendations are not intended to establish a legal standard of care that must be strictly adhered to by member institutions. In other words, these guidelines are not mandates that an institution is required to follow to avoid legal liability or disciplinary sanctions by the NCAA. However, an institution has a legal duty to use reasonable care in conducting its intercollegiate athletics program, and guidelines may constitute some evidence of the legal standard of care.[21]

The NCAA is in the best position to protect the health and safety of athletes because it is monitoring the injury rates of over 450,000 athletes on an annual basis. It has collected data since 1981–82, and in 2004–05 the NCAA entered into a partnership with the Datalys Center for Sports

Injury Research and Prevention, Inc., an independent, nonprofit research organization, to replace its paper-and-pencil system with a web-based Injury Surveillance System (ISS). The ISS provides data sets to researchers for study. Member institutions provide data on injuries incurred in "practices and competitions, the number of participating student-athletes, and time-loss injuries during the preseason, regular season, and postseason in 25 collegiate sports."[22] Numerous research studies use ISS data to examine the epidemiology of injuries in various sports and make recommendations for injury prevention.[23]

Using statistics from the NCAA's Injury Surveillance Program (ISP), researchers found that college athletes experienced 10,560 sport-related concussions annually, with one in eleven recurrent. In most sports, the majority of concussions occurred during practice sessions, while the actual rates of concussion were higher in competitions. Football led all sports in total incidents (3,417) because it has the most participants, but with regard to rates, men's wrestling was number 1, at 10.92 per 10,000 exposures, and men's ice hockey was next, at 7.91, followed by women's ice hockey at 7.52 and football at 6.71.[24] In another study of sudden cardiac death in NCAA athletes, the researchers concluded that the risk for sudden cardiac death is high, with males, black athletes, and basketball players at substantially higher risk.[25] Whether the issue is concussion, sudden cardiac death, or a host of other injuries tracked by the NCAA, the point is that it is the responsibility of a governance association to mandate that its member institutions do the most they can to protect the health of athletes.

This failure to mandate health protections for all college athletes as a condition of membership means the NCAA will tolerate member institutions that are willing to accept legal risk. It appears both necessary and eminently reasonable to require athletic program operations consistent with all guidelines contained in the NCAA *Sports Medicine Handbook*. It should not be optional to have rules that (1) prohibit subjecting athletes to intentional dehydration in order to meet weight requirements of any sport, (2) allow the use of local anesthetic injections only in the case of medical justification, or (3) require all coaches to be educated about severe exertional rhabdomyolysis, a condition most often caused by coaches directing athletes to perform excessive repetitions of extreme exercise or using exercise for physical punishment. It does not make sense to require institutions to have a concussion management plan in Divisions I and II and not in

Division III. It is inconceivable that National Football League teams are limited to two contact practices per week, while such restrictions on college football are left to the discretion of leagues or individual institutions.

Equally distressing is the NCAA's effort to protect itself and its member institutions from responsibility for not acting to protect athletes. When a group of college athletes sued the NCAA for its failure to act to protect athletes from concussions, the NCAA settlement sought blanket immunity from future litigation for itself and its members. The court refused to provide the sought-after immunity, ruling that current and former college athletes could still sue for personal injuries, including "class claims that do not relate in any way to medical monitoring or medical treatment of concussions or sub-concussive hits or contact."[26] As we write in April 2016, it is still unclear whether the NCAA will agree to its proposed settlement, which would create a "50-year medical monitoring program at $70 million to cover diagnostic medical expenses for athletes, not their actual treatment."[27]

Failure to Require Coaches to Adhere to Professional Standards of Sport Pedagogy

Simon Cvijanovic, a senior starter on the University of Illinois football team, reported that his coach pressured him to play with knee and shoulder injuries, the seriousness of which was concealed from him. When Cvijanovic resisted the coach's efforts to force him to play, the coach set out to embarrass him by making him observe practice while dressed in an opposing team's uniform.[28] University of Utah head swimming coach Greg Winslow was accused by his swimmers of five years of verbal, emotional, and physical abuse. Some examples included one swimmer being forced to swim underwater with a PVC pipe taped to his back and arms until he blacked out and another swimmer being forced to swim with a mesh bag over her head, eventually requiring counseling because of the experience.[29]

A coach's code of conduct demanding professional standards of sport pedagogy and maintenance of a safe instructional environment are responsibilities unaddressed by NCAA rules applicable to all member institutions. It is no longer appropriate to tolerate or protect an athletic culture in which any coach has the authority to treat an athlete disrespectfully; use physical punishment in response to losing games, skill errors, or lack of effort; or engage in conduct that would be totally unacceptable for a classroom teacher. The fear- and tradition-based code of silence and locker-room loyalty that prevents athletes from both recognizing and reporting mistreatment cannot be tolerated. Even the highly publicized case of Rutgers's head basketball coach Mike Rice being fired for abusive practices, such as throwing basketballs at his players and using homophobic slurs, might not have occurred if a disgruntled former basketball program administrator had not released a team practice video tape of the transgressions that eventually went viral. It wasn't until after Rice was fired that his players brought a lawsuit against him because of such treatment.[30] The use of intimidation, bullying, threats of nonrenewal of scholarships, or similar tactics not only creates educationally unsound environments for athletes but also effectively extinguishes athlete reporting of such behavior.

Another area of concern is coaches misusing their power over athletes to engage in inappropriate social or sexual relationships. Like other teachers on campus, coaches should be strictly prohibited from such misuse of their positions. It has only been since 2010 and because of national research revealing that one in five college women and one in sixteen men experience sexual abuse, harassment, and rape while in college that the federal government has become actively involved in preventing institutions from sweeping such conduct under the rug. While research on the frequency of athlete sexual abuse in the United States is nonexistent, anecdotal data from news reports within the United States abound and appear to represent the tip of the iceberg in sports.[31] For instance, 159 coaches, nearly all male perpetrators abusing girls, in Washington State public schools were fired or reprimanded over a period of a decade for sexual misconduct ranging from harassment to rape.[32] USA Swimming has declared seventy-eight coaches or others permanently ineligible for membership, with seventy-two listed as committing code of conduct violations.[33] USA Gymnastics has declared eighty-seven coaches or others permanently ineligible for membership because of conduct violations.[34] In open amateur sport, the U.S. Olympic Committee has established a Coach Code of Conduct and a Safe Sport program that is beginning to address these concerns.[35] No similar initiative is occurring with school and college sports, where there is a significant need for nationally mandated adherence to a coaches' code of conduct.

Clearly, all the elements of the athletics culture that result in the continued acceptance of the infliction of psychological and physical abuse on athletes need to be addressed and eliminated, and the athletic governance organizations must play a leadership role in this regard. Athletes must be educated not to accept such coach behavior. Athlete whistleblower protection should be required by the NCAA, but currently it is not. Strong sanctions that cut across institutional and conference lines of authority are required to ensure that coaches guilty of unprofessional conduct do not move from one institution to the next, simply changing the location of their transgressions.

Improper Restrictions on the Current and Future Earning Potential of College Athletes

Current NCAA rules improperly limit (1) a student's earning potential during his or her period of collegiate athletics eligibility, (2) sources of advice related to future professional sport employment, and (3) athletes' ability to test their marketability as professionals. Further, the NCAA and its member institutions have, in the past, pressured athletes into granting institutions and the NCAA use of their names, images, and likenesses (NILs) as a condition of their athletic eligibility, with such use extending beyond reasonable and educationally justifiable use. While the NCAA has dropped the NIL clause in its mandatory form, several conferences and schools continue to require NIL-use consent by athletes. In general, college athletes do not have the same rights to earn money or obtain career advice as other nonathlete students participating in school-sponsored performing arts or educational programs.

Overly Restrictive Definition of Professionalism and Barriers to Career Advice

The NCAA has created overly restrictive definitions of amateurism and barriers to career advice as conditions for athletic eligibility. Granted, it is properly within the authority of institutions of higher education and their national sports governance organizations to define a "professional athlete" and prohibit professional athletes from participating in college athletic programs because athletes like those in the NFL and NBA generally have skill and competitive advantages over college athletes. Indeed, maintaining a clear line of demarcation between college and professional sports is a stated purpose of the NCAA. Few would argue with a definition of a professional athlete as a person who has signed a professional employment contract, received remuneration (bonus or any other compensation) for participating in a professional sport, or, whether paid or not, participated as an athlete on a professional athletics team. The problem is that instead of the NCAA narrowly and clearly defining professional athlete in this manner, it has chosen to invent an overly broad definition of professionalization.

For instance, the NCAA limits college football and basketball players, but not athletes in other sports, from participating in professional drafts or tryout camps. Similarly, the NCAA does not allow college athletes to retain an agent or lawyer to provide advice, market the athlete's skills, or negotiate a professional contract, short of executing such an agreement. In the name of protecting the athlete from unscrupulous agents, the NCAA permits institutionally provided advisory panels in lieu of experts selected by the athlete, despite the institution's conflict of interest in retaining the athlete as eligible to compete for the institution rather than becoming a professional. The NCAA classifies many athlete activities short of actually becoming a professional athlete as eligibility disqualifiers in the name of "amateurism," a concept invented to control the college's athlete assets.

These excessive restrictions extend to athletes' use of their NILs to endorse products or become models, or to use their athletic knowledge or ability to provide sports lessons to individuals or to be paid as the coach of an amateur athletics team—clearly not part of what being a professional athlete means.

Treatment of College Athletes as Professional Athlete Employees

Until a 2015 reform that permitted the granting of four-year scholarships for the first time since 1973, the NCAA defined allowable athletics financial aid (that is, athletic scholarships) in a manner that permitted institutions to treat athletes as professional athlete employees rather than students receiving educational scholarships. The NCAA had crafted a one-year college athletic scholarship system that provided a relatively cheap and steady supply of highly talented athletes for the lucrative business of collegiate sports and had given coaches the kind of control over them that employers have over employees. In 2016, the vast majority of Division I and Division II institutions still grant only one-year athletic scholarships.

For an athletic scholarship to be analogous to an academic scholarship, as the NCAA contends, the grant-in-aid must meet the U.S. Internal Revenue Service (IRS) definition. For a scholarship to be tax-free and clearly not income by virtue of employment, the college athlete must be a candidate for a degree, the grant cannot exceed expenses, and it cannot represent payment for teaching, research, or other services (such as athletics) required as a condition for receiving the scholarship.[36] Thus, if one-year "scholarships" are administered in a way that requires the athlete to provide services as a condition for receipt, the IRS definition is not met.

"Under the common law definition, an employee is a person who performs services for another under a contract of hire, subject to the other's control or right of control, and in return for payment."[37] When the Region 13 Labor Relations Board examined the actual experience of Northwestern University football players, they found their treatment in conformance with this definition. Specifically, they performed services for the benefit of their employer, received compensation (in the form of a scholarship) in exchange, and were "subject to the employer's control in the performance of their duties as football players." These duties were unrelated to the players' academic studies or degree requirements. The fifty to sixty hours per week these players were required to spend on their football duties were in excess of the number of hours required of full-time employees working at their jobs and constituted more hours than the players spent on their studies. Further, coaches exercised extraordinary control over the lives of the players by using the actual and perceived threat of removal of their athletic scholarships.

In addition, the coaches have control over nearly every aspect of the players' private lives by virtue of the fact that there are many rules that they must follow under threat of discipline and/or the loss of a scholarship. The players have restrictions placed on them and/or have to obtain permission from the coaches before they can: (1) make their living arrangements; (2) apply for outside employment; (3) drive personal vehicles; (4) travel off campus; (5) post items on the Internet; (6) speak to the media; (7) use alcohol and drugs; and (8) engage in gambling. The fact that some of these rules are put in place to protect the players and the Employer from running afoul of NCAA rules does not detract from the amount of control the coaches exert over the players' daily lives.[38]

In light of the power and control of coaches, athletes receiving one-year scholarships are not adequately protected from the arbitrary or capricious withdrawal of aid. Because scholarships represent incentives for student attendance that greatly influence enrollment decisions and family financial planning, such protection is essential. It is perfectly acceptable to condition renewal of athletic aid on transparent academic standards such as cumulative GPA or on maintaining normal progress toward the degree, which is often true of academic scholarships or need-based aid received by nonathlete students. Such standards are directly related to the primary purpose of higher education institutions. Continuation of athletic scholarships for four or five years dependent on the college athlete's degree program, completion of a full-time course load each semester until graduation, and meeting minimum academic standards, such as a 2.0 GPA, would be both sensible and protect against an employment relationship in which a coach could simply not renew a player's grant whenever a better player is recruited or the coach is otherwise dissatisfied. Even a rule that says that a scholarship cannot be withdrawn for athletic performance reasons disregards the reality that a coach can make an athlete's life miserable in many ways, convincing the athlete to cease participation or transfer to another school, especially if the coach offers a release to transfer without eligibility penalty. It is not uncommon for a violation of team rules or athletics department policies to be misused as a justification for termination of financial aid. Thus, it is proper to contend that one-year athletic grants of aid should be considered de facto employment relationships, just as nonrenewal based on sport performance should be considered athletics employment.

In Division I of the NCAA, since 2014, multiyear scholarships may currently be awarded, but only at the option of the institution. Even though all characteristics of an employment relationship need to be addressed, an important first step is removing the equivalent of a one-year employee-at-will agreement and replacing it with a mandatory four- or five-year grant with academic rather than athletic conditions for renewal. Withdrawal of the scholarship because of nonparticipation resulting from injury, a participation factor not under the student's control, should be prohibited. Scholarships should also be protected from arbitrary or capricious withdrawal based on any violation of "team rules" or "athletics department policy" if such rules are more onerous than or inconsistent with rules of conduct applied to students generally or without due process hearings afforded to all students. Violations of such athletic policies may properly result in disciplinary action, but such action should not extend to the removal of financial aid.

At the heart of this issue is the inappropriate treatment of students participating in an extracurricular activity. NCAA rules allow coaches to treat athletes as employees. Such a climate of control can easily turn into intimidation and abuse because of the economic power the coach may exercise over the scholarship athlete. Further, because athletes understand the power of the coach and the economic stakes, they cannot be expected to challenge the authority or behavior of the coach. To say the least, this is not a healthy educational environment.

Improper Nonprofit Educational Institution Exploitation of College Athletes' NILs

The NCAA and its member institutions not only improperly gain rights to use college athletes' names, images, and likenesses, in many cases they exploit the commercial use of the athlete's NIL in a manner that is improper for nonprofit educational institutions. Extracurricular activities generally, and intercollegiate athletic programs among them, are considered important contributors to student development, allowing students to explore interests beyond the highly restricted nature of required and elective courses within specific degree programs. Many of these activities involve the performing arts (music, dance, theatre, athletics, and so on). These activities may or may not lend themselves to public performances for which admission is charged. If admission is charged, these revenues are used to defray the costs of the extracurricular program, accrue to the institution, or, in some cases, result in modest stipends to the student. Many of these extracurricular activities, including athletics, are subsidized by mandatory student fees. At some schools, students must pay participation fees or expenses to participate in these activities, even if they are partially funded by general student fees or institutional subsidies.

The mere fact of a student participating in a curricular or extracurricular activity does not and should not legally confer the student's NIL rights to the institution. If the institution wishes to use a student's NIL to advertise the institution or an extracurricular program event or wishes to televise, film, or otherwise commercially exploit the event, it should obtain permission from participating students. If the student does not wish to be in an advertisement or be part of a televised event, he or she should have the right to refuse such use of his or her NILs. Similarly, if the student says that he or she will only confer rights to the institution in return for pay or on terms to which the institution does not agree, the student should have no right to participate in the event. But this legal and common sense interpretation of how NIL rights should be handled is not the case for intercollegiate athletics, where athletes are pressured into giving up their NIL rights as a condition of athletic participation. While the NCAA has removed the requirement that college athletes sign away their NIL rights for no compensation on the annual NCAA Student-Athlete Statement,[39] which the student must sign to be eligible for regular season play, such statements are still being required by NCAA member institutions and conferences.[40]

Two NIL practices have a negative impact on student-athletes. First, the NCAA permits itself, conferences, and member institutions to condition athletic participation on the athlete waiving his or her NIL rights and restricts the athlete's rights to cede these rights to others during the student's period of collegiate athletics eligibility.[41] Use of the college athlete's NIL during this eligibility period is limited to institutional, charitable, educational, or nonprofit promotions, and the athlete is not permitted to receive any compensation, whereas NCAA member institutions, NCAA member conferences, or charitable, educational, or nonprofit agencies are allowed to profit from such use. Others may also profit from such use. The athlete regularly appears at intercollegiate athletic events for which his or her institution, or in the case of postseason championship play his or her conference or the NCAA, may receive millions in sponsorships or media rights fees. During these televised or otherwise electronically distributed events, the media rights holder sells advertising and sponsorships, extending benefits to numerous other entities. Further, many of these media agreements contain rights to rebroadcast or redistribute the property, or the institution will repurpose footage to create a documentary or commemorative property that is sold well beyond the graduation dates of college athletes who participated in the event. The point here is not that the athlete should be compensated for participation in athletic events from which the institution receives revenues. Rather, the issue is control of athletes' NILs beyond these live events or taped events rebroadcast in the current academic year.

This prohibition against athletes receiving compensation for use of their NILs when use does not involve the extracurricular activity or when electronic distribution of the event occurs for an unreasonably extended period must be examined. While it is arguably proper for nonprofit organizations to commercially exploit extracurricular performances by charging for admission or media rights fees for live or delayed carriage of extracurricular activity performances, it is not proper to allow nonprofit entities to use student NILs in perpetuity (that is, beyond the years of student enrollment) or to benefit from producing commercial products for which they must pay unrelated business income taxes, without specific athlete permission and donation or payment for use of their NILs.

In many cases, private individuals or corporations can benefit from use of the college athlete's NIL unrelated to the college or university for which he or she plays. For instance, the NCAA permits a college athlete's name, photograph, and other information to appear in a summer camp brochure, with revenues from the camp accruing to a coach or other owner. The NCAA also permits a private individual to write and publish a book or a company to produce a videotape, film, or other electronic publication on learning sport skills that contains photographs of the athlete demonstrating or giving instruction, as long as the book or video product is considered "educational." Such third parties can benefit monetarily from the publication, whereas the athlete cannot.

Second, the NCAA prohibits college athlete employment if it involves the use of the athlete's NIL, with a few exceptions, such as use of NILs in a summer camp brochure where the athlete works as a counselor. For instance,

- The athlete may establish his or her own business, but cannot use his or her NIL or athletics reputation to promote the business.[42]
- The athlete can accept fees for giving instructional lessons (teaching or coaching sport skills or techniques) provided institutional facilities are

not used, the athlete does not "play" during such lessons, member institutions keep records of such lessons (including the client and the fee), and fees are paid by the client and not by a third party, but the athlete is not allowed to use his or her NIL to promote or advertise the availability of these fee-for-lesson sessions.[43]

- The athlete is not allowed to accept employment as a model unless the athlete was previously employed as a model prior to enrollment in college, such employment was not based on any consideration of athletic ability, there is no commercial product endorsement, and the fee for such service is commensurate with normal rates.[44]

- The athlete is not permitted to accept any remuneration for or permit the use of his or her NIL to advertise, "recommend, or promote directly the sale or use of a commercial product or service of any kind, or to endorse a commercial product or service through the individual's use of such product or service."[45]

The issue is whether the NCAA has a right to restrict the employment of any student outside of participation in institutional properties as long as such participation is not payment to play professional athletics. This is the standard in USA open amateur and Olympic sports. If the NCAA's interest is to prevent third parties who support the athletic program from providing impermissible financial incentives under the guise of normal employment activities, it appears reasonable to simply have a rule that requires that outside employment be reported and remuneration under such circumstances be at market rates commensurate with the individual's athletic skills and experience, and not involve use of the institution's NIL rights.

Physical Isolation and Lack of Integration with the Student Body

One of the most distressing developments of the basketball and football Division I arms race is the common practice of building lavish facilities restricted for athletes' use only—residence halls, training tables, game rooms, study centers, computer labs, locker rooms, conditioning/weight rooms, barber shops, practice facilities, competitive facilities—that may not be used by nonathlete students. Some examples follow:

- The (Oregon) Ducks' Football Performance Center is a 145,000-square-foot building that cost a reported $68 million.[46] Amenities include a lobby with sixty-four 55-inch televisions that can combine to show one image, a weight room floor made of Brazilian hardwood, custom foosball tables where one team is Oregon and the other team has eleven players, each representing the rest of the Pac-12, a barber shop, and a coaches' locker room with TVs embedded in the mirrors.[47] Athletes already had access to an indoor practice field, an athletic medical center, a brand-new basketball arena, and an academic study center for athletes.[48] Oregon's new football program complex contains, among other things, movie theaters, an Oregon football museum, a players' lounge and deck, a dining hall, and private classrooms for top players.[49]

- Athlete-only practice facilities at West Virginia University, utilized only by the Mountaineer men's and women's programs, allow Mountaineer basketball players to have access to the best performance training tools available, top-tier practice areas, strength and conditioning space, sports medicine needs, team meeting and video rooms, and facility equipment.[50] Adding all the elements of performance training and providing first-class locker-room facilities, players' lounges, and study areas, the basketball practice facility provides a distinct advantage in recruiting top-tier student-athletes and showcasing the best that Mountaineer basketball and WVU can offer.[51]

- The Texas A&M University football players' lounge and academic center is 5,000 square feet and conveniently located one floor above the locker room, training room, and meeting rooms and across the hall from the new state-of-the-art, athlete-only academic center.[52] It is outfitted with ample leather seating, tables, and oversized leather lounge chairs that recline to a full prone position so players can watch the huge wide-screen, high-definition television.[53] Other amenities include Ping-Pong, foosball, pool, and gaming tables, as well as several arcade-style gaming stations that feature the latest video game systems.[54] Several flat-screen TVs are mounted in each corner of the room.[55] Immediately to the left of the lounge's entrance is a marble-top bar that contains soft drink and candy machines for the players' use.[56]

- Clemson University announced a $55 million facility for the exclusive use of football players that will include a laser tag area, a sand volleyball court, a miniature golf course, and a barber shop to serve a players' village.[57]

Academic support facilities for athletes are often of higher quality than those available to the student body. Weight training facilities are often larger and include higher-quality equipment than what is available to the student body. Gymnasiums or fields that are used only for basketball or other sports team practices are left unused for most of the day. Computer facilities are state of the art and, in addition, iPads or laptops are provided to individual athletes. Even though NCAA rules prohibit athletes-only residence halls, institutions have designed workarounds that conform to the rules and attract recruits with luxurious housing accommodations. For instance, at the University of Oklahoma, the athletics department fully funds the operation of Headington Hall, a $75 million, five-story facility, built with private funds. Headington Hall houses 380 students, 50 percent of whom are nonathletes, as required by NCAA rules. Headington Hall has apartment-style accommodations in two- and four-bedroom units with individual showers and restrooms for each unit, a central dining hall, computer labs, study rooms, a theater, a faculty-in-residence unit, and microwaves and refrigerators in the kitchen of each unit.[58]

These lavish facilities and practices not only create a double standard for the treatment of athlete and nonathlete students, they also effectively isolate athletes from the rest of the student body, creating a campuswide impression, which in turn shapes faculty and peer treatment of college athletes. This lavish treatment also increases the individual athlete's perception of self-importance and worth, contributing to expectations of special treatment in other aspects of student and community life. It is one small step to the athlete expecting different and advantageous treatment in the classroom, from community law enforcement officials, and from alumni and fans of the athletic program. Lack of integration with the general student body also creates the perfect environment for the development and acceptance of negative stereotypes that do a disservice to athletes and may create negative differential treatment. While coaches can argue in favor of the recruiting advantages of lavish facilities and treatment, it would seem the dysfunctional effect of such treatment on the individual athlete should take precedence.

Inadequate Protection of Due Process Rights

The power imbalance between athletes and their coaches, or the athletics department generally because of its political dominance on campus, leaves athletes particularly vulnerable to unfair treatment, ranging from suspension from playing to removal from a team to loss of athletics-related financial aid. Such unfair treatment may not be a reaction to athletes' breaking team rules, failure to follow the instructions of their coaches, or engaging in misbehavior. Even if the athlete is a model student and citizen, if he or she is in the unfortunate position of being less skilled than or performing not as well as an athlete the coach believes would be a better replacement, and if the coach wants to use the athlete's scholarship for the better prospect, the coach can engage in various schemes to get the athlete to leave the program or become ineligible to play. The athlete may be pressured to transfer with the promise of a full release (no athletic eligibility penalty). The coach may be less aggressive in seeking academic help for such an athlete if he or she is struggling in the classroom. The coach can inform the athlete that his or her scholarship will not be renewed. Thus, fair treatment protections are important.

Insufficient Protection from Improper Termination of Financial Aid

The only two protections provided by NCAA rules to assist an athlete in challenging wrongful termination of athletics-related financial aid are (1) an athlete's right to an institutional financial aid appeal when an athlete is informed that his or her scholarship will be terminated and (2) a requirement that any determination of "serious misconduct," a common reason for termination of aid, be made by the institution's regular student disciplinary authority. Both of these protections have serious flaws.

Unfortunately, with regard to the financial aid appeal, the athlete is not protected from conflict of interest on the part of the institution in the composition or deliberations of the financial aid appeals committee. While the athletics department or a faculty athletics committee is prohibited from handling the hearing process, there is no prohibition against members of the athletics department being present during the hearing or committee deliberations. Further, an athletics department member may be a member of the financial aid appeals committee. NCAA rules state the following:

15.3.2.3 Hearing Opportunity. The institution's regular financial aid authority shall notify the student-athlete in writing of the opportunity for a hearing when institutional financial aid based in any degree on athletics ability is to be reduced or canceled during the period of the award, or is reduced or not renewed for the following academic year or multiple academic years within the student-athlete's five-year period of eligibility. The institution shall have established reasonable procedures for promptly hearing such a request and shall not delegate the responsibility for conducting the hearing to the university's athletics department or its faculty athletics committee. The written notification of the opportunity for a hearing shall include a copy of the institution's established policies and procedures for conducting the required hearing, including the deadline by which a student-athlete must request such a hearing.

15.3.2.3.2 Athletics Department Staff as Member of Committee. An institution's athletics department staff member may be a member of a committee (other than an athletics department or faculty athletics committee) that conducts hearings related to the nonrenewal or reduction of a student-athlete's financial aid. Under such circumstances, the athletics department staff member must be a standing member of the committee and may not serve as a member of a committee only for a specific student-athlete's hearing.[59]

Even if an athletics department member is a standing member of the committee, common sense and fair due process demand that such a member recuse himself or herself for obvious conflict-of-interest reasons.

With regard to the handling of serious misconduct allegations, which can be grounds for termination of athletics-related financial aid and removal from the team, there is no NCAA requirement that the misconduct fall under behaviors prohibited for all students as opposed to violations of rules established by the athletics department. It appears reasonable to require that athletics departments conform to the same rules for termination or reduction of athletic aid that are applicable to any student receiving academic or other forms of aid. But the NCAA permits the athletics department to set standards that may be more stringent or arbitrary:

15.3.4.2.4 Misconduct. An institution may cancel or reduce the financial aid of a student-athlete who is found to have engaged in misconduct by the university's regular student disciplinary authority, even if the loss-of-aid requirement does not apply to the student body in general.[60]

Neither is there any NCAA requirement that athletics department rules and penalties be consistent with the rules of conduct or penalties applicable to all students. Coaches can establish team rules that are unreasonably restrictive. Students who are athletes should not be held to different standards than students who are not athletes.

No Protection of Eligibility Pending Completion of Fair Process

Institutional and individual stakes involved in the violation of NCAA rules are considerable. However, media coverage usually focuses on the impact penalties have on the institution and its coaches rather than on student-athletes. Institutions are publicly embarrassed by media coverage. In the case of Penn State, the school had to pay $60 million in cash penalties. In the case of the University of North Carolina, the venerable academic prestige of one of the country's most selective institutions of higher education was questioned. Television revenues are placed at risk. A coach's winning record may be damaged by sanctions that vacate wins. A coach may be suspended or have their employment terminated. The impact on student-athletes is less likely to be emphasized but is just as significant. The athlete may lose his or her eligibility to compete or may lose athletics-related financial aid. The team may be banned from postseason play because of the transgressions of their coaches, and this ban may be imposed many years after the affected athletes attend the institution. The athlete may be asked to pay restitution for receipt of impermissible benefits. Whether an individual or institution, the name and reputation of the accused are at stake. Thus, the potential outcome of the NCAA enforcement process has a considerable impact on both institutions and individuals.

Assuming the consequences are as serious as described above, at issue is whether the level of procedural due process afforded college athletes by the NCAA is at least as protective as due process used by higher education institutions in matters of student discipline or by national sport governing organizations (NGBs) in open amateur sport in dealing with the eligibility of athletes for competition or their treatment by the NGB. With regard to higher education standards, the following procedural elements are typically afforded:

- Notice of specific charges, including regulations allegedly violated and specific details (date, time, and place) forming the basis for the charges.
- Time to prepare an adequate defense.
- Right to a hearing before an impartial adjudicating body.
- Right to legal counsel in cases with serious consequences.
- Right to present evidence to refute allegations or support the student's position.
- Right to know the identity of witnesses.
- Right to cross-examine witnesses if the outcome of the hearing depends on the credibility of a sole witness, or access to witness statements and the right to refute such statement.[61]

With regard to standards required under section 220522 (a)(8) of the Ted Stevens Olympic and Amateur Sports Act, which are applicable in any case in which an athlete's eligibility to compete in amateur competition (not interscholastic or intercollegiate competition) is at issue, the following "due process checklist," adopted by the U.S. Olympic Committee at its April 7, 1984, meeting applies:

- Notice of the charges of alleged violations, with specificity and in writing, and possible consequences if the charges are found to be true.
- Reasonable time between receipt of the notice of charges and the hearing with respect to the charges, within which to prepare a defense.
- Notice of the identity of adverse witnesses proved in advance of the hearing.
- The right to have the hearing conducted at such a time and place as to make it practicable for the person charged to attend.
- The hearing to be held before a disinterested and impartial body of fact finders.
- The right to be assisted in the presentation of one's case at the hearing, including the assistance of legal counsel, if desired.

- The right to present oral and written evidence and argument.
- The right of the athlete to call witnesses to testify at the hearing, including the right to have individuals under the control of an adverse party attend, and the right to confront and cross-examine such individuals.
- The right to have a record (transcript) made of the hearing.
- The burden of proof shall be on the proponent of the charge, which burden shall be at least a "preponderance of the evidence" unless the rules of the NGB or tribunal require or provide for a higher burden of proof.
- A written decision, with reasons therefore, based solely on the evidence of record, handed down in a timely fashion.
- The right of written notice of appeal procedures, if the decision is adverse to the person charged, and the prompt and fair adjudication of any appeal.[62]

In addition to these procedural rights, the USOC recognizes that timely processing of eligibility appeals is important and that there is a high probability of conflict of interest on the part of the governing body seeking to penalize the athlete. As a result, athletes in open amateur sport benefit from a system of binding arbitration, conducted by trained arbiters, that protects athletes from biased treatment.

The NCAA affords none of these rights to individuals; rather, it substitutes a convoluted process of communication with the NCAA member institution that is devoid of procedural protections for the individuals affected. Neither athletes nor coaches (nor other institutional employees, for that matter) are required to be provided with information about the allegations against them. Individuals are literally left out of the process that occurs between the NCAA and their institutions. Athletes are particularly vulnerable because they are often left without unbiased third-party legal assistance while the institution is served by a cadre of lawyers and coaches and other employees have the independent financial means to obtain legal representation.

In addition to this failure to provide charged individuals with procedural due process, three basic principles of the NCAA enforcement process further undermine the prospect for fair treatment of athletes. First, the institution knows from the outset that if the athlete seeks and obtains court protection from unfair treatment, such court-afforded protection may later be reversed and held against the institution if the athlete is eventually determined to be in violation. Section 19.13 of the NCAA Manual defines "restitution" the following way:

> If a student-athlete who is ineligible under the terms of the constitution, bylaws or other legislation of the Association is permitted to participate in intercollegiate competition contrary to such NCAA legislation but in accordance with the terms of a court restraining order or injunction operative against the institution attended by such student-athlete or against the Association, or both, and said injunction is voluntarily vacated, stayed or reversed or it is finally determined by the courts that injunctive relief is not or was not justified, the Board of Directors may take any one or more of the following actions against such institution in the interest of restitution and fairness to competing institutions.[63]

The manual then lists actions ranging from vacating records, performances, wins, and championships to ineligibility of the institution for future NCAA championships, returning distributions of television income, or other financial penalties. For the institution to protect itself, this process of "restitution" in effect forces the institution to not allow an athlete to play even if the institution does not declare the athlete ineligible.

The second dampening agent is the NCAA's "cooperation principle," which on its face appears laudable but in practice encourages the institution to behave with extreme prejudice against those who the NCAA alleges have committed violations. This principle includes statements that "exemplary cooperation by an institution shall constitute a mitigating factor for purposes of determining a penalty"[64] and "failure to cooperate may result in an independent allegation and/or be considered an aggravating factor for purposes of determining a penalty."[65] The direct and indirect messages are that if the institution agrees with the NCAA charges and acts accordingly, penalties will be minimal. The not unreasonable implication is that if the institution disagrees and provides a vigorous defense that might be interpreted as lack of cooperation with the NCAA, the penalties may be more stringent. The cooperation principle also encourages institutions to throw someone under the bus, even if it is the wrong person, or to exact an institutionally imposed harsh penalty that may not be consistent

with the manner in which other students or employees are treated under
similar circumstances as a demonstration of its serious commitment to
conducting a reputable program. And, by the NCAA's dealing with the
institution and holding it responsible, the institution is more likely to consider its own reputation or the interests of its highest-ranking employees
before the interests of lower-ranking employees or athletes.

The third dampening agent is that while the institution is expected to
share all of its information with the NCAA and to get all of its representatives to cooperate, the NCAA investigations staff is not obligated to do like-
wise with the institution.

> The enforcement staff will usually share information with the institu-
> tion during an investigation, including information that may assist
> the institution in stopping an ongoing violation. However, to protect the
> integrity of the investigation, the staff may not in all instances be
> able to share information with the institution.[66]

While the NCAA is not allowed to use information from individuals
who ask not to be identified (so-called confidential sources) in the formal
charges brought at the hearing before its Committee on Infractions, it is
not prevented from using this information in any Notice of Preliminary
Inquiry, which marks the beginning of the pressure on the institution to
demonstrate it is hewing to the cooperation principle. A double standard
also exists with regard to leverage to obtain information. The NCAA does
not have the power to compel individuals to testify or provide information.
But the NCAA does have the power through its cooperation principle to
force institutions to use the threat of termination of employment or participation eligibility to compel athletes and coaches or other employees to
testify during its investigation.

The basic point of this criticism of the NCAA enforcement process is that
athletes are not fairly served. In fact, the institution is at high risk because
of the extraordinary rules of restitution and cooperation if it does not immediately declare an athlete ineligible when informed of a possible violation of NCAA rules. The institution knows it is better off waiting for the
NCAA to reinstate the athlete, keeping the athlete out of competition in
the interim, than it is waiting for the enforcement process to issue a finding. This is a system in which the athlete is considered guilty until proven

innocent and an insult in a society that prizes its protection of individual freedoms.

In summary, the absence of adequate protection of the health, educational, and psychological welfare of college athletes and the absence of fair treatment guarantees are easily demonstrated and must be addressed.

SIX

A Continuing Disgrace: Discrimination Based on Gender, Race, Ethnicity, and Disability

The general public was keenly aware of discrimination against women in sports because of the extensive 1970s media coverage of the athletics establishment's objection to Title IX of the Education Amendments of 1972, the federal law credited with opening the doors of interscholastic and intercollegiate athletics to females. It was a battle of epic proportion, with the president of the American Football Coaches Association charging that Title IX and women's athletics would be the death of big-time college football and the NCAA joining in to try to get Congress to amend Title IX to exclude football and men's basketball from gender equity assessments. Neither the public nor Congress bought into these efforts. Female physical education and athletics leaders used research-supported data to demonstrate the long-term career, social, psychological, and physical benefits of sports participation. Multiple national public opinion polls confirmed that parents wanted their sons and daughters to be treated equally, even if it meant cutting opportunities for men, and more than 70 percent wanted to see Title IX strengthened or left alone.[1] Unfortunately, some believe that gender equity has already been achieved. Not so. This chapter examines the current state of gender equity, why Title IX's progress has ground to a halt with regard to female opportunities to play sports, and why Title IX has not translated into increased coaching and other athletics department employment opportunities for females.

Similarly, while the public is somewhat aware of allegations of the academic exploitation of underprepared minority Division I football and men's basketball players (see chapter 2), few are aware that collegiate athletes are still predominantly white and predominantly male. Individuals of color are significantly underrepresented in the great majority of the NCAA's championship sports in Divisions I, II, and III and significantly underrepresented with regard to employment as coaches and in other athletics positions. This chapter, therefore, also examines the current state of college athletics participation and employment opportunities for minorities, as well as possible reasons why discrimination on the basis of race or ethnicity is not being successfully addressed.

The third civil rights pillar that should be addressed by the NCAA is opportunities for athletes with disabilities. This chapter explores why encouraging opportunities for athletes with disabilities or even tracking employment opportunities for individuals with disabilities does not appear to be on the NCAA's radar.

To the NCAA's credit, beginning in 2007–08, the organization required all member institutions and conferences to provide participation and employment data based on gender and race or ethnicity, with such data made publicly available online in the NCAA's Sport Sponsorship, Participation and Demographics Search database.[2] Data are available for athletes participating in all NCAA championship sports in all three membership divisions (Divisions I, II, and III). Data are also available on institutional employees—coaches, assistant coaches, and administrators. Within the administrator category are six different positions: director of athletics, associate director of athletics, assistant director of athletics, senior woman administrator, administrative assistant, and academic adviser/counselor. Data are available as well on NCAA member athletic conference employees: conference presidents (who is a college president in most cases), commissioners, associate commissioners, assistant commissioners, directors (for example, the director of compliance or the director of championships), and associate directors. Data include both the sex of the participant or employee and that person's race or ethnicity, categories that correspond to federal definitions. Unfortunately, the data are aggregated. There is no "report card" for each member institution or conference. Thus, this is not a resource that can be used by prospective college athletes or employees to assess the inclusivity climate of an institution or to create a public embarrassment incentive to address demonstrable discrimination.

Continued Sex Discrimination in Athletics Participation, Benefits, and Employment

Even though the passage of Title IX in 1972 clearly prohibited discrimination on the basis of sex in all educational activities, including athletics, progress in achieving gender equity in athletics participation, benefits, and employment has not been realized. Further, both Title IX and the Civil Rights Act of 1966 prohibit sex discrimination in employment. Yet females are still woefully underrepresented among employees in college and university athletics departments and athletic conference offices. Thus, the current state of female athletes and employees deserves careful examination.

Gender Equity for Female College Athletes in Athletics Participation, Treatment, and Benefits Still Unrealized

The growth of women's intercollegiate athletics participation since the passage of Title IX has been nothing short of extraordinary, but primarily because these opportunities were so miniscule in 1972–73 (see table 6-1).

TABLE 6-I: Growth of Female NCAA Athletic Participation, 1972–73 to 2014–15

	Male	Female
1972–73	170,384 (85%)	29,977 (15%)
2014–15	276,599 (57%)	212,479 (43%)
Growth	+ 62%	+609%
Female undergraduates= 57% Female athletes = 43% in 2014–15		

Source: NCAA, Sport Sponsorship, Participation and Demographics Search database, 2016 (http://web1.ncaa.org/rgdSearch/exec/main).

Although there are two exceptions, the basic Title IX participation stan-dard for gender equity is that the percentage of opportunities for males and females to participate in athletics must match their respective percent-ages in the undergraduate student body. Thus, forty-four years after the passage of Title IX, female athletes are still 154,176 participation opportu-nities short of their entitlement.[3] Insofar as more male sports participation opportunities (48,499) have been added than female participation oppor-tunities (41,948) during the ten-year period from 2005–06 to 2014–15, backsliding rather than a continued growth of female opportunities is a more likely future.

In 2012, on the occasion of the fortieth anniversary of Title IX, the NCAA Committee on Women's Athletics commissioned a "report to bring multiple research findings illustrating the status of women as student-athletes, coaches and administrators in NCAA athletics into one document."[4] Key findings of the report regarding the participation and treatment of female student-athletes included the following:

- The girls' high school participation rate is ten times what it was when Title IX was passed. However, the current girls' participation level has not yet reached the boys' 1971–72 level.

- More than 3.1 million female high school athletes are part of the re-cruiting pool to fill more than 191,000 roster spots on NCAA champi-onship sports teams.

- Over the past ten years, men's intercollegiate sports participation has grown by 48,499 opportunities, exceeding women's 41,948 new partici-pation slots by 6,551.

- Division I has the highest female participation rate, with 46 percent of opportunities for women, who on average constitute 53 percent of the undergraduate population on Division I campuses.

- Division I female participation is still seven percentage points away from matching the undergraduate female population. Division II has a seventeen-percentage-point difference between female athletes and fe-male undergraduates, while Division III has a fourteen-percentage-point point gap.

- Division II has the largest participation gap between men and women of all three NCAA Divisions. The twenty-percentage-point gap is the same as it was a decade ago.

- Since 2001–02, the Division III female participation rate as compared to the men's has actually decreased by one percentage point. Division III has the most member institutions but offers more than 6,000 fewer participation opportunities for women than Division I.
- Division I offers more equitable participation opportunities for male and female athletes but has the greatest difference in total expenses, at 60 percent for men and 40 percent for women.
- The largest gaps in expenditures between men's and women's programs in intercollegiate athletics occur in the Football Bowl Subdivision (FBS). Men's programs receive around 70 percent or more of resources in all areas except scholarships. The median budget for men's programs is more than 2.5 times the median budget for women's programs. FBS institutions spend twice as much on each male student-athlete.
- Resource allocations at Football Championship Subdivision (FCS) schools feature less of a gap between men's and women's programs than at FBS schools, but expenditures still favor male athletes by double digits in all areas.[5]

Well over forty years after the passage of Title IX legislation, it is apparent that most institutions of higher education are not providing female athletes with equal participation opportunities, treatment, or benefits.

Title IX Complaints and Lawsuits and Institutional
Self-Assessments: Why Enforcement Is Not Happening

While competitive division and overall NCAA membership data both reveal that the gender equity promise of Title IX is far from realized, it is important to note that Title IX applies to individual educational institutions, and no data are available on the compliance status of individual colleges and universities. Even though all educational institutions were required to perform a Title IX self-assessment in 1975 and are expected to be in continuous compliance with Title IX provisions, there is no federal, NCAA, or higher education regional accreditation agency requirement to regularly assess and report Title IX compliance. The federal Equity in Athletics Disclosure Act does require annual online public reporting of comparative gender data by individual institutions of higher education, but such data are insufficient to determine Title IX compliance. Even though participation numbers and numbers for undergraduate student male and female enrollment are required, which would enable the computation of athletics participation proportional to undergraduate male and female enrollment, there are acceptable Title IX exceptions to the proportionality standard, the data for which are not provided. Similarly, while Equity in Athletics Disclosure Act reports include the number of coaches by sport, athletics financial aid, aggregated salary expenditures, recruiting expenditures, and revenues and expenses by sport, Title IX compliance is qualitative rather than quantitative, is institution-specific, and has many acceptable reasons for differences in treatment such that these reports cannot be used to definitively determine compliance.[6] While the data can be used to determine those institutions suspected of noncompliance, only a detailed examination of actual institutional practice would be definitive.

This reality leaves the public in a position of looking at overall data and being fairly sure that most institutions are not in compliance with Title IX, but not being able to know with a reasonable degree of confidence, absent filing a Title IX athletics complaint with the U.S. Office for Civil Rights (OCR) or filing a lawsuit, or individual institutions voluntarily undertaking Title IX compliance assessments and making the results public. As previously explained, when the NCAA Division I Certification program was in effect, from 1993 to 2011 (it is now permanently discontinued), the gender equity assessment that was part of the program was a full Title IX assessment.

At the institutional level, college presidents are loath to commission a gender equity self-study, much less regularize Title IX athletics assessments, for fear the data, publicly accessible under state Freedom of Information Act requests, will be used to bring lawsuits against the institution. While Title IX cases have been few in number, defendant institutions have consistently lost and have been forced to pay millions for their own legal defense teams, the legal costs of successful plaintiffs, and the costs of coming into compliance as a result of judgments against them. The courts have generally not awarded damages to plaintiffs on top of forcing institutions to immediately come into compliance. Thus, college presidents can minimize the risk of litigation by hiding the existence of inequality—by making sure that such data are not easily accessible. It is not unreasonable to suggest that this is the real reason why the NCAA Division I Certification program was discontinued.

While the law requires that every educational institution have a Title IX coordinator and a complaint procedure, the function of the coordinator's position is more to handle Title IX grievances than to require athletic programs to regularly assess and report Title IX compliance status.[7] These positions are not focused on Title IX athletics compliance. Rather, compliance officers are almost exclusively focused on the OCR crackdown on the sexual harassment provisions of Title IX because campus rape and assault of females has reached epidemic proportions. As a practical matter, few Title IX compliance officers or athletics directors are trained in how to do a Title IX assessment, and even if they were, they would have to depend on the athletics department staff to gather all data and undertake a two- to three-month assessment effort. Title IX assessments are not complex in terms of level of difficulty, but they are extremely tedious and time-consuming. Not only does the assessment include participation, levels of competition, accommodation of interests, and financial aid, it also includes four to six variables under each of twelve other major elements:

1. The provision and maintenance of equipment and supplies.
2. The scheduling of games and practice times.
3. Travel and per diem allowances.
4. Athletes' opportunity to receive academic tutoring, and the assignment and compensation of tutors.
5. Athletes' opportunity to receive coaching, and the assignment and compensation of coaches.
6. The provision of locker-room, practice, and competition facilities.
7. The provision of medical and athletic training facilities and services.
8. The provision of housing and dining facilities and services.
9. Publicity.
10. Support services.
11. Recruiting.
12. Other issues, such as pregnancy and fundraising.[8]

Thus, is it reasonable to assume that Title IX compliance officers and college presidents will not be exercising their Title IX athletics compliance oversight responsibilities anytime soon.

So, who is left to blow the whistle? Athletics departments don't educate students or coaches about Title IX requirements, especially if they know they are not treating male and female athletes equally. While coaches and female athletes are in the best position to experience discriminatory treatment, they do not have access to overall program data to be able to confirm their suspicions. For instance, a female basketball player may see that the men's basketball team has four sets of uniforms compared to her two, travels farther to play more highly ranked teams, stays in better hotels, and receives extensive promotional support from the athletics department. But Title IX does not make same sport to same sport comparisons. Title IX examines whether all female athletes compared with all male athletes receive the same quality and quantity of uniforms, have access to the same quality of competition, are provided with the same quality of hotels and promotional support, and so on. For instance, in theory, an institution can choose to treat male basketball players like kings and female basketball players like paupers as long as an equal proportion of all male and female athletes are treated like kings and queens, respectively, and an equal proportion of all male and female athletes are treated like paupers. Therefore, while one might assume that the significant expenditure differences between men's and women's programs are indicative of noncompliance, it is simply not possible to know for sure without an individual institutional compliance analysis.

Even though retaliation is prohibited under Title IX, the female athlete is in an inferior power position, afraid that filing a Title IX grievance against the athletics department for inequitable treatment might affect athletic scholarship renewal or offers, the time and instructional attention of the coach, and the coach's decisions related to playing time. Even her parents will not file a formal OCR Title IX complaint or a lawsuit because they feel the institution might react negatively toward their daughter. Similarly, coaches of female teams are also in an inferior power position, often without multiyear employment agreements. They fear that such complaints will result in a less than supportive environment, more critical annual performance reviews, and even nonrenewal of employment agreements. While Title IX prohibits retaliation against whistleblowers, retaliation is often subtle and difficult to prove. Thus it takes an incredible level of unfair treatment and exceptional bravery for a student or coach of a female team to address gender inequities through the institution's internal Title IX grievance procedure or a formal OCR Title IX complaint. In fact, most lawsuits are the result of institutions dropping a women's sports team or firing a female coach who has raised Title IX issues. Only these extreme institutional actions appear to justify the cost, time, and adversarial intensity involved in students, parents, or coaches filing a Title IX lawsuit.

The OCR, in the U.S. Department of Education, is charged with enforcement responsibilities, but it barely has the staff and financial resources to respond to citizen complaints, much less undertake independent compliance reviews. It would be relatively simple for the OCR to undertake twenty to thirty such independent reviews (not the result of a submission of a formal complaint) based on the Equity in Athletics Disclosure Act reports, which can point the way to efficiently targeting the worst performers, but it lacks the resources or political impulse to do so.

Another dilemma related to OCR enforcement is that the penalty for Title IX noncompliance—loss of all federal funds—is so significant that it has never been used. The OCR's approach to resolving complaints is to enter into a resolution agreement with an institution. The agreement finds the institution in compliance with Title IX pending correction of identified deficiencies. No penalties are levied. While the OCR is legally obligated to investigate and resolve formal Title IX complaints within a certain time, the reach of the OCR will never extend to monitoring the athletic programs of more than 2,000 institutions of higher education, not to mention those of secondary education.

It is because of all of these factors that higher education institutions are taking their chances that if they are out of compliance, they will not be caught. Title IX OCR complaints and lawsuits are simply not numerous enough and the penalties are not strong enough to create a disincentive. College presidents are therefore taking a "don't ask, don't tell," look-the-other-way position. They are not going to look under the athletics rug.

Hiding behind Prong Three to Avoid Adding Women's Sports

The numbers of participation opportunities for males and females (for individual participants rather than numbers of teams) is at the heart of Title IX. There are three options to meeting Title IX participation standards:

1. The institution can show that participation opportunities for male and female students are provided in numbers substantially proportionate to their respective male and female undergraduate enrollments; or
2. Where the members of one sex have been and are underrepresented among intercollegiate athletes, the institution can show a history and

continuing practice of program expansion that is demonstrably re-
sponsive to the developing interests and abilities of the members of
that sex; or

3. Where the members of one sex are underrepresented among intercollegiate athletes and the institution cannot show a history and continuing practice of program expansion as described above, the institution
can demonstrate that the interests and abilities of the members of that
sex have been fully and effectively accommodated by the present
program.[9]

It is because of this three-part test that an observer cannot look at an
athletic program's simple count of male and female participants and determine whether the Title IX standard has been met. While the first option,
commonly referred to as the Prong One proportionality standard, is the
safest harbor, too many schools have not embraced this standard. Few
schools are able to rely on option two because it is very difficult to show a
history of "continuing expansion" of opportunities for the underrepresented sex over the forty-plus years since Title IX passed without reaching
the proportionality safe harbor. Option three is a different story because
"fully and effectively accommodating" the interests and abilities of the underrepresented sex has several loopholes. In making this determination,
the OCR, according to a policy guidance letter from the Department of
Education, "will consider whether there is (a) unmet interest in a particular sport; (b) sufficient ability to sustain a team in the sport; and (c) a
reasonable expectation of competition for the team."[10] If *all three* conditions are present, the OCR will find that an institution has not fully and
effectively accommodated the interests and abilities of the underrepresented sex.

More than 3.2 million girls participated in interscholastic athletics
at the high school level in 2014–15. While this is a large number, it is
smaller than the 3.6 million male high school athletes in 1972. In 2014–15,
there were 4.5 million male high school athletes.[11] While girls constitute
49 percent of all high school students, they receive only 42 percent of all
participation opportunities, a 1.1 million participation gap under the proportionality provision of Title IX. High schools are simply not adding new
girls' sports or expanding opportunities by adding junior varsity and freshman opportunities for existing sports. This is a function of administrative

choice and a lack of financial resources, neither of which is an acceptable excuse under Title IX. It is not because of a lack of interest: hundreds of thousands of additional females are competing in open amateur and Olympic sports that are not yet commonly offered at the high school or college level, such as wrestling, rugby, synchronized swimming, bowling, and water polo. The number of girls in the prospective athlete population is more than sufficient to fill the small number of intercollegiate athletic opportunities offered at the college level—212,000 NCAA athletes in 2014–15[12] and approximately 40,000–50,000 sponsored by the National Association of Intercollegiate Athletics (NAIA), the National Junior College Athletic Association (NJCAA), and several other small collegiate sports organizations. The authors, who have been heavily involved in collegiate sports for the last forty-five years, are not aware of a college or university that has added a new women's sport, hired a coach, and given the coach a recruiting budget, only to have that coach return his or her salary with the explanation of not being able to find a sufficient number of interested girls with the ability to play. The suggestion that there is a deficiency of sport interest or ability among females is a myth. Further, given the financial data from the Equity in Athletics Disclosure Act showing that women's sports are underresourced compared to men's sports, it would not be surprising to find girls with athletic interest and ability who choose not to play rather than be treated as second-class citizens compared to their male counterparts.

The real problem is with the third part, where OCR instructs the institution on how to take advantage of a loophole:

> In evaluating available competition, OCR will look at available competitive opportunities in the geographic area in which the institution's athletes primarily compete, including: competitive opportunities offered by other schools against which the institution competes; and competitive opportunities offered by other schools in the institution's geographic area, including those offered by schools against which the institution does not now compete.[13]

Thus there are institutions that maintain that the reason why they can't add a new women's sport is that there aren't enough women's teams in their normal competitive region to put together a regular season schedule. It appears that neither OCR nor any other entity is checking whether this contention is true. Further, schools are ignoring the additional Title IX requirement that requires institutions "to actively encourage the development of competition" within the region they claim has no women's teams to compete against.[14]

Let's consider several examples of the questionable use of Prong Three. For instance, all of the Ivy League Division I institutions have large sports programs, but they also have significant female participation gaps (see table 6-2). Every Ivy League institution has an existing women's rugby program at the club level. Only Brown, Dartmouth, and Harvard currently sponsor women's rugby as a varsity sport. How easy would it be for the other Ivy League schools to agree to add rugby, instantly solving the issue of being able to put together a competitive schedule?

Or consider the University of Texas at Austin, which has one of the richest athletic programs in the nation. Even though it has a female participation gap of 84 (see table 6-3), the athletics department maintains that it meets the Prong Three exception. Certainly the University of Texas can figure out how to add more women's sports and put together competitive schedules for those sports. Texas could first look to its conference, the Big Twelve (which consists of only ten institutions), as shown in table 6-4.

Half of the conference members are in the same position as Texas, needing to expand opportunities for women. Among the five institutions in compliance with the Prong One proportionality standard, three sponsor varsity gymnastics. Certainly all of the institutions with gaps could agree to add gymnastics, instantly creating a sufficient number of schools for regular season play and a postseason championship, and all of these schools have the financial resources to travel regionally or nationally to meet the best nonconference competition.

Hiding behind the Prong Three excuse of "not enough teams within the geographic competition area to compete against" is not just a Division I phenomenon, as a look at a typical Division III conference such as the Michigan Intercollegiate Athletic Association shows (table 6-5). All but one of these schools have significant participation gaps. At the very least, these schools should be expected to agree on adding the same women's sport(s) simultaneously so both regular season schedules and postseason conference competition could be realized. But it is not going to happen absent a

TABLE 6-2: Male and Female Athletes in the Ivy League, 2014–15

Institution	Undergraduate			Athletes			Total, duplicated count	Total female athletes required for proportionality	Female participation gap[a]
	Male	Female	Total	Male	Female				
University of Pennsylvania	5,005 49.0%	5,200 51.0%	10,205	624 57.4%	464 42.6%		1,088	648	184
Princeton University	2,688 51.1%	2,570 48.9%	5,258	753 59.0%	523 41.0%		1,276	720	197
Harvard University	3,624 52.7%	3,250 47.3%	6,874	734 57.8%	536 42.2%		1,270	658	122
Dartmouth College	2,120 50.7%	2,064 49.3%	4,184	583 55.4%	469 44.6%		1,052	568	99
Yale University	2,786 51.0%	2,681 49.0%	5,467	529 53.9%	453 46.1%		982	509	56
Cornell University	6,976 49.2%	7,206 50.8%	14,182	717 56.4%	554 43.6%		1,271	741	187
Brown University	3,041 48.7%	3,200 51.3%	6,241	530 50.6%	518 49.4%		1,048	558	40
Columbia University	3,926 52.4%	3,570 47.6%	7,496	493 56.7%	376 43.3%		869	448	72

Source: U.S. Department of Education, Equity in Athletics Disclosure Act database (http://ope.ed.gov/athletics/).
a. Computation of the female participation gap assumes the current number of male athlete participants remains constant and represents the proportion of males in the undergraduate student body. Male practice players on female teams are excluded.

TABLE 6-3: Male and Female Varsity Sport Participation,
University of Texas at Austin, 2014–15

Female participation gap = 84[a]

Percent

Sport	Male	Female
Baseball	39	0
Basketball	19	16[b]
All track combined	117	119
Football	126	0
Golf	13	8
Rowing	0	77
Soccer	0	28
Softball	0	21
Swimming and diving	43	27
Tennis	11	10
Volleyball	0	15
Total	368	321

Source: U.S. Department of Education, Equity in Athletics Disclosure Act database (http://ope.ed.gov/athletics/).

a. Computation of the female participation gap assumes the current number of male athlete participants remains constant and represents the proportion of males in the undergraduate student body (47.5 percent).
b. Excludes twelve male practice players.

lawsuit or a Title IX OCR complaint because campus leadership will continue to allow the athletics department to evade its responsibilities.

Use of Roster Inflation and Triple Counting in Cross Country and Track to Avoid Adding New Women's Teams

It is important to point out that current female participation numbers may be inflated because of a number of factors. First, the Title IX participation standard is a duplicated as opposed to an unduplicated count. In other

TABLE 6-4: Male and Female Athletes in the Big Twelve Conference, 2014–15

Institution	Undergraduate			Athletes		Total, duplicated count	Total female athletes required for proportionality	Female participation gap[a]
	Male	Female	Total	Male	Female			
Baylor University[b]	5,685 41.9%	7,892 58.1%	13,577	285 46.9%	323 53.1%	608	396	73
Iowa State University	15,275 56.2%	11,924 43.8%	27,199	274 53.9%	234 46.1%	508	214	−20
Kansas State University	9,387 52.3%	8,569 47.7%	17,956	291 49.5%	297 50.5%	588	266	−31
Oklahoma State University	9,190 50.7%	8,931 49.3%	18,121	342 52.5%	309 47.5%	651	332	23
Texas Christian University	3,317 39.8%	5,009 60.2%	8,326	304 56.4%	235 43.6%	539	459	224
Texas Tech University	14,035 55.0%	11,496 45.0%	25,531	335 59.1%	232 40.9%	567	274	42
University of Texas at Austin	17,167 47.6%	18,905 52.4%	36,072	368 53.4%	321 46.6%	689	405	84
University of Kansas	8,511 50.1%	8,484 49.9%	16,995	278 47.8%	304 52.2%	582	277	−27
University of Oklahoma	9,019 50.9%	8,692 49.1%	17,711	347 47.9%	378 52.1%	725	334	−44
West Virginia University	11,434 54.8%	9,429 45.2%	20,863	299 53.4%	261 46.6%	560	247	−14

Source: U.S. Department of Education, Equity in Athletics Disclosure Act database (http://ope.ed.gov/athletics/).

a. Computation of the female participation gap assumes the current number of male athlete participants, not including male practice players on women's teams, remains constant and represents the proportion of males in the undergraduate student body.
b. Does not include acrotumbling, a sport currently unrecognized by the Office for Civil Rights.

TABLE 6-5: Male and Female Athletes in the Michigan Intercollegiate Athletic Association, 2014–15

Institution	Undergraduate			Athletes			Total female athletes required for proportionality	Female participation gap[a]
	Male	Female	Total	Male	Female	Total, duplicated count		
Adrian College	812 52.5%	734 47.5%	1,546	429 58.8%	301 41.2%	730	388	87
Albion College	625 50.4%	614 49.6%	1,239	313 60.5%	204 39.5%	517	307	103
Alma College	614 45.4%	737 54.6%	1,351	368 58.5%	261 41.5%	629	442	181
Calvin College	1,684 44.9%	2,068 55.1%	3,752	271 51.4%	256 48.6%	527	333	77
Hope College	1,263 39.3%	1,950 60.7%	3,213	349 59.5%	238 40.5%	587	539	301
Kalamazoo College	521 39.4%	800 60.6%	1,321	219 59.2%	151 40.8%	370	336	185
Olivet College	561 60.9%	360 39.1%	921	382 68.6%	175 31.4%	557	245	70
Trine University	1,146 71.3%	461 28.7%	1,607	492 72.1%	190 27.9%	682	198	8
St. Mary's College	All female college—Title IX does not apply.							

Source: U.S. Department of Education, Equity in Athletics Disclosure Act database (http://ope.ed.gov/athletics/).

a. Computation of the female participation gap assumes the current number of male athlete participants, excluding male practice players on women's teams, remains constant and represents the proportion of males in the undergraduate student body.

words, a student-athlete who participates in two sports would be counted twice; a three-sport student-athlete would be counted three times. Further, cross country, indoor track, and outdoor track count as separate sports, even though cross country runners are distance runners who also often participate in indoor and outdoor track. The participants in indoor track and outdoor track are the same athletes. Thus, institutions first make sure they sponsor cross country, indoor track, and outdoor track for women and maintain large rosters, resulting in higher female participation numbers without the institution having to incur the expense of a new women's sport team with different coaches. The same coaching staff is involved in all three sports. Some schools try to achieve compliance by eliminating these same sports for men, or they just offer cross country and outdoor track for men but not indoor track. According to an NCAA sports participation report, "The men's sport that has been dropped the most since 1988–89 is indoor track and field with 319 teams discontinued in the NCAA."[15] Such solutions meet the letter of the law but not its spirit. As an example, data from a Division I FBS athletic program still not in compliance with Title IX's Prong One proportionality participation standard that has taken both of these actions are shown in table 6-6. The University of Nevada–Las Vegas (UNLV) dropped its men's cross country and indoor and outdoor track programs in 1981. The women's teams in these sports appear to have inflated rosters, insofar as the average team size for Division I women's cross country is 17.6, for indoor track 40.2, and for outdoor track 39.7.[16]

Roster inflation shenanigans abound. The institution can simply tell the coaches of women's teams to carry an extra five or six players on their rosters, easily expanding women's participation without having to add a new team or a new coach or worry about new facilities. But there are many Title IX questions concerning such practices. Are female teams overall subject to higher coach-to-athlete instructional ratios than men's teams? Do female athletes have the same chance to compete? For instance, when institutions add women's rowing and show a roster of 70 to 100 participants, is a large percentage of these participants rowing novice or lightweight boats that don't count in scoring, the equivalent of a junior varsity or freshman competition level, thereby not providing equal proportions of male and female athletes with the opportunity to compete at the varsity level?

TABLE 6-6: Using Triple Counting of the Same Female Athletes in Cross Country, Indoor Track, and Outdoor Track to Avoid Adding New Women's Sports

Example: University of Nevada at Las Vegas, 2014–15

	Athletes duplicated count	Undergraduate students
Male	230 (45.8%)	7,616 (43.9%)
Female	272 (54.2%)	9,724 (56.1%)

Female participation gap = 22 participation opportunities

Sports	Male	Female
Baseball	35	0
Basketball	15	15
Football	108	0
Golf	13	7
Soccer	27	31
Softball	0	22
Swimming and diving	23	28
Tennis	9	8
Track and field, indoor	**0**	**48**
Track and field, outdoor	**0**	**48**
Cross country	**0**	**47**
Volleyball	0	18
Total (duplicated count)	230 (45.8%)	272 (54.2%)
Total (unduplicated count)	230	176
Total multisport athletes	0	96

Source: U.S. Department of Education, Equity in Athletics Disclosure Act database (http://ope.ed.gov/athletics/).

a. Calculation of the female participation gap assumes male participation is constant and represents 43.9% of all athletics opportunities, matching the percentage of males in the undergraduate student body.

The Women's Rowing Scam

Title IX requires that male and female athletes be provided with an equal opportunity to participate at the same competitive levels. For instance, if an athletic program has varsity and junior varsity teams, an equal proportion of male and female athletes would be required to participate on varsity and junior varsity teams respectively. While most athletic programs have discontinued freshman and junior varsity programs, some so-called varsity sports operate at two different competition levels. Women's rowing is often a culprit in this regard, with team rosters between 60 and 100 participants and half the squad rowing in novice boats (first-year rowers, the equivalent of a freshman team). The other half of the rowing squad goes to meets and scores boats racing fours and eights—the equivalent of varsity competition. The coaches then row novice boats on an exhibition basis and may even do the same with lightweight boats.

Victims of the Arms Race: Men's Olympic Sports and Title IX Compliance

A look at table 6-6, regarding the UNLV athletic program, might lead to the opinion that the institution may lack the funds to add new women's sports and Title IX is forcing the elimination of men's sports as a solution. In fact, whenever men's sports teams are dropped from an athletic program, the causative factor most often suggested is Title IX compliance. NCAA sports sponsorship data simply do not support this conclusion. Men's and women's sports are added and dropped all the time for reasons such as declines and advances in the popularity of sports, injury rates and insurance costs, Title IX compliance, and budget limitations. Thus, it is important to look at net outcomes. Table 6-7 tracks sports teams added and eliminated in all three NCAA competitive divisions over a twenty-five-year period. The data clearly show that the richest NCAA institutions, those that are members of Division I, are dropping men's sports (not men's football and basketball, but other nonrevenue sports), and this phenomenon is not happening in Division II and III institutions with far fewer financial resources.

The previously discussed data on the growth of women's sports show that the savings from eliminating men's teams is not being used for increasing

TABLE 6-7: No Net Decline in Number of Men's Sports, 1988–2013

	Division I	Division II	Division III
Men's sports			
Men's sports added 1988–2013	623	1,185	1,819
Men's sports eliminated 1988–2013	943	739	1,184
Net outcome, 2013	**−320**	**+446**	**+635**
Net outcome, all men's sports, 2013			**+762**
Women's sports			
Women's sports added 1988–2013	1,198	1,602	2,300
Women's sports eliminated 1988–2013	440	549	1,046
Net outcome, 2013	**+758**	**+1,053**	**+1,254**
Net outcome, all women's sports, 2013			**+3,065**

Source: NCAA, *NCAA Sports Sponsorship and Participation Report 1981–82 to 2012–2013* (Indianapolis: NCAA, 2013).

female participation. Rather, both increased media and other revenues and the savings from dropped men's nonrevenue-generating sports are being used to fuel the Division I football and men's basketball arms race. The percentage of men's sports operating expenses spent on these two sports illustrates the point (see table 6-8).

Particularly notable is that Division I athletic programs without football are spending 41 percent of their annual operating budget on men's basketball, a program serving, on average, fifteen to sixteen college athletes. Thus, not only is Title IX compliance a victim of the Division I football and men's basketball arms race but men's nonrevenue-generating sports—mostly Olympic sports—are also suffering.

Erroneous Use of Unduplicated Count to Cheat Female Athletes Out of Millions in Athletic Scholarships

Another reason why it is in the interest of institutions to inflate women's cross country, indoor track, and outdoor track participation numbers (as opposed to adding a new women's sport) is that these multisport athletes

TABLE 6-8: Division I Football and Men's
Basketball Arms Race, 2012–13

Annual operating expenses by sport, as percentage of all sports

Subdivision	Football	Men's basketball	Football/men's basketball combined	Other men's sports
Division I FBS	62	21	83	17
Division I FCS	47	16	63	37
Division I, no football	0	41	41	59

Source: NCAA, *Revenues and Expenses 2004–2013: NCAA Division I Intercollegiate Athletics Programs Report* (Indianapolis: NCAA, 2014).

benefit the institution with regard to calculating the institution's Title IX athletics-related financial aid obligations. Title IX requires that athletics-related financial aid dollars be distributed to male and female athletes according to their percentage in the athletic program, with a 1 percent point difference allowed. Thus, in theory, if 50 percent of all athletes are female and 50 percent are male, no fewer than 49 percent of all scholarship dollars must be awarded to female athletes. The problem is that the OCR inexplicably instructs institutions to use unduplicated rather than duplicated participation counts in computations for scholarship equity. "Unduplicated" is not used for any other Title IX gender equity computation. The National Women's Law Center and the Women's Sports Foundation contend that both the OCR and the NCAA have erroneously instructed schools to use this standard from the OCR's *Investigators Manual:* "Review and adjust the participant count. . . . Participants who participate on more than one team are to be counted only once."[17]

It should be noted "that financial aid participation, unlike athletics participation described earlier, counts student-athletes only once, no matter how many sports they may play. Thus the athlete who runs cross country, indoor track, and outdoor track would count three times for participation generally and one time for purposes of financial aid analysis."[18]

The difference between using duplicated and unduplicated counts to compute athletics-related financial aid entitlement is highly significant.

TABLE 6-9: University of Nevada–Las Vegas, Difference in
Athletic Scholarship Obligation Using Duplicated versus
Unduplicated Male and Female Athlete Participation Counts

Total athletic financial aid awarded in 2014–15: $7,723,559

Unduplicated female athlete count	176 (43%)	$3,305,128
Unduplicated male athlete count	230 (57%)	$4,418,431
Duplicated female athlete count	272 (54%)	$4,170,722
Duplicated male athlete count	230 (46%)	$3,552,837

Female athlete shortfall as a result of using unduplicated count: $865,594

Source: U.S. Department of Education, Equity in Athletics Disclosure Act database (http://ope.ed.gov/athletics/).

Here the UNLV program depicted in table 6-6 is illustrative concerning the institution's financial aid obligation (see table 6-9). Using the publicly accessible Department of Education's Equity in Athletics Disclosure Act database,[19] we examined 2013–14 female athlete financial aid entitlements based on duplicated and unduplicated count percentages for 126 Division I FBS institutions (U.S. military academies exempt from reporting and all opposite sex practice players were removed from participation counts). If female athletes in 2013–14 actually received a financial aid distribution based on their *unduplicated* participation percentage, they would have received $32,151,151 less than if the distribution was based on duplicated count. When we looked at the financial aid actually awarded in 2013–14, female athletes received less than they should have been receiving under either duplicated or unduplicated count percentages.

Not only is the practice of using unduplicated counts commonplace to reduce the institution's financial aid liability for women and to inflate male athlete financial aid, duplicated counts almost always favor males and not females, which appears to support the presence of manipulation. For instance, 85 percent of the Division I FBS institutions showed women's unduplicated count percentages lower than men's unduplicated counts, most likely the result of the women's cross country and track triple counting or inflated roster practice previously described. And few FBS institutions were even awarding financial aid according to OCR instructions:

- Only fifteen (12 percent) institutions awarded financial aid to females within 1 percent of the athletic participation standard (duplicated count).

- Seventy-seven (62 percent) institutions awarded financial aid to females *below* the unduplicated count percentages.

- Twenty-one (17 percent) awarded aid somewhere in between the duplicated and unduplicated percentages.

- Twelve (9 percent) awarded more aid than the participation standard (duplicated count).

- Sixty-seven percent had female participation gaps larger than 50, which means that failure to add women's teams is further contributing to the female financial aid shortfall.

The OCR is currently considering a formal request from the National Women's Law Center and the Women's Sports Foundation to eliminate this "unduplicated count" instruction and practice, for the following reasons:

1. There is no legislative authority for the use of "unduplicated count" or the use of any definition other than "participation" in the Title IX regulations, the Policy Interpretation, Dear Colleague Letters, or any other official OCR advisory. Like the invalid Z test, an OCR enforcement manual instruction previously discarded, this interpretation is not the product of official government interpretation. Specifically, it should be noted that the Title IX regulation in the *Code of Federal Regulations*, 34, part 106.37(c), provides the following: "[Institutions] must provide reasonable opportunities for [athletic scholarship awards] for members of each sex in proportion to the number of students of each sex participating in . . . intercollegiate athletics." The definition of participation and the computation of participation in all OCR instructions have been clear. The 1979 Policy Interpretation explains that counted participants are those athletes:
   a. Who are receiving the institutionally-sponsored support normally provided to athletes competing at the institution involved (e.g., coaching, equipment, medical and training room services) on a regular basis during a sport's season; and

b. Who are participating in organized practice sessions and other team meetings and activities on a regular basis during a sport's season; and

c. Who are listed on the eligibility or squad lists maintained for each sport; or

d. Who, because of injury, cannot meet a, b, or c above but continue to receive financial aid on the basis of athletic ability.[20]

The OCR uses this "duplicated" count definition (athletes participating in multiple sports are counted in each sport in which they participate to determine the number of athletic participation opportunities provided), and this also becomes the definition for determining equal treatment in all aspects of Title IX—for instance, in determining whether equal proportions of male and female athletes are being provided with the same treatment and benefits in a host of other areas (equipment and supplies, uniforms, access to coaching, locker room, practice and competition facilities, and so on).

The Policy Interpretation also states that OCR will "examine compliance with this provision of the regulation primarily by means of a financial comparison to determine whether proportionately equal amounts of financial assistance (scholarship aid) are available to men's and women's athletic programs. [OCR] will measure compliance with this standard by dividing the amounts of aid available for the members of each sex by the numbers of male or female participants in the athletic program and comparing the results. Institutions may be found in compliance if this comparison results in substantially equal amounts or if a resulting disparity can be explained by adjustments to take into account legitimate, nondiscriminatory factors."

2. The use of an unduplicated count would be rational only if *both* of two conditions existed: (a) every athlete, male and female, received a full athletic scholarship and (b) no athlete was permitted to receive more than a full scholarship. Significantly, the federal government does not allow any national governance association rule to prevent gender equity under Title IX. Thus, if a rule limiting the amount of financial aid that could be received by an athlete (that is, no athlete could receive more than a certain amount) prevented gender equity, it would not be a justifiable defense. Second, the situation of

100 percent of all male and female athletes receiving full athletic scholarships has never existed in reality. The size of every athletic team exceeds the number of scholarships that the NCAA allows to be awarded to those team members. Thus there are far more athletes who are either not receiving any athletics-related financial aid or who are receiving partial athletics aid than athletes who are recipients of full athletic scholarships. If female athlete participants are entitled to receive higher amounts of financial aid, there will always be numerous female athletes who are not on scholarship or who are on partial scholarship who can receive increased amounts. Even if all athletes were on full scholarship and the school was meeting Title IX requirements with regard to numbers of participation opportunities, the use of multisport participation, the basis for the unduplicated count, should only be used to justify unequal distribution as one of many factors OCR admits it would consider.

3. The use of an unduplicated count to limit the total amount of aid to which female athletes are entitled is contrary to the total program nature of Title IX and invites abuse. Female athletes overall should be entitled to the same treatment as male athletes overall. Title IX does not make sport versus sport comparisons, and neither should it make multisport athlete versus single sport athlete comparisons. Given the above described practices and data, it appears reasonable to conclude that gender equity in the distribution of financial aid is currently highly deficient.

The Practice of Financial Tiering, and How It Is Being Used to Treat Female Athletes Unequally

One of the most common mechanisms used to discriminate against female athletes is athletics departments' practice of placing priority sports in higher funding tiers. For example, an institution will determine that football and men's basketball are its highest priority sports and therefore will provide large budgets that will allow participants in these sports to receive better benefits and treatment.

Table 6-10 depicts an example of how such tiered athletic programs are purposefully structured to provide different benefits to the athletes within each tier, funneling the bulk of athletic resources to the highest-priority

TABLE 6-10: Tiered Athletics Program Based on Five Primary Elements

Element	Tier I	Tier II	Tier III
Scholarships	• Maximum allowable • No restriction on in-state vs. out-of-state	• 50% of maximum • 1/3 out-of-state maximum	• None permitted
Coaching	• Full-time head coach • Full-time asst. coaches • Maximum no. of asst. coaches allowed	• Full-time head coach • 1 asst. coach (part-time)	• Part-time head coach • No asst. coaches
Recruiting	• National scope • 100% of team recruited	• Regional scope • 75% of team recruited	• Regional scope • 25% of team recruited
Facilities	• State of the art, exclusive access	• Top third in conference priority access	• Adequate, priority in season
Nonconference schedule travel	• National	• Regional	• State

sports. This is a primary enabling mechanism to advance the arms race between football and men's basketball. Rather than (1) eliminate sport programs and incur the wrath of alumni and parents, or (2) fall below NCAA minimum sports sponsorship standards to be eligible to compete in a particular division, or (3) risk dropping a women's sport and becoming the target of a Title IX lawsuit, the institution keeps all sports but funds the vast majority at exceedingly low levels.

Title IX requires that male and female athletes be equally treated within each tier, requiring that an equal proportion of the total male and female athletes be placed in each tier. Typically the institution places an equal number of men's and women's teams rather than an equal number of participants in each tier. Table 6-11 shows such a discriminatory placement of teams and the resulting lack of equal proportions of male and female athletes in each tier.

TABLE 6-II: Discriminatory Placement of Male
and Female Athletes in Financial Tiers

Total athlete population: 207 males (44%), 260 females (56%)

Tier I	Tier II	Tier III
Males	*Males*	*Males*
Football (85)[a]	Swimming (20)	Tennis (12)
Basketball (15)	Track (22)	
Soccer (24)	Fencing (15)	
	Volleyball (14)	
Females	*Females*	*Females*
Basketball (15)	Softball (25)	Track (22)
Lacrosse (27)	Volleyball (15)	Squash (14)
Soccer (24)	Swimming (20)	Cross country (12)
	Crew (12)	
	Field hockey (26)	
	Fencing (16)	
Totals:		
124 males/66 females	20 males/134 females	63 males/60 females
(60%/25%)	(10%/51%)	(30%/23%)

a. Numbers in parentheses indicate total number of scholarships allowed per team.

Current Status of Female Employment in NCAA Member Institutions and Conferences

With regard to the status of employment as head coaches, female coaches have virtually been shut out as coaches of men's teams, accounting for 4 percent overall but only 3 percent in Division I.[21] The small presence of women as head coaches in men's cross country, indoor track, outdoor track, and swimming is a reflection of combined men's and women's teams and coaching staffs in these sports.

The same situation exists with regard to assistant coaches for men's teams, with women holding 10 percent of all assistant coach positions for men's teams.[22] Again, female coaches are more likely to be included on men's coaching staffs when men's and women's teams and coaching staffs are combined. There is ample evidence to conclude that women are virtually excluded from the men's sports coaching marketplace.

Men also dominate employment as head coaches of women's teams (60 percent), with women dominating in sports that are traditionally not played by men (softball and field hockey) or in which women's rules are different from men's rules in the same sport (lacrosse).[23] The same NCAA database shows that women occupy 50 percent of all assistant coaching positions for women's collegiate sports teams.

LaVoi summarizes the excuses given by athletics directors for not hiring more women, reveals the extent of these blame-the-victim narratives, and points out the lack of empirical evidence to support any of these contentions:

- Women don't apply for open positions.
- The quality of women in the labor pool is thin and weak.
- Women choose other careers.
- Women aren't as interested in coaching as men.
- Women don't want to or are less willing than men to move/uproot their families for a job.
- Women "opt out" of coaching to start families.
- Women with children have less time to devote to coaching, due to time demands of the profession.
- Women with children are less committed.
- Women lack the knowledge and expertise.
- Women aren't confident or assertive enough.
- Women don't "lean in" and take responsibility for own careers.
- Women won't apply unless they feel they are 100 percent qualified.
- Women are too "whiny" and demand resources.
- Women don't support each other and "eat their own."
- Women don't have a strong network or an "old girls' club."
- Women burn out and leave coaching sooner than males.
- Women think they need to be overqualified to apply.

- Women don't perceive coaching as a viable career pathway.
- Women coaches are too "relational" (i.e., qualities that are devalued and naturalized as feminine).
- Women don't have thick skin and can't take the pressure.
- Female athletes prefer male coaches.[24]

So, what is the reality experienced by female coaches? The most recent and comprehensive national survey of 2,565 current and former male and female coaches of women's collegiate teams reveals a picture of subtle and not so subtle employment discrimination. The survey's findings included the following:

- Large majorities of current and former coaches (73 percent and 75 percent) reported that the person in charge of hiring them was a male athletics director (80 percent of all athletics directors at NCAA institutions were male in 2014–15), implying a possible favoritism toward men, a commonly recognized occurrence in male-dominated occupational fields.

- When coaches were asked questions about access to resources, a third of both female and male coaches of women's teams believed they did not have adequate access to the resources they needed to be successful (lack of access to suitable office space and financial resources), more than 40 percent reported that their departments did not invest in their professional development, and nearly half of all coaches reported not having a sufficient budget to be successful.

- Thirty-one percent of female coaches believed that they would "risk their job" if they spoke up about Title IX and gender equity; 20 percent of male coaches of women's teams also indicated that they worried about negative repercussions for pointing out Title IX and gender equity issues.

- LGBTQ female coaches were the most vulnerable in terms of fears regarding Title IX and gender equity, with 34 percent believing they would risk their jobs if they spoke up about Title IX or gender equity.

- Fifteen percent of female coaches and 9 percent of male coaches reported that they found a "noticeable level of homophobia" among some of their colleagues, with more than a third of female coaches (36 percent) and a quarter of male coaches (24 percent) indicating that it would be difficult to raise concerns about homophobia.

- Coaches who identified as sexual minorities were nearly twice as likely to report a "noticeable level of homophobia" in their immediate workplace, with a higher percentage of LGBTQ coaches (29 percent male and 21 percent female) expressing the belief that their athletics department hampered them from speaking up about homophobia compared to heterosexual colleagues (9 percent of males and 14 percent of females).

- There was range of issues associated with support areas and coaches' contracts, their retention, and their ability to move up and be promoted: (1) 65 percent of current coaches felt that it was easier for men to get top level-coaching jobs; (2) nearly three quarters of current coaches believed men had an easier time negotiating salary increases; and (3) more than half (54 percent) believed that men were more likely to be promoted, to secure a multiyear contract upon hiring (52 percent), and to be rewarded with salary increases for successful performance (53 percent).

- Respondents indicated that coaches of men's teams also wielded more influence in general with 56 percent indicating that coaches of men's teams had more influence with the director of athletics and 53 percent believing that coaches of men's teams had more influence on the allocation of fiscal resources.

- There was a clear difference along gender lines in viewpoints with regard to professional advantage: (1) while 80 percent of female coaches of women's teams believed it was easier for men to get top coaching jobs, just 33 percent of male coaches of women's team believed this was the case; (2) 91 percent of female coaches believed it was easier for men to negotiate for higher salaries (34 percent of male coaches thought this was true); and (3) female coaches (70 percent) held the belief that it was easier for male coaches to be promoted, while 19 percent of male coaches held that same belief.

- Coaches of female teams believed they were subjected to a double standard: (1) a quarter of female and male coaches of women's teams (25 percent and 27 percent, respectively) reported being criticized because of their coaching style; (2) three in ten female coaches indicated that they were vulnerable to potential retaliation should they speak up about gender bias, and another 27 percent reported that doing so could be perceived as a "weakness" by administrators and colleagues; (3) more than 40 percent of female coaches said they were "discriminated against because of their gender," compared to 28 percent of their male coaching colleagues; (4) almost half of the female coaches and just over a quarter of the male coaches (27 percent) reported "being paid less for doing the same job as other coaches;" and (5) female coaches were more than twice as likely than the male coaches in the study to believe that their coaching performance was evaluated differently because of their gender.

• Job security and the ability to advance are very different for female coaches in the collegiate athletics workplace: (1) 36 percent of female coaches agreed that their job security was "tenuous;" (2) more female coaches (46 percent) than male coaches (36 percent) reported being called on to perform tasks that were not in their job descriptions; (3) one in five female coaches (19 percent) indicated that male coaches at their institutions had access to more professional development opportunities; (4) nearly 25 percent of female coaches believed they had not gotten a coaching job because of their gender; and (5) less than half of female coaches (44 percent) said they would "apply to coach a men's team."[25]

It is clear that women coaches perceive injustice in their college sports workplace. Outside coaching positions, it is also clear that NCAA member institutions are not hiring women for top leadership positions, ones that provide the highest compensation and the most influence over the conduct of athletic programs.

It is interesting in table 6-12 to note the underrepresentation of females as NCAA faculty athletics representatives (FARs). These are faculty members rather than athletics department employees who are usually appointed by the president with the concurrence of the athletics director. They are commonly faculty members who support athletics and are inclined to follow the wishes of the athletics director or president. They attend NCAA conventions and conference meetings with the athletics director. They receive complimentary tickets to athletic events, often travel to postseason events with teams, and receive other perks. Thus they are generally not considered to be independent oversight appointments. The underrepresentation of females is inexplicable unless there is a fear on the part of the institution that a female FAR might be more likely to raise gender equity issues.

The NCAA mandates that a senior woman administrator (SWA), who must be a female, be designated by each institution and conference[26] and

TABLE 6-12: Women in Noncoaching Positions in
NCAA Athletics Departments, 2014–15

Percent[a]

Position	Division I	Division II	Division III	Divisions, all
Senior management				
Director of athletics	**9**	**19**	**29**	**20**
Associate director of athletics	**29**	**39**	46	**33**
Assistant director of athletics	**31**	**34**	**38**	**33**
Senior woman administrator	98	99	99	99
Athlete support services				
Life skills coordinator	71	67	80	72
Head athletic trainer	**18**	**31**	**39**	**30**
Asst./Assoc. athletic trainer	48	57	58	52
Strength coach	**14**	**10**	**20**	**15**
Academic adviser/counselor	62	60	51	61
Internal operations				
Business manager	59	68	69	62
Compliance coordinator/officer	51	58	52	53
Equipment manager	**11**	**12**	**18**	**13**
Fundraiser/development manager	**37**	**20**	**31**	**34**
Facility manager	**14**	**12**	**23**	**16**
Promotions/marketing manager	**39**	**34**	41	**38**
Sports information director	**12**	**10**	**13**	**12**
Asst./Assoc. sports info director	**23**	**20**	**26**	**23**
Ticket manager	**36**	58	67	43
Clerical and other support				
Administrative assistant	92	95	97	93
Graduate assistant (excludes football)	48	44	50	47
Intern	43	44	**39**	42
	42	44	47	44
Nonemployee position				
Faculty athletics representative	**34**	**28**	**34**	**32**

Source: NCAA, Sport Sponsorship, Participation and Demographics Search database (http:
web1.ncaa.org/rgdSearch/exec/main).

a. Values below 40 percent in bold.

uses this institutional classification to marginalize females, often specifying that an NCAA committee include at least one of these positions. NCAA regulations do not specify the gender or race of any other athletics department position. The SWA may or may not be considered a senior staff member in the athletics department. The NCAA demonstrates an almost perverse definition of inclusivity, arbitrarily requiring a minimum of one female and one racial or ethnic minority member on each committee and designating a 35 percent representation figure for gender equity and 20 percent for ethnic representation in the aggregate across all committees, far below U.S. census figures in both regards. The NCAA Manual states the following:

> **4.02.5 Gender and Diversity Requirements.** The Board of Directors membership shall include at least one person who is an ethnic minority and at least one person of each gender, and a single member shall not be considered to meet both minimums. The combined membership of the Council, Committee on Academics and other Division I governance entities (other than sport committees) shall include representatives who comprise at least 20 percent of persons who are ethnic minorities and at least 35 percent of persons of each gender.[27]

The same bleak picture of female representation is present among NCAA member conference staffs (see table 6-13). It should be noted that the conference president position is usually an elected or rotating position held by the college president, athletics director, or FAR, as specified in the conference governance documents. There is usually no significant compensation in addition to salary associated with the individual's full-time position within the member institution. An examination of the other paid positions within the conference reveals the same picture for women as employment in NCAA member institution athletic programs. The higher the status (competitive division) and compensation of the position, the less likely it is that a woman occupies the position.

Research supports the existence of homologous reproduction in the sport culture, just as in any occupational field that is dominated by a single gender.[28] The top of the administrative hierarchy is white male. In control of the hiring process, white men hire people who have similar characteristics. The characteristics of white men are valued, while different character-

TABLE 6-13: Women in NCAA Member Conference Offices, 2014–15

Percent[a]

Position	Division I	Division II	Division III	Divisions, all
Elected official				
Conference resident	**23**	**5**	**21**	**19**
Senior administrators				
Commissioner	**20**	**13**	**32**	**24**
Associate commissioner	**39**	56	55	42
Assistant commissioner	**33**	46	42	**38**
Program managers				
Director	49	36	55	49
Associate director	**31**	0	67	45
Assistant director	43	**0**	**29**	**39**
Supervisor/coordinator of officials	**31**	**19**	**19**	**24**
Administrative support				
Administrative assistant	92	100	77	89
Conference secretary	50	60	60	56
Intern	49	59	41	50
Student assistant	0	100	100	100

Source: NCAA, Sport Sponsorship, Participation and Demographics Search database (http://web1.ncaa.org/rgdSearch/exec/main).

a. Values below 40 percent in bold.

istics of race, gender, and culture are devalued within the organization. If women do access the organization, they are marginalized in many ways such as being placed in token positions such as SWA, discouraged from becoming head coaches, more likely to be hired for less visible, lower-paying, and financially less supported sports, and being funneled into assistant coach, recruiting, and athlete support positions—roles that do not supply the experience or training to move into top coaching or administrative positions.[29] These issues are not addressed by funding female coaches' academies or training academies for female administrators, programs that assume that the reason for sex discrimination lies with the victim. Yet that is exactly the approach adopted by the NCAA. Solutions must address the hiring process and activities of the white men who are perpetuating discrimination and must be tied to regulatory or certification standards related to model policies and hiring practices and transparency of employment data, recommendations that appear in the final section of this book.

Racism in College Athletics Participation and Athletics Employment Opportunities

Both sports participation and employment at NCAA member institutions and conferences are significantly more white and less racially or ethnically diverse than in the higher education undergraduate student population and the U.S. labor force. Table 6-14 gives the racial and ethnic composition of male and female undergraduate student populations at U.S. institutions of higher education according to the National Center for Education Statistics. For purposes of discussion and analysis in this section, under- and overrepresentation of white and racial or ethnic minority college athletes were determined based on comparisons with the percentages in table 6-14.

The 2014 Bureau of Labor Statistics percentages in table 6-15 were used for designations of under- or overrepresentation in employment. All participation and employment data were obtained from the NCAA Sport Sponsorship, Participation and Demographics Search database unless otherwise indicated.[30]

Underrepresentation of Racial and Ethnic Minority Athletes in NCAA Sports

Given the dominant exposure of Division I football and men's basketball, it is not surprising that viewers of college sports on television may believe that athletes of color are overrepresented in college sports. That is not so. Tables 6-16 and 6-17 depict the racial and ethnic diversity among NCAA 2014–15 male and female sports participants respectively by competitive division. With the exception of Division I male athletes, white athletes are overrepresented compared to their national undergraduate averages of 59.3 percent males and 56.7 percent females. In Division III, the competitive division with the greatest number of athletes, 75.1 percent of all athletes are

TABLE 6-14: Racial and Ethnic Composition by Gender,
Undergraduate U.S. Higher Education Population, 2012

Percent

	Male	Female
Race or ethnicity		
White	68.4	67.6
Black	9.1	11.9
Hispanic	15.0	12.8
Asian	4.8	4.9
Pacific Islander	0.3	0.3
American Indian/Alaska Native	0.9	0.9
Two or more races	1.5	1.6
Total undergraduates	100.0	100.0
All undergraduates	43.50	56.50

Source: U.S. Department of Education, National Center for Education Statistics, *Digest of Education Statistics, 2013,* NCES 2015-011 (2015), Table 306.10, "Total Fall Enrollment in Degree-Granting Postsecondary Institutions, by Level of Enrollment, Sex, Attendance Status, and Race/Ethnicity of Student: Selected Years, 1976 through 2012" (http://nces.ed.gov/fastfacts/display.asp?id=98).

white. Similarly, black athletes are overrepresented in Divisions I and II compared to their national undergraduate averages of 12.4 percent male and 16.2 percent female.

However, these aggregated data by competitive division do not tell the real story. Examining diversity data by sport, for all competitive divisions combined, reveals the strong concentration of male minority athletes in very few NCAA championship sports:

- White athletes are overrepresented in 92 percent (twenty-two of twenty-four) of all NCAA championship sports.

- Black athletes are overrepresented in 17 percent (four of twenty-four) of all NCAA championship sports (football, basketball, and indoor track and outdoor track, the highest participation sports).

TABLE 6-15: Racial and Ethnic Composition
by Gender, U.S. Labor Force, 2014

Percent

Race or ethnicity	Male	Female
White	68.4	67.6
Black	9.1	11.9
Hispanic	15.0	12.8
Asian	4.8	4.9
Pacific Islander	0.3	0.3
American Indian/Alaska Native	0.9	0.9
Two or more races	1.5	1.6
Total	100.0	100.0

Source: U.S. Bureau of Labor Statistics, Labor Force Characteristics by Race and Ethnicity, 2014, BLS Report 1057, November 2015, Statistics: Table I, "Employment Status of the Civilian Non-Institutional Population 16 Years and Older by Gender and Race, 2014 Annual Averages" https://www.google.com/#q=BLS+Report+1057.

- Hispanic athletes are overrepresented in none (none of twenty-four) of all NCAA championship sports.
- Asian athletes are overrepresented in 21 percent (five of twenty-four) of all NCAA championship sports (fencing, equestrian, gymnastics, squash, and tennis, with all but tennis being very low participation sports).

Because football, basketball, indoor track, and outdoor track are the top four sports with regard to men's participation, the skewed concentration of black athletes in these sports (no other racial or ethnic group exceeds single-digit representation), especially in Divisions I and II, is particularly noteworthy when one considers the 12.4 percent national average of black male students in the undergraduate population (see table 6-18).

The participation and research data regarding the Federal Graduation Rates (FGRs; the NCAA's use of its Graduation Success Rate metric does not permit comparisons with nonathlete students) of black male football and basketball players support the proposition that there is a serious racial

TABLE 6-16: NCAA Male Sports Participation by Race
and Ethnicity, by Competitive Division, 2014–15

Percent[a]

Male athletes—racial or ethnic category	Divisions, all	Division I	Division II	Division III
White/non-Hispanic	66.0	58.9	60.5	75.1
Black	20.1	26.5	25.6	11.5
Hispanic/Latino	5.5	4.8	6.8	5.3
Asian	1.4	1.3	0.9	1.9
American Indian/Alaska Native	0.4	0.3	0.6	0.3
Native Hawaiian/Pacific Islander	0.4	0.6	0.4	0.2
Two or more races	2.9	3.7	2.8	2.3
Other	3.4	3.9	2.4	3.5

Source: NCAA, Sports Sponsorship, Participation and Demographics Search database (http://web1.ncaa.org/rgdSearch/exec/main).

a. Nonresident aliens removed from ethnicity percentage calculations consistent with National Center for Education Statistics data.

component to the academic exploitation of Division I black male athletes, football and basketball players in particular. A breakdown of the 2007 entering class (six-year cohort) by FGR is depicted in table 6-19.

It is important to note that many NCAA Division I athletes are scholarship recipients who do not have to work, the beneficiaries of athletics-dedicated academic support programs (tutors, learning specialists, computer centers, study halls, and other amenities) that are not available to other students and receive summer school financial aid that enables them to address academic deficiencies. In addition, they have the incentive of having to maintain minimum grade point averages in order to maintain athletics eligibility. One would suppose that these advantages over nonathlete peers, other things being equal, should result in better graduation performances.

Because of the concentration of black athletes in football and basketball, examining FGRs from this perspective is important, especially among the most competitive members of Division I. In a 2016 study, Shaun R. Harper

TABLE 6-17: NCAA Female Sports Participation by Race
and Ethnicity, by Competitive Division, 2014–15

Percent[a]

Female athletes—racial or ethnic category	Divisions, all	Division I	Division II	Division III
White/non-hispanic	74.0	68.2	71.9	81.0
Black	11.5	16.2	13.3	5.8
Hispanic/Latino	5.0	4.8	6.9	4.1
Asian	2.0	2.0	1.3	2.6
American Indian/Alaska Native	0.4	0.4	0.7	0.3
Native Hawaiian/Pacific Islander	0.3	0.4	0.5	0.1
Two or more races	3.3	4.4	3.2	2.4
Other	3.3	3.6	2.4	3.5

Source: NCAA, Sports Sponsorship, Participation and Demographics Search database (http://web1.ncaa.org/rgdSearch/exec/main).

a. Nonresident aliens removed from ethnicity percentage calculations consistent with National Center for Education Statistics data.

TABLE 6-18: Black Male Athlete Representation in the NCAA
Sports with the Highest Participation Rate, 2014–15

Percent

Sport	Division I		Division II		Division III	
	White	Black	White	Black	White	Black
Basketball	27.0	62.6	36.2	54.2	57.6	31.4
Football	40.4	47.3	44.1	46.0	67.3	20.0
Track, outdoor	57.4	28.0	58.4	26.8	71.4	14.9
Track, indoor	57.6	28.9	63.6	25.1	72.4	14.7

Source: NCAA, Sport Sponsorship, Participation and Demographics Search database (http://web1.ncaa.org/rgdSearch/exec/main).

TABLE 6·19: Federal Graduation Rates of NCAA Division I
White and Black Male Athletes Compared with
Undergraduate Student Body, 2007 Entering Class

Percent

Racial category	Athletes	Student body
Overall (both sexes, all racial and ethnic categories)	66	65
White, male and female	70	67
Black, male and female	56	46
White males	64	65
Black males	52	41

Source: NCAA Research Staff, "Trends in Graduation: Success Rates and Federal Graduation Rates at NCAA Division I Member Institutions," PowerPoint presentation, October
2014.

is highly critical of the NCAA's use of aggregated Division I data to suggest
that black athletes are doing better than black nonathlete students:

> The Association has claimed in a television commercial that black male
> student-athletes at Division I institutions graduate at rates higher than
> do black men in the general student body. This is true across the entire
> division, but not for the five conferences whose member institutions
> routinely win football and basketball championships, play in multi-
> million dollar bowl games and the annual basketball championship
> tournament, and produce the largest share of Heisman trophy winners.
> Across these 65 universities, black male student-athletes graduate at
> nearly five percentage points lower than their same-race male peers who
> are not on intercollegiate sports teams. That an average of 46.4 percent
> of black male student-athletes on these campuses do not graduate
> within six years is a major loss. [31]

Harper's position is the result of taking a closer look at the graduation
rates of male football and basketball players participating in sixty-five athletic programs that are members of the wealthiest and competitively successful Division I athletic conferences—the Atlantic Coast Conference

(ACC), the Big Ten Conference, the Big Twelve Conference, Pac-12 Conference, and the Southeastern Conference (SEC). In his 2016 study of these institutions, Harper found the following:

- During the 2014–15 academic school year, black men were 2.5 percent of undergraduate students, but 56.3 percent of football teams and 60.8 percent of men's basketball teams.

- Across four cohorts, 53.6 percent of black male student-athletes graduated within six years, compared to 68.5 percent of student-athletes overall, 58.4 percent of black undergraduate men overall, and 75.4 percent of undergraduate students overall.

- Only the University of Miami and Northwestern University graduated black male student-athletes at rates higher than or equal to student-athletes overall.

- Two-thirds of the universities graduated black male student-athletes at rates lower than the graduation rates of black undergraduate men who were not members of intercollegiate sports teams.

- Only Northwestern University graduated black male student-athletes at a rate higher than or equal to the graduation rate of undergraduate students overall.[32]

Data also support the premise that minority athletes, and particularly black athletes in football and basketball, are significantly more likely to receive special admissions status (accepted for admission to the institution despite not meeting published admissions standards)[33] and are more likely not to graduate from college,[34] to perform academically more poorly than their athletic and general student peers, and to be be placed in less difficult courses and majors. These specially admitted athletes are ill-prepared to compete in the classroom with their better-prepared nonathlete peers. When they are provided with remediation programs, the focus of these efforts is often on maintaining athletic eligibility rather than on achieving demonstrable improvement in basic academic skills such as reading, writing, and mathematics.

A dangerous myth has started to gain traction in the predominantly white collegiate sport and higher education culture that should be vigorously rejected: simply rubbing elbows with the respected brand and attending a prestigious institution of higher education institution should be

appreciated for the future connections with prominent alumni. The implication of this belief is that this benefit is sufficient even if academically
underprepared athletes do not receive the education they were promised.

Two additional dangers of focusing on the academic underperformance
or low graduation rates of black male athletes should be emphasized. First,
it is important not to advance the myth that all black athletes, male or
female, are physically superior and intellectually incapable. Doing so supports the unethical practices of academic clustering—pushing black athletes into a limited number of less demanding majors, selecting less academically demanding classes, or selecting courses with professors known
for generous grading—in order to maintain their athletic eligibility. Second, the impact of the experience of black athletes attending predominantly white institutions must be acknowledged and carefully examined.
Eighty percent of black students are now attending predominantly white
institutions compared to 10 percent just before the beginning of World
War II. According to Hawkins, research has not examined "how the
black athletes' experience with racism, racial isolation, and alienation
may contribute to their academic success and graduation."[35]

The picture with regard to female minority participation is similar to
that of males, but slightly less academically distressing. Examining diversity data by sport, all competitive divisions combined, reveals a similar
concentration of female minority athletes in very few NCAA championship sports:

- White female athletes are overrepresented in 96 percent (twenty-three
  of twenty-five) of all NCAA championship sports.

- Black female athletes are overrepresented in 16 percent (four of twenty-
  five) of all NCAA championship sports (basketball, outdoor track, indoor track, and with only 572 total participants in bowling, which is a
  popular women's sport in historically black colleges and universities).

- Hispanic female athletes are overrepresented in 4 percent (one of
  twenty-five) of all NCAA championship sports (only synchronized
  swimming, which has thirty-nine total participants).

- Asian female athletes are overrepresented in 20 percent (five of twenty-
  five) of all NCAA championship sports (synchronized swimming, fencing, squash, golf, and rifle—all low-participation sports except golf).

TABLE 6-20: Black Female Athlete Representation in the NCAA
Sport, with the Highest Black Participation Rates, 2014–15

Percent

Sport	Division I White	Division I Black	Division II White	Division II Black	Division III White	Division III Black
Basketball	33.9	53.6	50.4	37.1	70.8	17.1
Bowling	58.2	28.2	55.3	35.1	87.8	7.8
Track, indoor	58.4	28.5	68.1	19.9	77.5	9.9
Track, outdoor	58.5	28.1	63.0	22.1	76.5	10.0

Source: NCAA, Sports Sponsorship, Participation and Demographics Search database (http://web1.ncaa.org/rgdSearch/exec/main).

As with male athletes, black female athletes are concentrated in basketball, indoor track, outdoor track, and bowling (see table 6-20). No other racial or ethnic group exceeds single-digit representation in any other NCAA sport except volleyball (10.1 percent black). The FGRs for female black athletes are eleven percentage points higher than for male black athletes but thirteen percentage points lower than the FGRs of their white female athlete counterparts (see table 6-21).

The concentration of minority athletes, whether male or female, in a minimum number of sports and the dominant position of white athletes in all but a few NCAA sports shape the sport culture and demand attention. Inclusivity within athletic programs at the institutional level is almost impossible when the majority of time spent by student-athletes interacting with other athletes is within their own relatively homogeneous teams—either white overrepresented or nonwhite overrepresented. And when these concentrations of black athletes in particular are celebrated by the media, the aspirations of generations of young athletes are shaped by these images, perpetuating the imbalance. We also know that minority groups are overrepresented at lower socioeconomic levels and in major metropolitan population centers, access to many sports is dependent on access to financial resources, and the availability of local facilities is inadequate. Do the NCAA and higher education athletic programs have a role to play in correcting these sport access imbalances? If inclusivity is important, the answer is yes.

TABLE 6-21: Federal Graduation Rates of NCAA Division I
White and Black Female Athletes Compared with the
Undergraduate Student Body, 2007 Entering Class

Percent

Racial category	Athletes	Student body
Overall (both sexes, all racial and ethnic categories)	66	65
White, male and female	70	67
Black, male and female	56	46
White females	76	70
Black females	63	50

Source: NCAA Research Staff, "Trends in Graduation: Success Rates and Federal Graduation Rates at NCAA Division I Member Institutions," PowerPoint presentation, October
2014.

*Employment of Racial and Ethnic Minorities in NCAA Member
Institutions and Conferences*

First, it is important to understand that full-time and part-time higher
education faculty members are predominantly white (see table 6-22). Minority athletes and nonathletes participate in a college and university
environment in which the vast majority of decisionmakers in the academic classroom are white.

This lack of diversity is also reflected among athletic program employees at the institution and conference levels. Even though these higher
education employees operate nonacademic programs, they have a disproportionately more significant impact on the experience of nonwhite athletes because they exert control over the athletes' financial support and
time outside the classroom. Thus, the lack of nonwhite coaches at NCAA
institutions has significant implications for the treatment of minority athletes at predominantly white institutions. It is clear white coaches are recruiting predominantly white athletes (with the exception of Division I
and II football and basketball), the classic example of homologous reproduction. But when we look at the sports in which minority athletes are
concentrated, we uncover another culture in which predominantly white
coaches and athlete support staff members are treating minority athletes

TABLE 6-22: Racial/Ethnic Composition of Full-Time and Part-Time Postsecondary Education Faculty, Fall 2013

Race/Ethnicity	Percent
White	79
Black	6
Hispanic	5
Asian	10
American Indian/ Alaska Native	>1
Two or more races	>1

Source: National Center for Education Statistics, "Fast Facts: Race/Ethnicity of College Faculty—Fall, 2013" (2015) (https://nces.ed.gov/fastfacts/display.asp?id=61).

in very different ways. One driver of this differential treatment is the employment retention pressure on coaches of Division I football and basketball to recruit the very best players, even if those players are underprepared to compete in the classroom. Then it is common practice for NCAA member institutions to grant waivers of admissions standards for such athletes, who are disproportionately black compared to their nonathlete undergraduate peers and their numbers in this specially admitted student population. When students matriculate and begin classwork, the pressure on athletics department support staff members to keep them academically eligible is intense. The resulting academic disaster is obvious, and predictable. It doesn't take a rocket scientist to predict how the dominoes are going to fall, and the signs are clear: the clustering of athletes in less demanding academic majors and courses, learning specialists seeking disability accommodations for an academically underprepared population, an army of tutors controlled by the athletics department rather than by academic authorities, and so on.

But there is a more insidious impact that is not as evident: the predominantly white athletics department staff composition is part of the problem in that staff members are more likely to promulgate minority athlete stereotypes of physical superiority and intellectual inferiority. Research demonstrates that there is a gap between white and black student performance under white teachers. White teachers are not immune to "powerful social conditioning that cultivates actual negative attitudes . . . which also predisposes them to have lower expectations of black students and lack of respect for the students' families and primary culture."[36] There is also research-supported evidence that predominantly white male coaches are more likely to treat minority athletes, female athletes, and LBGTQ athletes with a lack of civility and differently from how they treat white athletes.[37] It is within this context that athletics employment statistics should be critically examined. The issue is not employment discrimination, although such practices may exist. The critical issue is the treatment of minority athletes within predominantly white academic institutions and athletics departments, and the predominantly white actors within the NCAA national office, institutional and conference representatives who are making and implementing the rules. The extent to which these athletic and educational administrators and leaders are predominantly white is depicted in tables 6-23 and 6-24.

The NCAA national office employment picture is similarly distressing with regard to minority employees. *The 2014 Racial and Gender Report Card: College Sport,* issued by the Institute for Diversity and Ethics in Sports at the University of Central Florida, reported the following employment picture at NCAA headquarters:

- The number of people of color and women in the positions of chief operating officer, executive vice president, senior vice president, and vice president remained the same, four each in 2013 and 2014. African Americans were the only people of color to hold these positions.

- The percentage of executives in managing director/director positions who were people of color increased from 17.1 percent in 2013 to 18.1 percent in 2014. African Americans represented 15.7 percent in 2014, which was a decrease of 0.2 percentage points from the 2013 total. The 2014 data showed there was one Latino in these positions, which was an increase of 1.2 percentage points, while the percentage of Asians remained the same from 2013 at 1.2 percent.

- At the professional administrator level, the percentage of people of color decreased slightly from 20.4 percent in 2013 to 20.2 percent in 2014. The percent of African Americans remained the same, or 15.8 percent in

TABLE 6-23: Racial and Ethnic Composition of NCAA Member Institution Athletics Department Employees, 2014–15

Percent

Position	White	Black	Hispanic	Asian	Other[a]
Coaches					
Head coach	86.9	8.7	1.9	0.9	1.6
Assistant coach	78.5	14.7	2.5	1.0	3.3
Senior management					
Director of athletics	87.3	9.8	1.7	0.5	0.7
Associate director of athletics	87.1	9.5	1.6	0.6	1.2
Assistant director of athletics	86.0	9.4	2.3	0.9	1.4
Senior woman administrator	85.5	10.4	2.0	0.8	1.2
Athlete support services					
Life skills coordinator	74.1	21.3	2.3	1.0	1.3
Head athletic trainer	91.3	3.4	2.6	1.5	1.1
Assistant/Associate athletic trainer	87.0	4.9	3.1	2.6	2.3
Strength coach	81.9	11.5	2.2	1.2	3.3
Academic adviser/Counselor	69.8	22.8	3.2	1.8	2.4
Internal operations					
Business manager	84.4	8.8	3.3	1.8	1.8
Compliance coordinator/officer	82.6	12.8	2.7	0.7	1.2
Equipment manager	82.0	10.4	4.7	1.2	1.7
Fundraiser/Development manager	88.4	7.1	1.9	1.2	1.4
Facility manager	84.1	9.5	4.6	0.6	1.1
Promotions/marketing manager	84.5	8.4	2.4	2.0	2.7
Sports information director	92.0	4.9	1.1	1.4	0.7
Assistant/Associate sports information director	91.5	3.3	1.9	1.6	1.7
Ticket manager	84.9	9.4	2.5	1.4	1.9
Clerical/Other support					
Administrative assistant	83.9	9.7	3.7	0.9	1.7
Graduate assistant (excludes FB)	82.4	10.5	2.7	1.2	3.2
Intern	79.1	13.2	2.7	1.3	3.7
Nonemployee position					
Faculty athletics representative	89.7	7.4	1.1	0.9	0.9

Source: NCAA, Sport Sponsorship, Participation and Demographics Search database (http://web1.ncaa.org/rgdSearch/exec/main).

a. Includes Hawaiian/Pacific Islander, American Indian/Alaska Native, Two or More Races, and Other.

TABLE 6-24: Racial and Ethnic Composition of NCAA
Member Conference Employees, 2014–15

Percent

Position	White	Black	Hispanic	Asian	Other[a]
Nonemployee position					
Conference president (N = 108)	91.7	7.4	0.9	0.0	0.0
Senior management					
Commissioner (N = 136)	93.4	3.7	0.7	2.2	0.0
Associate commissioner (N = 175)	82.9	16.0	0.6	0.0	0.6
Assistant commissioner (N = 141)	87.2	8.5	2.1	1.4	0.7
Middle management					
Director (N=146)	84.2	10.3	2.7	1.4	1.4
Associate director (N = 22)	100.0	0.0	0.0	0.0	0.0
Assistant director (N = 71)	78.9	12.7	4.2	1.4	2.8
Coordinator of officials (N = 514)	87.4	8.2	3.7	0.6	0.2
Clerical/Other support					
Administrative assistant (N = 63)	81.0	9.5	4.8	4.8	0.0
Conference secretary (N = 52)	92.3	3.8	1.9	1.9	0.0
Intern (N = 135)	69.6	22.2	5.2	1.5	1.5
Student assistant (N = 4)	25.0	75.0	0.0	0.0	0.0

Source: NCAA, Sports Sponsorship, Participation and Demographics Search database (http://
web1.ncaa.org/rgdSearch/exec/main).

a. Includes Hawaiian/Pacific Islander, American Indian/Alaska Native, Two or More Races, and
Other.

2014. The percent of Latino and Asian representation decreased from
1.8 percent and 2.8 percent in 2013 to 1.4 percent and 2.7 percent, respectively, in 2014. The percentage of white administrators increased
from 79.6 percent in 2013 to 79.8 percent in 2014.[38]

NCAA staff members do have an impact on the student-athlete experience in that they investigate rules-compliance issues, from academic integ-

rity to recruiting and eligibility violations. Their perceptions and beliefs shape these responsibilities.

It is within the "impact on minority student" context, as well as employment discrimination, that we should question the judgment of predominantly white decisionmakers and hold them accountable for the demonstrated academic exploitation of the most vulnerable college-athlete population subset, Division I basketball and football players. We must also take a more careful look at the graduation rates and academic performance of minority athletes in other sports, in addition to those with higher than average concentrations of minority athletes.

The Forgotten Players—Opportunities for Athletes with Disabilities

The Rehabilitation Act of 1973 is identical in structure to Title IX of the Education Amendments of 1972. Education programs and activities receiving federal financial assistance are prohibited from discriminating against individuals with a disability or they will suffer loss of federal funding. The Department of Education issued general regulations implementing the law in 1980, specifying, with regard to postsecondary education, its application to all extracurricular activities, including athletics:

104.43 Treatment of students; general

(a) No qualified handicapped student shall, on the basis of handicap, be excluded from participation in, be denied the benefits of, or otherwise be subjected to discrimination under any academic, research, occupational training, housing, health insurance, counseling, financial aid, physical education, athletics, recreation, transportation, other extracurricular, or other postsecondary education aid, benefits, or services to which this subpart applies.[39]

However, unlike the Title IX athletics provisions, there was no detailed guidance issued with regard to athletics until a 2013 Dear Colleague letter reminded schools and colleges of their athletics obligations.[40] The Dear Colleague letter was precipitated in part by a U.S. Government Accountability Office report that found that students with disabilities were not being provided with extracurricular athletic activities.[41] Similar to Title IX, which requires that females be allowed to try out for men's teams, the Dear Colleague letter noted that athletes with disabilities must be given the opportunity to try out for varsity athletic teams and to participate in an integrated manner to the maximum possible extent. The student with disabilities must be given an "individual inquiry" if not satisfied with the athletics department's proposed accommodation and, if necessary, rules of the sport must be adjusted to accommodate the participation of such athletes as long as the adjustment doesn't result in "a fundamental alteration to the nature of the extracurricular activity" or give the individual with disabilities a competitive advantage (noting that a prosthesis does not represent a competitive advantage).[42] As examples, a deaf athlete would have to be provided with a visual cue to start a race, a swimmer with one arm would not be required to end a breaststroke event with a two-hand touch, a blind cross country runner must be provided with a guide, and deaf athletes should be provided with interpreters. Decisions not to permit a student with a disability to compete cannot be based on an unfounded fear (for example, the wheelchair will damage the gym floor) or stereotype (such as a student with a learning disability can't play in a game because he or she can't make a fast enough decision under pressure).

And, like Title IX (which requires that separate and equal teams be provided for girls if trying out for boys' teams does not provide girls a legitimate opportunity to compete), separate, "adapted" sports teams (that is, wheelchair basketball, sled hockey, and so on) must be provided for athletes with disabilities if they cannot be integrated or mainstreamed into existing varsity athletic programs.

It wasn't until 2011 that the issue of opportunities for athletes with disabilities was addressed at the NCAA convention informational session. In 2012 the NCAA appointed a Student-Athletes with Disabilities Subcommittee. Currently there is only one individual with disabilities who serves on this committee. In 2013 the NCAA sponsored an NCAA Student-Athletes with Disabilities Think Tank. Despite a series of recommendations that were generated by both groups, the NCAA has been slow to take action to provide championship opportunities for students with disabilities or even to strongly encourage their members to do so.

In 2014, at the May NCAA Regional Rules Seminar in Atlanta, Chris Ruckdaschel, a staff member of the NCAA's Office of Inclusion and Leadership Development, presented a session on the inclusion of student-athletes with disabilities. Commenting on the prospects of the NCAA offering national championships in adaptive sports, he indicated that the addition of adapted sports as new NCAA sport was a "long-term initiative" with "no formal plans on the horizon." He also suggested that institutions being required to offer adaptive sports programs would be "a catalyst for NCAA sponsorship," implying that this is not a current member obligation and that the NCAA would play a follower rather than a leader role.[43] Currently, to be a member of any NCAA competitive division, an institution must sponsor a minimum number of men's and women's sports. In light of the recent guidance provided by the OCR in 2013, it would seem appropriate to expect a national governance organization such as the NCAA, NAIA, and the NJCAA to give its respective member institutions sufficient notice and lead time to meet a requirement for a minimum number of individual and team adaptive sports opportunities.

Currently, only two NCAA member institution athletic programs, both in Division II, are funding adaptive sports teams as integral parts of their varsity athletic programs (men's wheelchair basketball teams) at Edinboro University in Pennsylvania and at Southwest Minnesota State University. Even though the University of Illinois, the University of Arizona, the University of Alabama, the University of Texas at Arlington, the University of Missouri, and Pennsylvania State University have well-established and exemplary adaptive sport programs, these are all club-based programs that are not presently under the aegis of a national collegiate athletic association (the NCAA, NAIA, or NJCAA) or recognized by their primary conferences for varsity sports (for example, the Big Ten, the PAC-12, the Southeastern Conference, or the Sun Belt conferences). Although these programs, along with a handful of other university-based club programs, are well developed and seem poised to be elevated to varsity status, they remain not recognized as bona fide varsity programs sponsored by the athletics department.

The National Wheelchair Basketball Association has a men's (nine teams) and women's (four teams) intercollegiate division that enforces academic eligibility rules, similar to the NCAA, and conducts national championships in each division.[44] It would not be unreasonable to expect the NCAA to partner with adaptive sport governing organizations currently running national collegiate championships and to recognize the winners as NCAA champions while working cooperatively to advance the expansion of championship opportunities for students with disabilities.

There is one really bright light at the end of the tunnel that can demonstrate the way forward to expand opportunities for students with disabilities. In January 2015 the Eastern Collegiate Athletic Conference (ECAC, the largest NCAA member conference, with more than 300 members spanning Divisions I, II, and III) adopted a four-pronged "inclusive sport strategy" fully consistent with the spirit and letter of the Rehabilitation Act of 1973[45] and more fully articulated in the Dear Colleague Letter of January 2013. ECAC has outlined the following principles of sport inclusion:

Inclusion principle 1: The inclusion of athletes with a disability on existing teams and in competitions and championships without any sport-specific accommodations required. This already occurs within the purview of the NCAA, NAIA, and NJCAA.

Inclusion principle 2: The inclusion of athletes with a disability on existing teams and competitions and championships with reasonable sport-specific accommodations provided. This already occurs within the purview of the NCAA, NAIA, and NJCAA.

Inclusion principle 3: The inclusion of athletes with a disability on existing varsity teams through the addition of specific adaptive events in swimming, track and field, rowing, and tennis to existing competitions and conference championships.

Inclusion principle 4: The inclusion of athletes with a disability through the creation of specific adaptive team sports in new leagues, competitions, and championships, such teams permitting the participation of inclusion athletes with and without disabilities from neighboring institutions that do not have sufficient numbers to support a full adaptive team.[46]

Led by Ted Fay, a Paralympic sport expert and now the ECAC senior adviser on inclusive sport, the ECAC Inclusive Sport Initiative strategy was developed with the engagement of former and current Paralympic athletes, coaches, intercollegiate sport administrators and athletics directors, as well as key officials from disability sport organizations and national sport governing bodies.[47] Fay noted that there was a large enough pool of students with disabilities who would benefit from the ECAC program: students currently on-campus, high school students who would be inspired to follow in the footsteps of ECAC athletes, international students, and military veterans with disabilities recently incurred during their service, many of whom are former athletes returning to complete undergraduate degrees.[48] Fay and ECAC are to be congratulated for leading the way. Although the NCAA has endorsed and assisted in the implementation of this ECAC strategy, many feel that the NCAA has a responsibility to assume a more proactive leadership role beyond hosting a national think tank and creating a Student-Athletes with Disabilities Subcommittee. Some skeptics believe this is simply following the same lip service modus operandi the NCAA has used for race or ethnicity and gender equity issues. The last chapter of this book offers recommendations to advance participation opportunities for students with disabilities.

SEVEN

The NCAA's Unsustainable Economics

Contrary to common impressions, operating a big-time intercollegiate athletics program is neither profitable nor sustainable under current conditions for over 90 percent of the schools in the top NCAA subdivision, the Football Bowl Subdivision (FBS) of Division I.

Financial deficits and fiscal excess are conditioned by the absence of stockholders in intercollegiate athletics departments. Unlike company directors in other sectors of the economy, who seek profitability each quarter to drive the stock price upward or to enable dividend payments to shareholders, athletics directors seek competitive success on the playing field. Hence, even at the most successful programs, when copious flows of new revenue appear from television deals, corporate sponsorships, or donations, athletics directors put these funds at the service of building winning teams.

Over the decades, as intercollegiate athletics has become more and more commercialized and the financial stakes have sharpened for participating schools, there has been a clear trend toward larger deficits and greater revenue inequality—a trend that was accelerated by the 1984 Supreme Court decision in *Board of Regents*. This growing inequality, in turn, is making it increasingly expensive and untenable for the vast majority of schools, even those in Division I, to pursue athletic glory.[1]

Sources of Revenue Inequality

With the NCAA's long-standing national TV policy struck down in 1984, schools and conferences were left to fend for themselves. The NCAA television cartel was broken. The leading football colleges and conferences were cut free, and the weaker football colleges lost the protection of the previous NCAA national television policy.

The data in table 7-1 illustrate the revenue distributional impact of the 1984 Supreme Court decision and the conference restructuring of the 1990s. During the eighteen years between 1962 and 1980, there was a steady increase in relative revenue inequality across the top 150 college athletic programs, with the ratio of the top revenue program to the average (mean) revenue program increasing by 0.67 points. During the next seventeen-year period, 1980–97, the ratio increased at a 50 percent faster rate or by 1.00 point.

TABLE 7-1: Revenue Inequality among the Approximately Top 150 Athletic Programs, 1962–97

Year	Ratio, top school/ average school
1962	1.81[a]
1970	1.92
1980	2.48
1989	3.04
1995	3.29
1997	3.48

Source: Mitchell Raiborn, *Financial Analysis of Intercollegiate Athletics* (Kansas City: NCAA, 1970); Mitchell Raiborn, *Revenues and Expenses of Intercollegiate Athletics Programs, 1970–1977, 1978–1981, 1981–1985, 1985–1989* (Overland Park, Kan.: NCAA, 1978, 1982, 1986, 1990); NCAA, *Revenues and Expenses of Intercollegiate Athletics Programs, 1993* (Overland Park, Kan.: NCAA, 1994); NCAA, *Revenues and Expenses of Divisions I and II Intercollegiate Athletics Programs, 1995, 1997* (Overland Park, Kan.: NCAA, 1996, 1998).

a. Shown is the ratio of the top revenue program to the average (mean) revenue program, revenues from all sources, including television deals, other media rights, corporate sponsorships, and donations.

It is also noteworthy that the Supreme Court ruling was largely coincident with the explosion in popularity of cable television in the United States. Whereas in 1980 there were 15.5 million cable TV homes (or 19.9 percent of all TV households), by 1990 there were 52 million cable TV homes (or 56.4 percent of TV households). Cable TV added a second revenue stream (monthly subscription fees) to the traditional advertising stream, and hence its expansion helps to explain the rapid growth in television contracts for the elite football conferences in Division I.

Other factors promoting inequality include the former Bowl Championship Series (BCS), the Football Championship Playoff (FCP), skewed revenue distributions from the NCAA, the emergence of conference-owned regional sports channels, the explosion of network conference television contracts, and the construction of professional grade sports facilities at institutions with the big-time programs. Since its inception in 1998 through 2014, the BCS allowed preferential bowl access and sharply differential revenues to flow to the six original BCS (aka automatic qualifier, or AQ) conferences. The FCP extends the unequal distribution of revenue flows, but it roughly triples the amount of money distributed. Of course, if the FCP is ever extended to an eight-game playoff series, this pattern will be exacerbated.

Once subjected to market forces, revenue inequality becomes self-perpetuating. High revenue schools have more funds to renovate or build new stadiums and arenas, which generate more revenue, which allows the hiring of more renowned coaches and makes more funds available for recruitment and athlete support, which leads to more competitive success, which leads to larger media contracts, and so on.

Revenue distribution data prior to 2000 are scarce, and the data that are available are generally tabulated with different metrics than those commonly used since 2000. It is therefore difficult to get an accurate picture of how much inequality has increased over the decades. Further, because of inconsistent and incomplete accounting practices within athletics departments and because a good deal of revenue and cost information is treated as proprietary, it is impossible even today to acquire a full and accurate picture of the extent of inequality. Nonetheless, it is possible to compile pieces of information from the periodic NCAA's *Revenues and Expenses* reports,[2] the Equity in Athletics Disclosure Act (EADA) reports, and other

TABLE 7-2: FBS Football and Men's Basketball Revenue, 1997–2003

	High	Average	Ratio, top school/ average school
1997	$37,400,000	$10,500,000	3.56
1999	$44,700,000	$12,200,000	3.66
2003	$67,300,000	$17,300,000	3.89

sources to assemble a broad outline of the trends and the status quo in revenue inequality among FBS programs.

Table 7-1 presents data on the highest to average revenue ratios for roughly the top 150 athletic programs between 1962 and 1997. A clear trend toward greater inequality is evident, with some acceleration in the trend after the 1984 Supreme Court decision. The post-2003 data are for the FBS (128 schools in 2014–15) and refer to the highest revenue to the median revenue ratio. With the skewed revenue distribution that prevails in the FBS, the mean typically is considerably above the median, so these two data series are not comparable.

Although the top/average revenue ratio series ends in 1997, it is possible to extend the trend through 2003 by reference to NCAA data for football and men's basketball programs. Table 7-2 shows that the ratio of the highest revenue program in football and men's basketball to the average revenue program steadily increased from 3.56 in FY1997 to 3.66 in FY1999 and to 3.89 in FY2003.

After 2003 the average (mean) program is no longer reported; only the median is reported. As shown in table 7-3, the ratio of the highest revenue program to the median revenue program in both football and basketball continues its steady ascent between FY2004 and FY2014.[3]

Finally, the numbers for entire athletic programs during 2004–14, given in table 7-4, indicate that while relative inequality has stabilized (as defined by the top revenue to median revenue athletic program), the absolute amount of inequality (the dollar difference between the top revenue and the median revenue program) has continued to grow rapidly.

This pattern of inequality is underscored by what emerges from a decile breakdown of revenues in football and men's basketball within the 124 FBS schools in FY2014. In football, 40 percent of the programs had

TABLE 7-3: FBS Football and Men's Basketball Revenue, 2004–14

millions of dollars

	Median generated revenue	Top generated revenue	Top divided by median	Top minus median
Football				
2004	8.3	46.2	5.6	37.9
2010	16.2	93.9	5.8	77.7
2014	21.7	151.0	7.0	129.3
Men's basketball				
2004	3.2	16.5	5.2	13.3
2010	4.8	25.9	5.4	21.1
2014	5.8	40.6	7.0	34.8

revenues below $7.56 million in FY2014, while in basketball 40 percent had revenues below $3.2 million. Meanwhile, even the bottom half of FBS schools are trying to remain competitive and expanding their spending on athletics. The average annual athletics spending per student-athlete in FBS went from $63,000 in 2004 to $85,000 in 2008, $105,000 in 2012, and $116,000 in 2014.

Accordingly, the median FBS athletic programs run a substantial and growing operating deficit. As depicted in table 7-4, these operating deficits (median net revenues) have grown steadily from $5.9 million in 2004 to $14.7 million in 2014. In 2013–14, only twenty-four athletic programs showed an operating surplus, and that without including most capital costs (which an NCAA study separately estimated to average more than $20 million per year per FBS school), as well as certain indirect costs.[4]

These mounting deficits have impelled most universities to raise student athletic fees. According to a 2015 study by the *Washington Post*, of the sixty-five schools in the Power Five conferences within the FBS, the combined athletic fees at thirty-two of the schools totaled $125 million in 2014, roughly double what it was ten years earlier.[5] And these are among the wealthiest athletic programs in the country. The less wealthy athletic programs have even greater need for subsidies from student fees.

TABLE 7-4: Athletic Programs, 2004–14

millions of dollars

	Median generated revenue	Top generated revenue	Top divided by median	Top minus median	Median net revenues
2004	22.9	103.9	4.5	81	−5.9
2010	35.3	143.6	4.1	108.3	−9.4
2012	40.6	163.3	4.0	122.7	−12.3
2014	44.5	193.9	4.4	149.4	−14.7

According to a 2010 *USA Today* study of the then 119 NCAA Division I-A (or FBS) schools, on average, 60 percent of athletics department income came from student fees and other institutional subsidies. That figure represented an increase of more than 20 percent on average over four years. In 2011–12, subsidies for all of Division I athletics rose another 10 percent, by nearly $200 million, compared to 2010–11, reaching a total of $2.3 billion.[6] The $2.3 billion in subsidies is for the 227 public institutions in Division I. More than 120 private institutions belong to Division I. When these private institutions are included, the athletic subsidies for all of Division I are most likely between $3.3 billion and $3.5 billion annually. When Divisions II and III are included, the total athletic subsidies annually for NCAA institutions exceed $4 billion. That is, nationwide, student athletic fees are adding $4 billion to the student debt burden.

In 2015, it was revealed that the athletics departments at several public institutions in Virginia received almost 80 percent of their funding from student fees and institutional subsidies. This reality prompted Virginia state representative Kirk Cox to propose a bill that would limit subsidies from student fees and from the institution to 20 percent of the total athletics department budget.

Technological change in telecommunications is likely to further complicate the financial picture of intercollegiate athletics. Much of the impressive increase in media revenues over the past ten years has been the product of national networks' (such as ESPN) and regional sports networks' (such as the Big Ten Network) ability to be incorporated into expanded basic or tiered cable packages. The networks charged the cable distributors, which themselves faced no or limited competition in their areas, a handsome monthly fee, and the cable distributors passed this fee on to television households in their bundled monthly service. Technological change has created a multitude of video entertainment options, such that content may be received over the Internet, through over-the-top video services, and through personal devices such as tablets and smart phones. These options are leading increasing numbers of households to "cut the cord" of cable television or "shave the cord" by purchasing reduced channel bundles. Meanwhile, younger households increasingly are opting to never install the cord of cable television. In consequence, the sports contests are unable to command the same audience and the same price points that they did in the past. This trend, though complicated and difficult to predict, will likely lead to either stagnant or lower media revenues for both college and professional sports in the future. The budget cutbacks at ESPN and Fox Sports during 2015, as well as the large losses of the Longhorn Network of the University of Texas, may be a harbinger of what awaits the Power Five conference networks and future media rights deals.[7]

The current financial situation for the NCAA, then, is particularly tenuous. On the one hand, as a few dozen schools rake in tens of millions of dollars of additional revenue,[8] the remaining schools in FBS and throughout Divisions I, II, and III, are experiencing increasing subsidies to athletics during a period of budgetary stringency. On the other hand, star athletes at the leading programs witness the new massive inflows of revenue and feel cheated by their below-market compensation and the absence of a true college education. This perceived exploitation, in turn, has led to a variety of actions and litigations.

Calls for Reform and Initial Efforts

Largely in response to the White, Keller, O'Bannon, Berger, and Jenkins lawsuits and the aborted attempt by the football players at Northwestern to unionize, the NCAA has reorganized itself to allow modest reform to benefit athletes materially. These reforms include: in 2014 the NCAA allowed expanded food service for athletes and for the resumption of multiyear scholarships, which had been banned since 1974, and in 2015 it reintroduced cost of attendance stipends in Division I, and basically allowed the Power Five conferences within FBS of Division I to chart their own financial course.[9] These reforms will only exacerbate the trend toward growing inequality and the provision of school subsidies to athletics.

When capital expenses and indirect costs are included in the accounting analysis, the number of college athletic programs running a true surplus in any given year dips below ten. Many economists argue that most FBS schools have profitable athletic programs but don't show a surplus because there is no market discipline to contain costs. The second part of the contention is accurate. College athletic programs do not have stockholders who demand to see a profit at the end of every quarter in order to boost the price of the stock; rather, they have stakeholders—boosters, alumni, students, sponsors, media companies—who demand victories. The consequence is that the cost side is paid little attention and programs' athletics directors spend freely on facilities, coaches, administrators, recruitment, tutors, and travel to build winning teams.

As total coaches' compensation has soared from an average of $8.54 million per public school in the Power Five conferences in 2004 to $16.1 million in 2014, noncoaching staff compensation has also increased rapidly, from $9.38 million per school in 2004 to $16.0 million in 2014.[10] Absent a competitive labor market for athletes, the money that would otherwise go to athletes goes instead into other aspects of the program. Rather than attracting star athletes with higher salary offers, schools offer as inducements more famous coaches, along with more lavish facilities and better services. The typical pattern is that the athletics director's objective is to maximize wins, and the vast majority of programs run in deficit.

A word of clarification is in order here. It is common for more than half of FBS football teams (55 percent in 2013–14) and roughly half of FBS men's basketball teams (50 percent in 2013–14) to run an *operating* surplus[11]—that is, a surplus before capital and certain indirect costs are included. (In recent reporting, many schools have reported facility debt service when the debt was held by the athletics department. Properly reckoned, capital costs include not only the debt service on the sunk construction costs of facilities when they were built but also the money that would have to be set aside for replacing these facilities as they depreciated.)[12] But typical FBS athletic programs support fifteen to thirty sports, virtually all of which run a substantial operating deficit. When all the sports are considered together (that is, when the entire athletics department budget is considered), on an operating basis in a typical year there are roughly twenty FBS programs showing a surplus and roughly 100 showing a deficit.

The massive amounts of new television money that have poured into the Atlantic Coast Conference, the Southeastern Conference, the Big Twelve, the Big Ten, and the Pac-12—the Power Five conferences—provide the necessary resources for roughly half of the sixty-five universities in these conferences to cover the added expenses from the 2014 and 2015 reforms. The remaining ninety-odd schools in the FBS either will have to accept growing deficits or will have to opt out of the arms race of top-level intercollegiate athletics. Those schools facing larger athletic deficits, in turn, will have the options to (1) eliminate Olympic sports, (2) raise student activity fees, (3) cut back student financial aid[13] or substitute loan aid for grant aid, further increasing student debt, or (4) otherwise reduce the academic budget.

Thus the current state of finances and operations of intercollegiate athletics is in flux, in the red, and not sustainable. Change will come. The only question is whether college administrations, the NCAA (or another governing body), or the U.S. Congress will take part in deliberately shaping this change or whether these institutions and organizations will allow the laissez-faire and unpredictable litigation process that has been unfolding to continue.

The recent Northwestern University case, in which the National Labor Relations Board (NLRB) Regional Office in Chicago first opined that scholarship football players are employees and could unionize, and then the national NLRB in Washington D.C. asserted that it did not have jurisdiction, left the players without the possibility of unionizing. But in its decision the national NLRB called on the U.S. Congress to clarify the institutional structure of college sports. In particular, the NLRB declined to assert its jurisdiction and made three key observations: (1) intercollegiate athletics was in a transitional phase in 2015; (2) allowing unionization would have engendered systemic instability by permitting the seventeen private colleges out of 128 FBS schools in FY2015 to unionize; and (3) there was a need to resolve the labor market issues and academic tensions in the current system.

The NCAA has been responding, with various degrees of alacrity and seriousness, to the call for reform ever since its founding in December 1905.

Whatever reforms it has promulgated have failed to reverse the tides of academic hypocrisy, commercialization, inequality, and financial loss. Through various internal restructurings, the NCAA has functioned essentially as a trade association of athletics directors, coaches, and conference commissioners. Further, it has been consistently dominated by the power conferences within Division I-A or the FBS. The 2015 convention decision to allow the Power Five conferences to legislate autonomously on certain economic matters underwrites this control, even as it begins a more decisive bifurcation of the NCAA into two distinct groups of colleges. As long as a smaller and smaller group of athletically successful colleges increasingly dominates the NCAA, the association will be even less able than it has been historically to implement meaningful reform.

PART III

A Return to Sanity

EIGHT

Two Paths to Meaningful Reform

Intercollegiate athletics has long been caught in the ambiguous space between professional and amateur sport. As a hybrid and immensely popular system run by the NCAA, intercollegiate athletics has been critiqued as ethically hypocritical, educationally corrosive, materially exploitative, and economically unsustainable. Political and legal pressure has been building over the last ten years to reform the system. Such reform will ultimately require a choice between the professional and the amateur models, or a bifurcation whereby a select group of a few dozen schools chooses a professional paradigm while a thousand-plus schools opt for the official NCAA vision of academically centered amateur athletics. After considering the arguments for a market-oriented reform in the direction of professionalism, in this chapter we argue for an educationally based reform accompanied by a constrained and conditional antitrust exemption for the NCAA or an alternative governing body.

Marketization

There are two possible paths to meaningful reform: (1) toward marketization and professionalism or (2) toward educationally centered athletics and amateurism. The first is embodied in Jeffrey Kessler's antitrust suit, filed in the Third Circuit, on behalf of Martin Jenkins against the NCAA. It claims that the NCAA functions as a cartel that artificially and injuriously colludes to preclude the development of a labor market for college athletes and to prevent them from receiving fair compensation given their revenue contribution to the schools. If successful, Kessler's suit would compel a marketization of labor markets in intercollegiate athletics. While this suit has much economic logic to commend it, in our judgment the remedy *Jenkins* proposes would make sense only if it were accompanied by a separation of big-time intercollegiate sports from the university. Such a schism, in turn, would have serious consequences for the continuation of college sports as we know them.

If an open labor market forms within college sports, it will engender several intractable problems. First, though it seems clear that today's top college football and men's basketball teams do exploit their star players (some have marginal revenue products of well above $1 million,[1] but they receive full scholarships valued in the range of $30,000 to $70,000 annually), introducing a labor market would be a complicated affair. For instance, the average Football Bowl Subdivision (FBS) football team has eighty-five full scholarship players and thirty-five walk-on players. The majority of the scholarship athletes probably produce a value well inferior to the value of their scholarships. A few dozen produce a value close to their scholarship value. The starters probably produce a value from a little above to far in excess of their scholarship value for the superstars. (Of course, the scholarship value itself holds only if the athletes are truly being educated and if they receive a degree—two conditions that often are not met.) So, given this variation in player value, how would labor market rules be constructed to fairly reward each player? Would the AD negotiate individually with each player, with the result that each high school prospect ended up talking to a dozen or more schools? Would the prospective stars be allowed to have parents or lawyers or agents in the room to assist them? Or would there be rules that constrained how the negotiations unfolded? And, if there were rules, what would they be, and who would set them? It would be difficult to impose rules (such as a salary cap) that constrained a free and open players' market without invoking a nonstatutory labor exemption, which wouldn't be invocable without collective bargaining (or an antitrust exemption enacted by Congress). Collective bargaining, in turn, would be impossible because public sector unions are not permitted in many states.[2]

To be sure, a new player compensation scheme could result from the imposition of a "less restrictive alternative" emerging out of an antitrust lawsuit against the NCAA. The plaintiffs in O'Bannon v. NCAA argued for a less restrictive alternative of paying all players on a team the same salary. So, of the eighty-five scholarship players on a football team, if the salary of one player was raised by $1, then the salaries of the eighty-four other players would also have to be increased by a $1. Such an arrangement would amount to an 84 percent luxury tax on player salaries, lifting the marginal player cost by 84 percent. Teams would pay players in such a market up to the point where the player's expected marginal revenue product equaled the player's marginal cost. A reasonable estimate is that the football players in such a system would be paid roughly $20,000 above their cost of attendance scholarship. This income (including the value of the room and board coverage) would then be subjected to federal and state income taxes, as well as social security taxes. Colleges would be subjected to social security contributions and workmen's compensation and unemployment insurance payments. One can imagine a variety of permutations of this scheme. Such schemes would be imposed by the courts or the litigants (and approved by the courts) as the result of an antitrust suit. In either case, the resulting system would be the product of a few individuals rather than of democratically elected members of Congress and a president accountable to their constituents.

Second, to the extent that such an open labor market for players did function, how would the resulting player incomes affect the student culture at the university? The NCAA constitution states clearly that the student-athlete is to be integrated into the general student body. Having players deriving incomes of hundreds of thousands of dollars or millions of dollars (or even tens of thousands of dollars from a less restrictive alternative ruling or settlement) would even more clearly create two classes of "students" at the school.

Third, as noted earlier, the median operating deficit of FBS athletic programs in FY2014 was more than $14 million. The corresponding figure in the rest of Division I was more than $11 million.[3] These numbers leave out large capital expenditures and certain indirect costs, so that the actual deficit or university subsidy can typically surpass $20 million or $30 million annually—and it has been growing over time.

Fourth, according to current interpretation, if the football and men's basketball programs remained under the aegis of the university, payments to athletes on these teams would have to be matched by payments to female athletes, compounding the costs of a pay-for-play system.

Hence the question naturally emerges: if FBS programs are to begin paying some athletes millions of dollars a year in salaries (along with social security, unemployment, workmen's compensation, and other benefits) and others hundreds of thousands of dollars, where will the money come from? One source of funds would likely reflect the forces of supply and demand. As player costs escalated, head coaches and schools would suddenly realize they didn't need 120 players on the team. The number of scholarships would fall by two or three dozen.

Another partial source of funds is evident: today college coaches are paid for the value of the athletes they recruit. The top-paid college coaches are compensated on a par with their counterparts in the NFL and NBA, yet their teams generally generate one-fourth to one-tenth as much revenue. These discrepancies would not make sense in a normal market, and they make sense in college sports only because compensation to the players is artificially suppressed. So, if the athletes were paid a salary, the salaries of head and assistant coaches (and athletics directors) would come down, but only after a transition period as current multiyear contracts played out and the culture of the marketplace was transformed. A similar dynamic would occur with stadiums, arenas, fitness facilities, tutoring buildings, and so on. There would be less need to invest in these auxiliary attractions because schools would be able to bid for athletes directly with higher compensation. But here too, these facilities have already been built and financed with long-term bonds. Money would not be freed up until these bonds were paid off. The upshot is that some funds would become available to help defray the higher costs of athletes in an open labor market, but these funds would become available only gradually, over time. In the protracted interim, there would be a significant new cost burden falling on athletic programs.

The competitive forces fostering the drive to success would be expected to compel higher salaries, higher costs, and greater commercialization. Further, the continuation of various tax preferences that currently go to college sports (such as no payroll tax payments, tax-exempt debt issuance for facility construction, favorable unrelated business income tax IRS interpretations, the categorization of purchase of seat tickets as "donations," deductible up to 80 percent of the amount paid) would come under greater scrutiny, and political pressure for their elimination would increase. Academic fraud would proliferate, and schools would find it increasingly in their interest to end the charade of amateur and educationally centered college athletics. Thus, it seems likely that this marketization process would ultimately result in the formation of a professional minor league in both men's basketball and football.

Whether these new professional leagues, severed from their educational ties to the university, would diminish the iconic branding associated with college sports is another matter of concern. While the new minor league teams could continue to play at university facilities and attempt to elicit the interest of existing fans and boosters, the leagues might devolve into little more than minor league associations in the public's mind. While media pundits and opposing lawyers have argued stridently on both sides of this branding issue, the reality is that no one knows how the public will react.

(Among those who don't know are the judges in the Ninth Circuit Court of Appeals. The fact that they relied on a poorly designed survey by the NCAA and off-the-cuff remarks by Neal Pilson and ignored more robust historical evidence from the Olympics, Major League Baseball, and tennis, among other sources, should inspire little confidence in their judgment in *O'Bannon*. The flimsy empirical and dubious legal reasoning in its review of the district court's ruling in *O'Bannon*, however, promises to keep this matter open for some time to come, especially if it is left to the courts to decide. While the courts may precipitate scattered reform, courts should not and cannot guide the needed reform because their nature is to deal with narrow and esoteric issues rather than devise coherent systemic solutions.)

Equally troubling is that the financial support that the big-time football and men's basketball programs currently contribute to Olympic sports and to women's sports would be gone. Nonrevenue-generating sports in all three divisions would lose funding, as would the implementation of Title IX.[4] Thus, while there is a certain logic to opening a labor market for college athletics, there are many reasons to resist this development.

Reinforcement of Educationally Centered Amateur Athletics by Revisiting the Antitrust Treatment of College Sports

A major factor that facilitated, accelerated, and deepened the commercialization of college sports was the 1984 Supreme Court decision in NCAA

v. Board of Regents of the University of Oklahoma. The majority of justices in that case ruled that the commercial activities of the NCAA were subject to antitrust law and that the NCAA's existing national television contract with ABC, CBS, and TBS was an illegal restraint of trade. The ruling set the stage for subsequent conference contracts with the television networks, a mergers and acquisitions phase of conference growth, which redrew geographic conference lines to maximize the value of media deals, and heightened incentives to compromise academic integrity in pursuit of athletic glory.

One logical way to confront this tendency toward the subordination of academics to athletics is to revisit the major source of the post-1984 commercialization juggernaut: the antitrust treatment of college sports. By legislating a partial and conditional antitrust exemption for the governing body of college sports, it would be possible not only to blunt the incentives that are corroding academic integrity but also to arrest the runaway expenses that are burning a deep hole in the pockets of athletic programs, and therefore also of university budgets.

That is, on the condition that the governing body enacted certain reforms to promote academic integrity and the fair treatment of athletes, the governing body would be granted an antitrust immunity in certain commercial areas and in others that overlap commercial and academic areas. Because the Sherman Act was designed to focus only on commercial decisions, it is very difficult to apply it to activities that are a hybrid, with both commercial and noncommercial effects, as is the case with many NCAA policies. Most of the former and current antitrust lawsuits filed against the NCAA fall in this hybrid, gray space, where the key question is whether the rules such as controlling compensation to athletes, the compensation to coaches, the value of athletic scholarships, and so on are necessary to protect the separation between college and professional sport. There are no clear-cut balancing tests or other mechanisms to make these policy judgments cleanly. The answers end up depending on the judgment of the particular court and not on any clear objective standards. A limited antitrust exemption in this hybrid space would seek to define neatly those actions of the NCAA or other governing body that could not be questioned under the Sherman Antitrust Act on the grounds that they are controls necessary to achieve the priority purposes of higher education in the conduct of intercollegiate athletics as an extracurricular activity.

This pattern was illustrated clearly in the September 2015 ruling of the Ninth Circuit Court of Appeals in *O'Bannon*. The NCAA appealed the district court decision by Judge Wilken, who had ruled that there were two less restrictive ways that the NCAA could still maintain amateurism and yet improve the compensation of athletes, to wit: first, by allowing member schools to offer scholarships that included a cost of attendance allowance, and second, by allowing member schools to offer a deferred payment to athletes of up to (a limit not allowed to be set below) $5,000 annually for use of their names, images, and likenesses (NILs). Judge Jay Bybee, Judge Gordon Quist, and Chief Judge Sidney Thomas heard the NCAA's appeal and ruled in a two-to-one decision that the NCAA did not have to allow a deferred NIL payment to athletes because it would amount to pay for a noneducational function and would violate the norms of amateurism. To arrive at this conclusion, Judge Bybee and Judge Quist opined that consumers of college sports would lose interest in the product if athletes received NIL payments, even on a deferred basis (that is, payment were not made until after the athletes had left college). Curiously, they made this judgment without any solid empirical evidence whatsoever. Applying the same logic, the judges would have concluded that if college sports had been based on a system of slavery and if the consumers found this appealing, then slavery would have been legal as far as the antitrust laws were concerned. They compounded their error by never engaging in a balancing test regarding the anti- and pro-competitive aspects of the NCAA's prohibition against NIL payments to athletes. The decision of the three appellate judges was appealed for an en banc review by the full Ninth Circuit, but the appeal was denied. The *O'Bannon* plaintiffs have appealed the Ninth Circuit ruling to the Supreme Court. The NCAA also appealed to the Supreme Court.[5]

Bybee and Quist further opined that if deferred NIL payments were allowed, it would open the door to other non–educationally based forms of remuneration and would eventually destroy the amateur basis of intercollegiate athletics. Their logic appears to overlook the fact that the Amateur Athletic Union, the United States Golfers Association, and other amateur sport organizations have considerably looser rules to define amateurism. These rules essentially proscribe compensation for playing the sport, not for activity such as endorsements off the playing field. Even the NCAA allows student-athletes to play on national Olympic teams, which offer broken-time payments to athletes to compensate them for lost income from jobs while participating on the national team. In essence, the NCAA defi-nition of amateurism is arbitrary and has morphed multiple times over the years. The one common element in all sports associations' definitions of amateurism is that the athlete cannot be paid for *playing* the sport. Any other restriction is not basic to the common understanding of amateurism.

A limited antitrust exemption in the hybrid space between profession-alism and amateurism would seek to define clearly those actions of the NCAA that could not be questioned under the Sherman Antitrust Act on the grounds that they are controls necessary to achieve the priority pur-poses of higher education in the conduct of intercollegiate athletics as an extracurricular activity.

A fundamental function of the NCAA is to maintain a clear line of de-marcation between college sports as an extracurricular activity secondary to the academic responsibilities of students and professional sports, which place a time and effort priority on athletics excellence and revenue pro-duction inappropriate for a nonprofit educational institution. Actions that should be considered the legitimate functions of a nonprofit national inter-collegiate athletics governance association typically include, among others, those that (1) control the cost of athletics (athletic programs are heavily subsidized by student fees and general funds), so that the support of athletic programs does not damage the ability of the institution to support its pri-mary academic programs; (2) prevent the operation of varsity sport programs from conflicting with student academic responsibilities (for example, control of sport schedules so that they don't conflict with class attendance, restrict-ing athletic participation for students not performing academically, limit-ing time spent on sports activities to allow sufficient time for study); and (3) protect the health and welfare of college athletes (such as by providing in-surance and instating protections related to return to play following injury).

Some of these actions also have commercial implications and can be-come the target of antitrust lawsuits. A limited antitrust exemption that applied only to these legitimate categories of control would enable higher education institutions to collectively enact needed reforms without fear of legal liability, and would be both justifiable and necessary. Antitrust lawsuits represent huge costs, in the tens of millions of dollars, for legal representation, participation in court cases, and payment of damages. Those are funds that would otherwise be available to advance the NCAA's and its member institutions' nonprofit educational purposes. In what follows, we first elaborate on what areas might be granted an antitrust exemption and then on the conditions the governing body would have to follow to qualify for the partial exemption.

Potentially Exempt Areas

First, the NCAA would be exempt from imposing limits on the salaries paid to head football and men's basketball coaches, which often exceed the salaries of the member universities' presidents by a factor of five to ten.[6] More than one hundred and ten college football and basketball coaches received salaries exceeding $1 million in 2014; three dozen received salaries exceeding $3 million, and fifteen received salaries exceeding $4 million. The highest-paid coach was Nick Saban at Alabama, who received a salary of $7.2 million plus potential bonuses of $700,000. His contract is guaranteed with increases through the 2021–22 season. Saban's staff earned an additional $5.2 million in salary in 2014. Thus, total football coaching compensation at Alabama before handsome benefits and rich perquisites exceeded $13 million. Perquisites generally include the free use of cars, housing subsidies, paid country club memberships, private jet service, and exceptionally generous severance packages.[7] The coaches also have attractive opportunities to earn outside income through apparel or sneaker endorsements, giving speeches, participating in or running summer camps, and signing book contracts. In forty states the head football or basketball coach of a college team makes more than the state's governor.[8]

Back in 1924, Centenary College in Shreveport, Louisiana, the nation's first liberal arts college west of the Mississippi, was denied accreditation by the Southern Association of Colleges and Schools because, in the association's opinion, the school placed an "undue emphasis on athletics." The primary evidence of Centenary's misplaced priorities, in the eyes of the Southern Association, was that the college paid its football coach more than it paid its college president. The next year the football coach was fired, and the college gained accreditation.[9]

In more recent times, Bear Bryant, the legendary head football coach at the University of Alabama (1958–1982), adhered to a firm policy of always keeping his salary $1 below that of the school president. Bryant believed that it was symbolically important for the university president to be paid more than the head football coach.[10]

Defenders of multimillion-dollar head coaches' salaries are wont to repeat the mantra, "Coaches' compensation packages are driven by market
forces." Fair enough, but what drives the market forces? It is clear that the
market for coaches is sustained by several artificial factors: (1) no compensation is paid to the athletes; (2) intercollegiate sports benefit from
substantial tax privileges; (3) no shareholders demand dividend distributions or higher profits to bolster stock prices at the end of every quarter; (4)
athletics departments are nourished by university and statewide financial
support; and (5) coaches' salaries are negotiated by athletics directors,
whose own worth rises with the salaries of their employees.

In a normal competitive market, college football and basketball coaches
would not be getting compensated almost at the same level as NFL and
NBA coaches. The top thirty-two college football programs generate revenues in the $35 million to $150 million range; the revenue range for NFL
teams is $296 million to $620 million.[11] The top thirty college men's basketball teams generate revenue roughly in the $10 million to $40 million
range, while NBA team revenues go from $110 million up to $293 million.
Thus, NFL team revenues are 8.4 times college football team revenues at
the lower end and 4.1 times at the top end, while NBA team revenues are
11 times those of college basketball teams at the lower end and 7.3 times at
the top end. Yet the compensation packages of college and professional
coaches in football and basketball are strikingly similar.

What's wrong with this picture? Basically, it is that the coaches are being
paid the value created by the players they recruit. Much recruiting is done
by assistant coaches, and much of the allure of the recruitment effort has
to do with the school's history and brand and its facilities. Moreover, the
coaches' bloated compensation packages are almost all economic rent. That
is, they are being paid way beyond what they would have to be paid to in-
duce them to offer their labor in the college coaching market. If the Nick
Sabans and John Caliparis of the college coaching world did not coach in
an FBS program, their next best alternative employment opportunity likely
would be coaching at Football Championship Series or Division II or III
schools, or high school. Thus, if the NCAA placed, say, a $400,000 limit on
coaches' compensation packages, it would not affect the quality of coaching or the level of intercollegiate competition one iota. Stated differently, it
would not affect the allocation of coaching resources or diminish the entertainment value of college sports. Further, it would address the Bear Bry-

ant concern of sending a twisted signal to undergraduate students about the importance of the college president or the professoriate relative to the head football or basketball coach.

A second exempt policy would be the size of FBS football teams. As of April 2016, there were two active antitrust suits against the NCAA over its scholarship limits on football teams. FBS football teams are allowed eighty-five scholarships. Sixty (or fewer) would do fine.[12] NFL teams have a maximum active roster of forty-five, plus a maximum inactive roster of eight additional players.[13] The average FBS team has thirty-five walk-ons plus eighty-five scholarship players—120 players in all![14] If football scholarships were cut to sixty, the average college would probably save close to $1.5 million annually[15]—easily enough to finance an average FBS soccer team plus an average FBS golf team, or an FBS tennis team plus gymnastics team, and have several hundred thousand dollars left over.[16] Even assuming the number of walk-ons would not increase with the lower scholarship limit, the average squad size would still be over ninety. What rational coach would dare to argue that ninety-plus players on a football team is inadequate?

A third exempt policy would be restrictions on the payment of salary to athletes for the performance of their sport. Athletes could continue to receive full scholarships for participating on their team, along with a cost of living allowance and other elements to be discussed shortly, but they could not be paid directly for what they do on the football field or basketball court. This is basically the concept of amateurism (that is, no compensation for *playing* a sport) that is applied by the Amateur Athletic Union and other amateur sports organizations in the United States.

Other areas of antitrust immunity that lean more toward the academic integrity end of the spectrum include restrictions on weeknight football and basketball games, the length of competitive seasons, the number of in-season and out-of-season practice and game hours per week, and academic eligibility standards.

Conditions for Granting Partial Exemption

One can imagine a variety of conditionality stipulations geared toward ensuring that athletes are treated fairly and that academic fraud is, if not extirpated, minimized. For the NCAA or an alternative governing body to be granted a partial antitrust exemption, the association would have to enact and implement certain pro-educational reforms. A suggested, noninclusive list follows and is discussed at greater length in chapter 9.

Initial eligibility standards need to be strengthened. Since the 2003 sliding scale was introduced, it has been possible for athletes to gain full initial eligibility and still receive the lowest possible score on standardized tests by raising their grade point average (GPA) to a 3.55.[17] If, however, the high school rigs the athlete's classes and teachers to achieve this GPA, then the initial eligibility standard is a mockery. Similar issues apply to the continuing eligibility standards and to the Academic Progress Rate metric. New, more meaningful standards need to be set and become conditions for the areas of antitrust immunity.

The governing body should also be required to put in place appropriate due process procedures for all schools, administrators, and athletes who are accused of transgressions before penalizing them.

Athletes' rights must be fortified. Health and safety protections, as well as broader injury insurance and loss of value coverage, should be instituted, along with legal aid for athletes around eligibility issues. Allowable scholarships should be expanded to include cost of attendance and publicity rights income, and athletes should have the right to work with counsel or an agent before deciding to enter a professional draft or participating in a sports league combine. All academic support programs for athletes should be removed from the athletics department and put entirely under academic control. Athletes should be allowed to transfer to other institutions without athletic eligibility penalties.

The national championship football playoff system, inaugurated in 2014–15, generates more than $600 million in revenue, over three-fourths of which is distributed to the Power Five conferences. This skewed distribution at once enhances the financial incentives to achieve victory at any cost and, importantly, diminishes funding for Olympic sports and women's sports throughout the NCAA's three divisions. The NCAA controls all national championships except the FBS football playoff. A condition for receiving a partial antitrust exemption should be to bring the football playoff into the fold.

Other conditionality reforms might include whistleblower protection, Title IX compliance, and defined controls over game scheduling.

Courts or Congress?

Intercollegiate athletics is at a tipping point. The status quo is not stable, and change is coming. This change can move college sports further toward commercialization and quasi-professionalism or it can endeavor to reinforce the historical vision of college sports as an extracurricular activity subordinated to the educational mission of U.S. colleges. The former path will lead to increasing academic scandals, widespread financial insolvency, and diminishing support for Olympic sports and Title IX. The latter path, while not without its own challenges, may succeed in restoring a proper balance between athletics and academics.

Congress could play a significant role in restoring this balance by adopting a constrained and conditional antitrust exemption for intercollegiate athletics. Without congressional action, the court system will equivocate without producing clarity. In addition to uncertainty, the status quo will perpetuate the exploitation of athletes and the undermining of academic integrity. It will also waste hundreds of millions of dollars on needless litigation. The plaintiffs' bill alone through the district court proceedings in *O'Bannon* was $46 million. The NCAA is responsible for that sum[18] as well as for its own, much larger legal expenses in the case. A congressionally conferred, conditional, and constrained antitrust exemption would provide a clear, productive way forward and in the process would at once blunt incentives to academic fraud and fortify college finances.

NINE

Anchors for Reform: Guidelines and Conclusion

Extracurricular activities generally, and intercollegiate athletic programs among them, are important contributors to student development. Most colleges and universities have an educational mission that includes development of the "whole student." A broad range of extracurricular activities is available on most campuses to deliver on this individual student development promise. These activities meet a variety of student interests, including entertainment and social purposes, and often provide laboratory-like settings for students to gain, improve, and test various skills from dance, sport, and music to drama and debate. Extracurricular programs enable students to explore a wide range of activities and interests beyond the highly restricted nature of required and elective courses within specific degree programs. In cases where the extracurricular activity has a direct relationship to the student's degree program, course credit may even be awarded for such participation. Suffice it to say that extracurricular programs are valued student development activities and integral parts of the college experience.[1] Many of these programs also involve public event performances attended by nonparticipating students and alumni that contribute to the development of a sense of community and institutional affinity. Athletic programs are valued contributors in all of these spaces.

223

Necessity of a National Governance Association Compact

As the reader has most likely inferred by this point, we believe that as long as intercollegiate athletics resides in the higher education environment, these programs must be academically compatible with their larger institution, subordinate to the institution's educational mission, and defensible from a not-for-profit organizational standpoint. The issue is not whether intercollegiate athletics belongs in higher education as an extracurricular offering. Rather, the perennial challenge has been how these programs have been governed and conducted. These conduct and governance issues have revolved around nine consistent themes: (1) the eligibility of athletes to compete; (2) protecting the health, safety, and general well-being of athletes; (3) crossing the line that separates educational sport, properly in the higher education milieu, and professional sport, participation in which violates both the educational purpose and the nonprofit legal protections such as tax preferences afforded college athletic programs; (4) excessive demands on participants related to time spent on athletics-related activities, which has a negative impact on academic performance; (5) excessive control of the lives of college athletes, which prevents them from being treated as regular students, unfairly limits sport-related outside employment, isolates athletes from the typical higher education experience, and interferes with normal institutional and community disciplinary processes; (6) the recruiting of academically underprepared athletes, mismatched to compete in the classroom with their peers, who are disproportionately black male participants in football and basketball; (7) institutionalized academic fraud and misconduct intended to keep athletes eligible to compete; (8) insufficient control of expenditures, creating excessive pressure to increase student fees and institutional and state government funding of athletics; and (9) failures of due process and conflicts of interest, resulting in a selective and unfair enforcement system. While these issues must be addressed by each higher education institution, the interinstitutional nature of college sports, in which hundreds of diverse educational institutions sponsor sports teams that compete against each other, also requires a compact among the institutions on how these programs are to be conducted. Thus the existence of an effective national organization that effectively controls the conduct of member institutions is a necessity.

Clear Rules and Regulations That Effectively Implement Principles

It is incumbent, therefore, on the higher education community to have a sound philosophy of educational sport with regard to purpose, clear principles that govern the sport's conduct and rules, and regulations that implement these principles. To ensure that extracurricular intercollegiate athletic programs are conducted as an integral part of the educational program, the moral compass must be reset in the most educationally and legally defensible manner. Thus, it is important to do more, and better, than stating vague generic principles. More detailed guidelines and a stronger national governance organization are called for if repeating past mistakes is to be avoided. It is from this perspective that the following guidelines are proposed for institutional policy and athletics governance association rules and regulations. They must be adopted as a package because they are interrelated. They should not be rank ordered, implying that just a few choices can be made.

Alternative to NCAA Reform

While the bulk of this book has been a critique of the operation of the National Collegiate Athletic Association, the following guidelines do not necessarily represent a prescription for reform of the NCAA. Insofar as the NCAA is controlled by a small number of the wealthiest Football Bowl Subdivision (FBS) members, we doubt that NCAA reform is possible. We believe Congress should consider the establishment of a federally chartered replacement organization, taking action comparable to its passage of the Amateur Sports Act of 1978, which replaced a similarly flawed Amateur Athletics Union with the United States Olympic Committee to create a more just organization to govern open amateur sports in the country.[2] We also believe that congressional action is necessary to tie compliance with these guidelines to either Higher Education Act funding of the larger institution or the continued enjoyment of tax preferences by athletic programs, or both. Compliance with these guidelines should also be tied to Congress's granting (1) a limited antitrust exemption that would allow the national governance association and its members to control costs and (2) legal discovery powers to enable an effective enforcement system administered by objective third parties and guaranteeing college athletes and institutions of higher education due process.

The purpose of this chapter is to clearly state what the purpose of intercollegiate athletics should be and the components of a model governance structure that would dictate a return to sanity. What follows are recommended guidelines for the conduct of intercollegiate athletics.

GUIDELINE NO. I
Statement of National Governance
Organization's Purpose

National athletic organizations should perform the following functions:

1. Establish eligibility rules for student participation in athletic programs that are consistent with higher education academic standards related to good academic standing and normal progress toward the baccalaureate degree, and draw a clear line of demarcation between collegiate and professional sports.
2. Formulate, copyright, and publish rules of play that permit fair and safe athletic competition between member institutions.
3. Require members to conform to sports medicine policy and treatment standards established by medical authorities that protect the health and well-being of participating athletes.
4. Establish organization and competitive division initial and continuing membership rules consistent with federal laws that prohibit member institutions that are recipients of federal funds from discriminating on the basis of gender, race or ethnicity, or disability in the conduct of educational activities.
5. Operate a rules enforcement program that affords due process to member institutions and individual athletes and conforms to the highest standards of integrity, fairness, and objectivity.
6. Conduct national championship events for members and establish standards for the participation of member athletic teams and individuals in postseason events not sponsored by the national governance organization.

7. Establish rules that control the costs of intercollegiate athletics to ensure that the student fee and institutional subsidization of such programs does not diminish the primacy of member institutions' academic programs.

8. Collect and preserve intercollegiate athletics records.

9. Collect and make available for association and academic research and analysis financial, academic, and athletic injury data, as audited by member institutions.

10. Study all phases of competitive intercollegiate athletics for the purpose of establishing standards whereby members conduct programs in a respectful educational environment that enhances the efforts of college athletes to successfully pursue their degrees and participate as integral members of the student body.

11. Cooperate with other amateur athletics organizations in promoting and conducting national and international athletic events.

12. Legislate on any subject of general concern to the members related to the administration of intercollegiate athletics.

GUIDELINE NO. 2
Majority Independent Board of Directors

National governance associations should be governed by a board of directors, which should be the highest governing authority of the organization and should have the fiduciary responsibility to act to advance the best interests of the entire organization, college athletic programs, and college athletes generally, as opposed to the special interests of membership divisions, subdivisions, or conferences. The majority of board members should be "independent," meaning that the individual member should not concurrently, during the two years preceding commencement of or at any time during his or her term as a director, hold a position as a member institution's president, trustee, faculty, college athlete, athletics director, or other paid employee of a higher education institution or as a commissioner of an athletic conference that includes member institutions. The composition of the board should reflect diversity in gender, race or ethnicity, and disability and should include a majority of former college presidents and others who are former college trustees, tenured faculty, college athletes, and athletics directors. The board should be equally balanced with regard to members formerly employed by or having participated at institutions in different competitive divisions.

The board should be expert in intercollegiate athletics, with noncollege-athlete directors having served no less than five years in a leadership position directly related to the oversight of intercollegiate athletics or, in lieu of such leadership experience, demonstrating expert knowledge of intercollegiate athletics. Former college athletes should have completed four years of eligibility, earned a baccalaureate degree, and completed his or her eligibility within ten years of beginning service as a director.

The board should have the sole legislative authority to promulgate policies, rules, and regulations in the following specific areas:

1. Establish various competitive divisions that differ based on the maximum number of athletic grants-in-aid that may be awarded in each sport, the minimum dollar amount of total athletic grants-in-aid awarded overall, maximum sport program operating expenses, maximum salary and wage expenditures commensurate with the not-for-profit educational marketplace, minimum number of sports sponsored, and maximum numbers of allowable coaches and support personnel in each sport (accompanied by a limited antitrust exemption in order to fulfill these responsibilities).

2. Establish for each sport in which it conducts championships or recognizes championships conducted by others limits on the number of contests, the length of competitive seasons, the conditions for member institution participation in pre- or postseason collegiate athletic events conducted by third parties, and limits on the number of hours per week spent on athletics-related activities and other scheduling constraints to enable college athletes to devote sufficient time to their primary academic responsibilities. Such rules and regulations should include a limit of no more than twenty hours of athletics-related activity per week for eligible athletes during their competitive season and ten hours per week outside the competitive season and for any athlete academically ineligible to compete.

3. Establish athletic grants-in-aid policies consistent with the *Federal Student Aid Handbook* guidelines and Title IX of the Education Act Amendments of 1972.

4. Establish other rules that limit athletic program expenditures to be consistent with expenditures on other extracurricular student activities.

5. Establish conduct requirements or other limitations or conditions to be included in contractual agreements or appointments between a coach and a member institution.

6. Determine insurance, academic support program subsidies, and other college athlete benefit programs financed by the organization.

7. Determine the distribution of revenues to members, which should not be based on the athletic performance or athletic event qualification of any individual or team and should be consistent with the purposes of the organization and its stated principles.

8. Establish academic conditions for individual college athlete eligibility for regular participation and team eligibility for conference and national championship participation and other pre- or postseason competitions.

9. Establish and maintain provisions for reasonable representation of institutional and other members in decisionmaking or recommending structures regarding the adoption of legislation not otherwise under the exclusive jurisdiction of the board of directors. Representation or voting on such other governance committees should not be weighted to advantage any membership or competitive division subgroup.

GUIDELINE NO. 3

Commitment to Campuswide Assessment
and Peer Review

National athletics governance associations should require their member institutions to conduct periodic athletic program self-assessments by campuswide committees with expert third-party peer reviews. Such assessments should examine compliance with model standards regarding academic integrity; governance and commitment to rules compliance; gender, race or ethnicity, and disability inclusion; and student-athlete educational success and well-being. If deficiencies are identified, they should be remedied within a certain time or constitute cause for institutional penalties, including ineligibility for postseason championships or revocation of membership. The assessments should be part of the public record and should be submitted to the faculty senate or a parallel body at each institution.

Such athletic program certification programs should follow the accepted higher education methods of regional accreditation agencies and are necessary additions to these larger institutional processes. Accreditation agencies simply have not been able to accomplish the depth of analysis required to examine complex multimillion-dollar athletic programs capable of hiding transgressions beneath layers of aggregated data. The cost and time consumed in undertaking certification assessments are warranted for highly commercialized athletic programs in which the financial stakes and pressures to win pose the greatest risk of college athlete exploitation and academic fraud. Institutional members of less competitive divisions could be required to go through the same process but without the external peer review aspect of the program.

GUIDELINE NO. 4

Ownership and Proper Use of Assets for Educational Purposes

All national collegiate championships in which members participate should be owned by the national governance organization, and the proceeds from such events should advance the purposes of the association. Priorities as to the use of national championship and other association revenues should be restricted to the reasonable cost of association operations, reimbursement of reasonable expenses for the conduct of national championships and the participation of athletes therein, the provision of catastrophic and other injury insurance benefiting all athletes, the funding of research and other activities that advance the health, safety, and academic success of all athletes, and grants to member institutions that are restricted to use for special athlete needs, athlete academic support, athletic scholarship support, and sport operating expenses. No portion of governance association proceeds should be returned to member institutions based on winning or qualification for national championships or for unrestricted use.

GUIDELINE NO. 5

Code of Ethics

National governance associations should promulgate and enforce codes of ethics to guide (1) the conduct of its board of directors, councils, and committees, (2) the professional conduct of coaches and the respect coaches should afford college athletes, (3) sportsmanlike conduct by all those involved in athletic events, and (4) the proper conduct of institutional staff members with regard to admissions, academic support, and proper relations with the athletes and employees they supervise. Violations of such codes should subject employees to penalties, including termination of employment.

GUIDELINE NO. 6

Specific Prohibitions against Lavish Expenditures and Facilities or Policies That Isolate Athletes from the General Student Body

National governance associations should establish guidelines for financial prudence in the conduct of athletic programs consistent with commonly accepted standards for nonprofit organizations, including appropriate compensation of employees and prohibitions against lavish expenditures. Further, capital expenditures for facilities used by athletes only or policies that restrict athletes from accessing experiences or services available to all students should be prohibited because they unnecessarily isolate athletes from the general student body. (The implementation of this and other guidelines may require application of the conditional antitrust exemption.)

GUIDELINE NO. 7

Whistleblower Protection

National governance associations should establish and implement policies and procedures that enable individuals to come forward with information on illegal practices or violations of organizational policies without fear of retribution. Such whistleblower protection policies should be adopted by the national governance association and be required of all member institutions and conferences, and should specify that both the organization and its member institutions will not retaliate against, and will protect the confidentiality of, individuals who make good-faith reports.[3]

GUIDELINE NO. 8
Transparency

National governance associations should mandate that their member institutions produce an annual report fully disclosing audited financial and academic data specified by the association, including comparisons with the academic performance of nonathlete students and the demographic composition (gender, race or ethnicity, disability) of athletes and employees, to allow the campus community and the general public to determine the efficacy of its programs.

Athletic programs greatly benefit from student fees and general fund subsidies, tax preferences (because they are part of a nonprofit institution), the use of tax-free bonds and government subsidies. Insofar as most students leave college with considerable debt and taxpayers are directly and indirectly subsiding multimillion-dollar athletic programs, it is important that athletics department financial data be transparent to the public. Thus, in addition to the regularized certification program, each member institution's athletic program should be required to publish a comprehensive annual report in a standardized format to include audited academic, financial, and student and staff demographic (gender, race or ethnicity, disability) data, which should be available to the general public. All academic data should include comparisons to the nonathlete student population whenever possible. Acknowledging that some data are currently available in the Equity in Athletics Disclosure Act database, the Knight Commission's Athletic and Academic Spending Database for Division I, various NCAA databases, and elsewhere, this information should be consolidated into an annual report published by and available from each NCAA member institution.

GUIDELINE NO. 9

Institutional Control and Responsibility

Each member institution's president or chancellor should be ultimately responsible for the administration of all aspects of the athletics program, which should minimally include the following activities or areas:

1. Rules compliance oversight by a senior-level employee paid for and reporting to the Office of the President.
2. Budget oversight and execution of an independent audit of all expenditures by the senior financial officer of the institution.
3. Provision of academic advising and support programs administered by academic authorities assigned that function for all students.
4. Oversight of athletics financial aid practices by the Office of Student Financial Aid.
5. Determination of initial academic eligibility by the director of admissions and the determination of continuing eligibility by the registrar.

The institution's responsibility for the conduct of its intercollegiate athletics program should include responsibility for the actions of its staff members and for the actions of any other individuals or organizations engaged in activities promoting the athletics interests of the institution.

GUIDELINE NO. 10

Academic Integrity

Admissions, academic advising, course grading, the creation of special courses or independent study opportunities, or tutoring practices that place athletic eligibility above academic integrity, as indicated by athlete versus nonathlete grading differences and enrollment patterns, should be considered academic fraud and should constitute cause for institutional penalties, including ineligibility for postseason play and revocation of membership.

GUIDELINE NO. II

Academic Eligibility for Athletics Participation
and Postseason Events

Academic standards for initial athletic eligibility should be pegged to institutional academic profiles that ensure a match between the athlete and the nonathlete with regard to classroom competitiveness. If institutions choose to recruit underprepared college athletes who are more than one standard deviation below the academic profile of the nonathletes with whom they must compete in the classroom, freshman ineligibility for athletic competition should be mandated. Further, institutions admitting such athletes should be required to provide (1) athletic scholarship assistance to support these athletes during a year of transition; (2) academic skills and learning disability testing; (3) a remediation program supervised by academic authorities; and (4) a ten hour per week participation restriction applicable to all athletics-related activities (practice, meetings, and the like).[4] Reductions in course load should be permitted for athletes requiring remediation.

Academic standards for continued eligibility for athletic participation in any semester should be 2.0 (the common minimum 2.0 cumulative GPA required to be above probationary status or for graduation). Any athlete not meeting the 2.0 standard should not be permitted to participate in practice more than ten hours per week, should be prohibited from traveling with the team or engaging in other team activities, and should be required to participate in an academic support program. Students should not be eligible for participation when they are on probation. A student-athlete who is in a four-year degree program and entering his or her third year of collegiate enrollment should have completed successfully at least 50 percent of the course requirements in the student's specific degree program. A student-athlete who is in a four-year degree program and entering his or her fourth year of collegiate enrollment should have completed successfully at least 75 percent of the course requirements. A student-athlete who is in a five-year degree program and entering his or her third year of collegiate enrollment should have completed successfully at least 40 percent of the course requirements in the student's specific degree program. A student-athlete who is in a five-year degree program and entering his or her fourth year of collegiate enrollment should have completed successfully at least 60 percent of the course requirements. A student-athlete who is in a five-year degree program and entering his or her fifth year of collegiate enrollment should have completed successfully at least 80 percent of the course requirements in the student's specific degree program. For athletes completing a year of freshman ineligibility and remediation, computation of normal progress should begin effective their second year of enrollment.

GUIDELINE NO. 12
Meaningful Graduation Expectations:
Penalizing the Correct Party

Each team of a member institution should be required to maintain a Federal Graduation Rate (FGR), without any exceptions, that equals or exceeds the national average FGR or the institution's own FGR, whichever is lower. Failure to achieve this benchmark should not be used to declare a team ineligible for postseason play, which penalizes the student-athlete as well as the institution. Rather, institutions should absorb the penalties for such failure, which might be yearlong coaching suspensions, financial aid reductions, recruiting limitations, or exclusion from receiving NCAA or conference financial distributions derived from postseason championship media rights fees or NCAA nonsports-specific revenue distributions.

Because more than 1,100 institutions offer academic programs of varying academic rigor, the institutional comparator FGR is of critical import. The optional use of the national average FGR in lieu of the institutional FGR gives reasonable leeway to highly selective institutions with traditionally high FGRs. Use of the FGR, which emphasizes athlete retention and graduation from the athlete's original institution, would reduce the current practice of discarding athletes for whom an institution finds more talented replacements. Most important, it would require institutions to recruit student-athletes capable of competing academically with other students attending and graduating from that institution. This standard would create academic expectations of athletes that are equal to those the institution has for the rest of the student body.

Coaches should be held responsible for the academic success and graduation of every athlete the coach recruits. A Coach Graduation Rate (CGR) should be established, with one point earned for every recruit who graduates within six years of initial enrollment from the institution to which the coach recruited him or her. The graduation number would be divided by the total number of athletes recruited. The institution should be required to publish the Coaches' Graduation Rate (that is, graduation percentage) for each head coach or former head coach (one who has been fired or has moved to another institution) in its program. The graduation rate performance should be carried by the head coach to each institution at which the coach subsequently serves, thereby providing the public and prospective recruits with a head coach's track record for recruiting athletes who have successfully completed their degrees.

GUIDELINE NO. 13
Highest Standard of Academic Oversight

Each member institution should be required to establish an Academic Oversight Committee comprised of tenured faculty elected by the faculty senate or the highest faculty governance authority. This committee should meet annually with the head coach of each team to review the academic progress of all athletes on that team. The committee should also be required to report to the faculty senate (or other highest faculty authority) annually on the academic progress and admission qualifications of college athletes and, when possible, to compare athletes' academic qualifications and performance to those of nonathletes. The methods of comparison should include average SAT and ACT scores by sport, FGRs by sport, independent studies undertaken by sport, the professors offering the independent studies and their average grade assigned, admissions profiles, athletes' progress toward a degree, trends in selected majors by sport, average grade distributions of faculty by major, incomplete grades by sport, grade changes by professors, and the name of each athlete's faculty adviser.

GUIDELINE NO. 14
Recruiting Prospective College Athletes

National governance associations, in conjunction with eligibility center operations, should be responsible for educating prospective athletes about the following: (1) the importance of matching the academic ability and academic interest of the prospective student with the academic profile of the student body and the course offerings of the institution, (2) the importance of matching the athletic ability and sport interest of the prospective student with the competitive level and sport offerings of the institution, and (3) rules related to initial eligibility. Member institutions should be required to provide all prospects with team FGRs and Academic Progress Rates of the sport programs in which they are interested, head coach CGRs among all athletes previously recruited at any institution, the academic profile of the institution's previous year's freshman class, and a copy of the institution's most recent Equity in Athletics Disclosure Act report. Rule-making related to recruiting should restrict recruiting activities to coaches, admissions office recruiters, or other appropriate institutional employees, prudently limiting the staff time and cost of recruiting activities and reducing recruiting pressures on prospective students to minimize interference with the academic or athletic activities of the prospective student-athletes or their educational institutions.

GUIDELINE NO. 15

Full Access to Academic and Education Choices

College athletes should have full access to the academic and education choices available to all other students, including the right to select courses and academic majors without regard to athletics eligibility or conflicts with athletics practice times, the right to be advised by counselors available to all other students, and the right to transfer to other institutions without an athletics eligibility penalty. Athletics-related time demands should be limited so as not to interfere with the ability of athletes to meet academic demands.

GUIDELINE NO. 16

Protection of Athletes' Health, Freedom, and Well-Being

The rules of national governance associations should minimally include the right of every college athlete, regardless of sport or scholarship status, to the following:

1. Receive institutionally financed prevention education and baseline or monitoring assessments for sports-related injuries and risks (such as neurological baseline assessments related to concussion, the presence of sickle cell trait, a review of susceptibility to dehydration, and the like), for college athletes predisposed to injury risk owing to the nature of their sports participation, as recommended by the American College of Sports Medicine, the U.S. Centers for Disease Control and Prevention, or other national associations of specialist physicians.

2. Receive athletics program–adopted exercise and supervision guidelines for identified potentially life-threatening health conditions.

3. Receive a licensed physician's determination of ability to return to play following any injury or other medical decision affecting the college athlete's safe participation.

4. Receive initial and continuing treatment for any injury directly resulting from participation in his or her institution's athletic program at no cost to college athletes or their parents or legal guardians, with such requirement not applicable to any preexisting medical condition that predates the college athlete's participation in the institution's athletic program.

5. Be treated with respect and be protected from sexual or professional relationship misconduct and physical, verbal, or mental abuse or other pedagogical practices that endanger the athlete's health and welfare.

6. Be covered by long-term disability and catastrophic injury insurance at no cost to the athlete that ensures coverage of all medical expenses related to athletic injuries sustained while participating in intercollegiate athletics, including loss of future earnings in the case of a limited number of exceptional college athletes who choose to complete their college education before entering a professional draft and who are listed as having the potential to be selected in the first or second round of such drafts. Such coverage should include permanent total disability (PTD) and loss of value (LOV) insurance of no less than $10 million.

Further, national governance associations should be required to compile, and member institutions should be required to adhere to, all sports medicine policies and practices recommended by medical authorities. The governance association should fund an independent ombudsman to assist athletes in filing complaints about institutional or employee practices, their legal rights, or other issues. Such an ombudsman should have the power to immediately intercede to prevent the practices of any institutional employee from endangering the health and well-being of an athlete.

GUIDELINE NO. 17
Treatment of Athletes as Integral Members of the Student Body

College athletes should be treated as other members of the general student body are and should not be segregated with regard to access to dining, housing, academic support, study areas, computer laboratories, entertainment areas, and other nonsport-specific student services. Such student services should be administered by those entities responsible for the provision of such services to all students. Athletes should be subject to the same disciplinary and conduct rules and treatment as all other students. Athletes' time involved with athletic activities should be limited to a specified number of hours per week and a maximum number of weeks during a regular competition season, as well as a maximum number of hours per week and a maximum number of weeks in the off-season. Such off-season limits should permit an athlete to fully experience nonathletics-related college activities, spend sufficient time with family, or pursue work and internship interests.

GUIDELINE NO. 18
Due Process Protections of Member Institutions

National governance associations should enforce the following or similar conditions providing for due process before suspending a coach or other athletics personnel from representing a member institution in athletics events, suspending the athletics events telecommunications privileges of a member institution, or suspending a member institution from participating in a collegiate athletics event:

1. Member institutions should be required to self-report rules violations, investigate themselves, and assist the national association in its own investigation or face enhanced penalties for not cooperating or taking appropriate corrective action.

2. The association should hire professional judges from among candidates with experience as arbitrators, magistrates, trial or appellate judges, or administrative law judges, and should hire experienced investigators, as independent contractors. These judges and investigators should participate in enforcement cases involving severe and significant breaches of conduct but should be excluded from participating in breaches-of-conduct determinations and incidental issues for which penalties are not onerous. They should preside at hearings and appeals, issue subpoenas or other compulsory processes when necessary (assuming congressional authority is granted to do so), and possess exclusive authority to adjudicate, resolve, and issue final judgments, including penalties, in enforcement cases under their jurisdiction.

3. In severe or significant breach-of-conduct cases, a prehearing discovery process should be instituted, including depositions, requests to admit interrogatories, and document production, during which process association staff and counsel for accused parties may gather and exchange pertinent information.

4. In severe or significant breach-of-conduct cases, accused parties, including coaches, athletes, institutional employees, and institutions themselves, should be permitted to confront and cross-examine opposing witnesses at hearings.

5. At the discretion of the hearing judge, a nonparty whom the association or the accused institution has identified as having engaged in wrongdoing, or having enabled wrongdoing to occur, should be required to present an oral or written statement at the hearing, subject to rebuttal by the institution. The judge should require the statements to be given under oath or affirmation.

6. Member institutions should be prohibited from firing or permanently reassigning employees or disassociating themselves from representatives of the institution's athletic interests whom the association or the accused institution has identified as having engaged in or enabled wrongdoing under association rules and regulations until after the case has been resolved and the party's role in it has been determined.

7. All hearings and appellate proceedings should be open to the public, except the judge may make special accommodations depending on circumstances. This rule should not apply to the posthearing deliberations of the appellate panels, which should be closed to the public.

8. No employee, faculty member serving on any athletics oversight committee or other representative of the athletics department of any member institution should interfere in the investigation or adjudication of athletes or staff members alleged to have committed violations of institutional rules or federal laws related to sexual harassment or to have assault or engaged in misdemeanor or felonious behavior.

GUIDELINE NO. 19

Due Process Protections for College Athletes

National governance associations should enforce the following practices in the case of reductions to an athlete's financial aid dollar amount or award period or in cases of claims for reinstatement of athletic eligibility:

1. Athletes declared ineligible for competition by their respective educational institutions or the association owing to violations of association rules for reasons other than an insufficient GPA, failure to make satisfactory progress toward a degree, or similar academic failure or nonathletics-related institutional determinations related to sexual abuse, sexual harassment, academic discipline, or other instances of improper student behavior should have the right to appeal the eligibility determination and seek reinstatement by means of binding arbitration only.

2. A panel of arbitrators certified by the American Arbitration Association (AAA) and approved by the athlete and the association should conduct the arbitration process in accordance with the AAA's commercial arbitration rules and mediation procedures.

3. Binding arbitration should replace an appeal to any committee of the association that reviews an institution's requests for the reinstatement of athletic eligibility in accordance with the association's rules. The arbitration panel's decision should be final and should bind the athlete(s) involved, the athlete's educational institution, and the association.

4. The involvement of athletics department personnel as voting or non-voting members of an Office of Student Financial Aid appeals committee reviewing the termination of athletics-related financial aid should be prohibited.

5. The association's board should hire and provide salary, benefits, and administrative expenses for, and member institutions should provide all athletes with contact information for, an athlete welfare advocate(s) who would provide independent legal advice to college athletes at no cost regarding the application of association rules and due process rights.

GUIDELINE NO. 20
Clear and Reasonable Distinction between Professional and College Athletes

Professional athletes should be prohibited from participating in college athletics in the sport in which they are professional. The definitions of professional athlete should be limited to (1) a person receiving compensation for the use of his or her athletic skill to play a sport in excess of actual and necessary expenses to participate in the practice or competition; (2) a person receiving, directly or indirectly, a salary, reimbursement of expenses, or any other form of financial assistance from a professional sports organization as payment for sport participation; or (3) a person competing on any professional athletics team.

Accordingly, college athletic scholarships should not be considered professional athlete payment as long as such grants are clearly educational, meaning that they should be guaranteed for four or five years, depending on the student's degree program, or until graduation (whichever occurs first), conditioned on maintenance of a minimum cumulative GPA and not on athletics performance, and limited in total value, consistent with *Federal Student Aid Handbook* requirements.

GUIDELINE NO. 21

No Employment Restrictions Other Than Actual Employment as a Professional Athlete

College athletes should not be prohibited from obtaining career-related advice from any individual, hiring an agent, participating in professional drafts, or engaging in athletics-related or other employment in the same manner as nonathlete students other than those activities described above as constituting professional athlete employment. College athletes own and should be able to control the use of their names, images, and likenesses, just as other students do. As long as college athletes can demonstrate that (1) their compensation for nonplaying sports employment and remuneration for the commercial or charitable use of their names, images, or likenesses in advertisements are commensurate with marketplace value, (2) the activities for which compensation and remunerations were received were not arranged by employees or others engaged by the athlete's institution for that purpose (thereby constituting extra benefits), and (3) the name or affiliation of the athlete's institution is not utilized as a part of such employment, such activities should not be interpreted as being a professional athlete.

CONCLUSION:

In Search of a Higher Education

From the vantage point of the football player settling for a less desirable major, or of the illiterate basketball player with or seeking a college degree, or of the less-than-elite minority athlete with sound academic credentials whose athletic scholarship and access to higher education went to an athlete poorly prepared for college academics, the current state of college sports with regard to academic integrity is in need of serious reform. College athletes must be provided with a reasonable opportunity to earn an education. Anything less fosters exploitation of a group of students, who have only recently begun to use the legal system to address the broken academic promises of their institutions.

Academic standing, admissions, and academic progress must be consistent with the standards expected of the student body. Yet in each of the three components, the NCAA rules depart from the association's stated principle of maintaining the athletic program as a vital component of the university's educational program. The NCAA has developed lower standards for academic standing, admissions, and academic progress than those applied to enrolled nonathlete students. The NCAA is controlled by its most commercialized athletic programs. The intent of these Division I institutions of higher education is to place the most talented athletes on the field or court, regardless of academic skills level.

Each institution of higher education has a unique mission and philosophy, a high level of independence with regard to curricular offerings and academic priorities, and different prospective student population targets. This is a strength of American higher education. However, when it comes to athletics, in the case of highly talented athletes, especially in the revenue sports of football and men's basketball, these standards are discarded. Schools cannot continue to recruit underprepared athletes who cannot compete against peers in the classroom. At the very least, schools must match the academic abilities of athletes with the academic profiles of their classroom peers. If institutions are going to continue their current practice of waiving normal admission requirements for high-academic-risk athletes (special admissions), those athletes' participation in athletics should be delayed (freshman ineligibility) until they demonstrate successful remediation of marginal academic skills.

The promise of admission to a university, whether tendered to an athlete or a nonathlete, a revenue or a nonrevenue sport participant, is that of a meaningful education. If athlete academic standards are not firmly anchored to the institutional academic standards and expectations applicable to all students, athlete academic standards will float with the tide of institutional greed and the will to win—as they are now. In the process, not only is the athlete's educational experience diminished but the experience of other students is vitiated as the norms of intellectual rigor at the school are defrauded. If intercollegiate athletics is ever to be restored as a valued enhancement of a college athlete's higher education experience, college presidents and institutional faculty must insist on a reasonable balance of athletic time demands with academic life, ensuring adequate academic preparation and progress regardless of wins and losses.

The academic integrity challenges of the current system are significant. Many college athletes feel forced to cheat to maintain eligibility and keep their athletically related financial aid. Coaches feel pressure to sign high school recruits at all costs. Athletics department academic support staff members charged with trying to maintain athletes' eligibility as part of their employment agreement see few alternatives to selecting less challenging classes, professors friendly to athletics, and academic majors that will not interfere with athletic demands or be so academically challenging as to place athletes at risk of ineligibility. Tutors earning good wages and faced with unrealistic classroom expectations of academically underprepared athletes believe they are expected to cut corners. A return of academic integrity to college sports does not appear imminent in this climate. There are few tenured faculty activists, and seemingly none in any position of power. College president leadership on meaningful athletic reform at present is practically nonexistent. Athletics directors, powerful coaches, and conference commissioners, who are garnering the bulk of financial benefits from college athlete exploitation, show no signs of guilt or motivation to fundamentally change the system or to use the riches accrued to enhance the health and well-being of college athletes as opposed to their own pockets. The changes they support are the minimum ones necessary to ward off the critics and potential legislative or judicial action.

The NCAA is controlled by the FBS plutocracy, which has a vested interest in maintaining an elite athlete pipeline, regardless of academic preparation, to bolster the quality of its revenue-generating products. Athlete activism through the courts may serve as a catalyst for real reform. A string of courtroom successes may result in higher education asking for congressional involvement to provide relief. If that call is heeded, hopefully Congress will act only with quid pro quo demands to ensure academic integrity.

Appendix

NCAA Academic Fraud Cases

Since 1990 the NCAA has processed forty-one cases of academic fraud. The following information on these cases is based largely on Bradley David Ridpath, Gerald Gurney, and Eric Snyder, "NCAA Academic Fraud Cases and Historical Consistency: A Comparative Content Analysis," *Journal of the Legal Aspects of Sport* 75 (2015), p. 25.

Georgia Southern University
Conference: Southern Conference
Penalty year: 2016
Findings: Former compliance assistant director and assistant director of student-athlete services performed academic work for three football student-athletes.
Penalties: Two years probation; reductions in scholarships, recruiting limitations, three-year show cause orders, financial penalty.

University of Southern Mississippi
Conference: Conference USA
Penalty year: 2016
Findings: Former head men's basketball coach directed staff to engage in academic misconduct; fabricated document for payment of student-athletes.

Penalties: Three-year probation; two-year postseason ban; reductions in scholarships, recruiting limitations, show-cause orders for head coach and others.

University of Louisiana–Lafayette
Conference: Sun Belt Conference
Penalty year: 2016
Findings: Former assistant football coach arranged for prospects to get fraudulent entrance exam scores.
Penalties: Two-year probation; financial penalty; recruiting restrictions.

Southern Methodist University
Conference: American Conference
Penalty year: 2015
Findings: Men's basketball committed academic fraud, academic misconduct, failure to promote an atmosphere of compliance; assistant coach and staff member performed academic work for a student-athlete.
Penalties: Three-year probation; postseason ban; scholarship reduction, recruiting limitations, coach suspension for 30 percent of season.

Syracuse University
Conference: Atlantic Coast Conference
Penalty year: 2015
Findings: Director of basketball operations, academic services personnel, and office receptionist did substantial academic work for athletes.
Penalties: Five-year probation, vacation of all wins in which ineligible students played men's basketball; $500 fine per contest played by ineligible students; return of all funds received from NCAA Men's Basketball Tournament; suspension of head basketball coach from the first nine conference games of 2015–16; reduction of men's basketball scholarships by three for the 2015–16, 2016–17, 2017–18, and 2018–19 academic years. The NCAA accepted the school's self-imposed postseason ban for the 2014–15 season.

University of of North Carolina
Conference: Atlantic Coast Conference
Penalty year: 2012
Findings: Violations stemmed from a former tutor constructing significant parts of writing assignments for three football student-athletes.

Penalties: Public reprimand and censure; three-year probation; postseason ban for the 2012 football season; reduction of football scholarships by a total of 15 during three academic years; vacation of wins during the 2008 and 2009 seasons (self-imposed by the university); $50,000 fine (self-imposed by the university); dissociation of former tutor.

Arkansas State University
Conference: Sun Belt Conference
Penalty year: 2011
Findings: Director of technology in the institution's College of Agriculture and Technology changed a final grade in a course for a men's basketball student-athlete without the consent of the professor.
Penalties: Public reprimand and censure; two years of probation (from March 11, 2011, through March 10, 2013). The institution was to reduce the amount of athletically related financial aid in the sports of football and men's basketball by one full scholarship each for both the 2011–12 and 2012–13 academic years. The institution was to vacate victories for participation by ineligible student-athletes in the following sports: football (2006), six wins, (2005), four wins; men's basketball (2006–07), 15 wins, (2005–06), 12 wins; baseball (2006–07), three wins; women's soccer (2005–06), five wins. In January 2009 the institution paid a fine of $43,500.

East Carolina University
Conference: Conference USA
Penalty year: 2011
Findings: Self-reported academic fraud violations after a women's tennis player working as a tutor wrote papers for four baseball players.
Penalties: Public reprimand and censure; one year of probation (May 19, 2011, through May 18, 2012); two student-athletes ruled ineligible for competition for the remainder of the 2009–10 baseball season and the entire 2010–11 season; the three remaining involved student-athletes ruled permanently ineligible and removed from the baseball and women's tennis teams; vacation of all wins in which the four baseball student-athletes competed during the 2009–10 season and the women's tennis student-athlete competed during the spring 2010 season.

Georgia Southern University

Conference: Southern Conference

Penalty year: 2010

Findings: A former assistant coach provided substantial portions of course work, and in some instances completed course work, for two men's basketball student-athletes.

Penalties: Public reprimand and censure; two years of probation (January 20, 2010, to January 19, 2012); five-year show-cause order for the former assistant coach (January 20, 2010, to January 19, 2015); two-year show-cause order for the former director of basketball operations (January 20, 2010, to January 19, 2012); reduction of basketball scholarships by one for the 2009–10, 2010–11, and 2011–12 academic years. During the 2009–10 academic year the number of official recruiting visits for men's basketball was reduced by four from a maximum of 12 (self-imposed by the university). Vacation of all wins in which the two academically ineligible student-athletes competed during the 2007–08 and 2008–09 men's basketball seasons.

Florida State University

Conference: Atlantic Coast Conference

Penalty year: 2009

Findings: Learning specialist, academic adviser, and tutor gave improper assistance to student-athletes, resulting in academic fraud.

Penalties: Public reprimand and censure; four-year probation (March 6, 2009, to March 5, 2013); scholarship reductions in football, men's and women's basketball, men's and women's swimming, men's and women's track and field, baseball, softball, and men's golf (additional details are available in the public report). Vacation of all wins in which the 61 student-athletes competed while ineligible during 2006 and 2007; five-year show-cause order for the former academic adviser (March 6, 2009, to March 5, 2014) (additional details are available in the public report); four-year show-cause order for the former learning specialist (March 6, 2009, to March 5, 2013) (additional details are available in the public report); three-year show-cause order for the former tutor (March 6, 2009, to March 5, 2012) (additional details are available in the public report).

Alabama State University

Conference: Southwestern Athletic Conference

Penalty year: 2008

Findings: Staff members arranged for fraudulent academic credits for eight football student-athletes when their original letter grades were changed without approval from the appropriate university administrators; six of these student-athletes avoided ineligibility status owing to the grade changes.

Penalties: Public reprimand and censure; five years of probation; two-year show-cause order for the former head coach; no postseason competition for the 2009 football season; reduction of official paid visits in football; all football coaches withheld from engaging in recruiting activities for two weeks in December; reduction in football scholarships to 58.74 during the 2004–05 academic year and 54.11 during the 2005–06 academic year from the limit of 63 (self-imposed by the institution); vacation of all football contests won by the university in 2000 and 2001, including the conference championship.

Purdue University

Conference: Big Ten Conference

Penalty year: 2007

Findings: Assistant coach admitted to conducting research and reading a textbook to assist a former women's basketball student-athlete with an assigned paper but denied committing academic fraud. She also admitted typing, correcting, and revising the paper.

Penalties: Public reprimand and censure; two years of probation; reduction in women's basketball program scholarships by three. The former assistant coach received a three-year show-cause penalty.

McNeese State University

Conference: Southland Conference

Penalty year: 2007

Findings: Assistant men's basketball coach facilitated academic fraud for two junior college prospective student-athletes when he arranged for a third party to complete quizzes and a test for a math correspondence course the young men were taking in an effort to gain admission and athletic eligibility at the institution.

Penalties: Public reprimand and censure; two years of probation; reduction in women's track and field and cross country program scholarships by two full equivalencies; reduction from twelve to ten official visits for men's basketball; recruiting ban for men's basketball; reduction by one in available men's basketball scholarships. The former assistant men's basketball coach and the former head track coach both received a five-year show-cause penalty.

University of Kansas
Conference: Big Twelve Conference
Penalty year: 2006
Findings: The graduate assistant football coach gave two recruits answers to a test they were taking in the coach's dorm room.
Penalties: Public reprimand and censure; three years of probation; reduction in number of recruited two-year college students; reduction of three initial scholarships in football. The former graduate assistant football coach who committed academic fraud received a three-year show-cause order.

Ohio State University
Conference: Big Ten Conference
Penalty year: 2006
Findings: Prospects received impermissible academic assistance when a booster wrote academic papers for the student-athletes.
Penalties: Public reprimand and censure; three years of probation; the institution's men's basketball team withheld from postseason competition; former head coach terminated by the institution on June 8, 2004; reduction in the number of financial aid awards in men's basketball; distributions received by the institution for participation in the 1999, 2000, 2001, and 2002 NCAA Division I Men's Basketball Championship ordered reimbursed. A copy of the report was to be sent to the institution's regional accrediting agency.

Texas Christian University
Conference: Conference USA
Penalty year: 2005
Findings: Former head coach directed or condoned the use of academic fraud by several former assistant coaches who were assisting student-athletes and prospects with their academic work.

Penalties: Public reprimand and censure; probation through September 21, 2007; vacation of all individual results of ten student-athletes who should have been declared ineligible; team results adjusted accordingly. For the next eight years, the former head coach was to be subject to the NCAA's show-cause procedures. If the former head coach sought athletics-related employment at another NCAA institution, he and the hiring institution would have had to appear before the Committee on Infractions to determine whether his duties should be limited.

Baylor University
Conference: Big Twelve Conference
Penalty year: 2005
Findings: Part-time tutor wrote papers for three players. English professors apparently uncovered the violation when three players in different course sections submitted identical papers.
Penalties: Although the Committee on Infractions found academic fraud among three football student-athletes, the case penalties largely dealt with unrelated repeat penalties in men's basketball; there were no discernible penalties related to fraud.

Nicholls State University
Conference: Southland Conference
Penalty year: 2005
Findings: Head basketball coach, an assistant football coach, and an athletics academic adviser committed academic fraud using online correspondence courses from Brigham Young University. The fraud involved 28 student-athletes and one prospective student-athlete.
Penalties: Public reprimand and censure; four-year probation; exclusion from the conference television packages in football and men's basketball; loss of one scholarship in men's basketball.

University of Georgia
Conference: Southeastern Conference
Penalty year: 2004
Findings: Assistant coach conducted the class in such a manner that the grades of A he awarded to three men's basketball student-athletes constituted academic fraud.
Penalties: Public reprimand and censure; four years of probation; reduction in number of grants-in-aid in men's basketball by one during each of

the 2005–06, 2006–07, and 2007–08 academic years; vacation of wins as well as of team and individual records of the three student-athletes; suspension by the university of former assistant men's basketball coach. Because this case involved academic fraud, the report was to be forwarded to the appropriate regional academic accrediting agency. The chair of the Physical Education and Sports Studies Department received a letter of reprimand from the university.

California State University at Northridge
Conference: Big West Conference
Penalty year: 2004
Findings: An assistant basketball coach arranged for a student-athlete to be enrolled in and receive course credit in two kinesiology courses, even though the student-athlete never attended class or otherwise completed the course requirements.
Penalties: Public reprimand and censure; a continuance of probation; for the 2004–05 and 2005–06 academic years the permissible number of grants-in-aid for initial and overall counters in the men's basketball program were to be reduced by one. Because this case involved academic fraud, the NCAA president was to forward the report to the appropriate regional academic accrediting agency in accordance with NCAA Bylaw 19.5.2.7.

California State University at Fresno
Conference: Western Athletic Conference
Penalty year: 2003
Findings: Academic adviser arranged for a statistician to prepare 17 pieces of course work for two other student-athletes who were completing their last semesters of eligibility, as well as for a men's basketball prospective student-athlete.
Penalties: Public reprimand and censure; four years of probation; the university's men's basketball team prohibited from participation in postseason competition for one year; reduction of grants-in-aid in men's basketball by a total of three for the 2004–05 and 2005–06 academic years, with at least one grant cut in each of those years. The university elected to forfeit all wins by the men's basketball team for any games in which student-athletes participated while ineligible (for record-keeping purposes, the NCAA deemed these forfeited wins as having been

vacated); vacation of wins and return of revenues from NCAA Men's Basketball Tournament. The university issued a written reprimand to a former assistant men's basketball coach and a written reprimand to the faculty athletics representative.

University of Utah
Conference: Mountain West Conference
Penalty year: 2003
Findings: Tutor provided student-athletes with a paper for a writing class.
Penalties: Public reprimand and censure; three years of probation; reduction in number of men's basketball scholarships.

University of California at Berkeley
Conference: Pacific-10 Conference
Penalty year: 2002
Findings: Two football student-athletes received credit for courses they did not attend. In August 1999, the two enrolled retroactively in spring semester classes and received passing grades from the professor who taught the courses.
Penalties: Public reprimand and censure; five-year probation; ban from preseason competition; reduction in number of football scholarships; vacation of team record as well as of any individual records of the two student-athletes who participated in football contests while academically ineligible during the 1999 season. The university president was required to forward a copy of the public infractions report to the appropriate regional accrediting agency.

University of Kentucky
Conference: Southeastern Conference
Penalty year: 2002
Findings: During two academic years, the recruiting coordinator committed academic fraud by completing or assisting with course work for student-athletes.
Penalties: Public reprimand and censure; three-year probation (beginning January 31, 2002). No study hall or other types of academic support allowed to be provided outside the direct supervision of the appropriate personnel. The former recruiting coordinator's resignation was accepted

on November 20, 2000. The former head football coach's resignation was accepted on February 9, 2001. The former administrative assistant to the recruiting coordinator was dismissed from her position; one student worker was reassigned.

Marshall University

Conference: Mid-American Conference

Penalty year: 2001

Findings: An assistant professor at the university, who also served as a volunteer flexibility coach in the athletics program, provided advance copies of a final examination to football student-athletes.

Penalties: Public reprimand and censure; four years of probation (beginning December 21, 2001). Whether a specific penalty related to academic fraud was applied is not discernible from the records.

Howard University

Conference: Mid-Eastern Athletic Conference

Penalty year: 2001

Findings: Baseball student-athlete was enrolled in six hours of summer course work at the university even though he had returned to his home in another state for the summer.

Penalties: Five-year probation; show-cause penalties imposed on three former coaches.

University of Southern California

Conference: Pacific-10 Conference

Penalty year: 2001

Findings: Violations included three separate instances over a two-year period from the summer of 1996 to the spring of 1998. Employees of the university's Student Athlete Academic Services (SAAS) substantially composed academic papers for three student-athletes. In addition, the tutors involved in the fraud misrepresented their role in preparing the papers.

Penalties: Public reprimand and censure; two-year probation; reduction in number of total athletically related financial aid awards in the sport of football reduced by two; show-cause order for the former tutor coordinator. A copy of the report was to be sent to the appropriate regional accrediting agency.

New Mexico State University

Conference: Sun Belt Conference

Penalty year: 2001

Findings: A men's basketball coach helped prospective student-athletes complete course work and answered questions on final examinations.

Penalties: Public reprimand and censure; four years of probation; show-cause order for basketball coaches.

Mississippi Valley State University

Conference: Southwestern Athletic Conference

Penalty year: 2001

Findings: An assistant men's basketball coach, athletic trainer, and the student union director arranged for individuals to take college entrance exams for others. The assistant coach or athletic trainer recruited nine students or student-athletes on various occasions to take the entrance examination.

Penalties: Public reprimand and censure; two years of probation; NCAA show-cause penalties imposed on three former staff members.

Southern Methodist University

Conference: Southwest Conference

Penalty year: 2000

Findings: An assistant football coach arranged on two occasions for other individuals to use the identity of the prospective student-athlete to take the ACT, a college entrance exam, on his behalf.

Penalties: Probation for two years and reductions in the number of coaches permitted to recruit off-campus and the number of official visits allowed in football. A former assistant football coach was placed under a seven-year show-cause order, and the university was required to vacate its team record for ten games.

University of Minnesota–Twin Cities

Conference: Big Ten Conference

Penalty year: 2000

Findings: A former secretary in men's basketball office completed approximately 400 items of course work for at least 18 men's basketball student-athletes. The secretary's involvement was arranged primarily by the academic counselor with the knowledge of the head men's basketball coach.

Penalties: Public reprimand and censure; four years of probation (beginning October 24, 2000); reduction in the total number of grants-in-aid in men's basketball by five for the 2001–02, 2002–03, and 2003–04 academic years, with a reduction of at least one, from 13 to 12, in each of the years; reduction in number of official paid visits in men's basketball; show-cause orders for head basketball coach and former secretary.

Texas Tech University
Conference: Big Twelve Conference
Penalty year: 1998
Findings: An assistant coach committed academic fraud by completing course work for a student-athlete.
Penalties: Public reprimand and censure; four years of probation (the institution had proposed three years); reduction by four (from 25 to 21) in the number of initial financial aid awards in football during the 2000–01 academic year; reduction by five (from 85 to 80) in the number of total financial aid awards in football; reduction by seven in the number of total financial aid awards in men's basketball; reduction by one (from 15 to 14) in the number of total financial aid awards in women's basketball during the 1999–2000 academic year; reduction by three (from 11.7 to 8.7) in the number of equivalency scholarships in baseball; vacation of the institution's performance in the 1996 NCAA Division I Men's Basketball Tournament.

Montana State University
Conference: Big Sky Conference
Penalty year: 1996
Findings: Prospective student-athlete received fraudulent academic credit and the assistant coach was aware that the student-athlete did not complete the course work.
Penalties: Two years of probation; reduction in number of scholarships in men's basketball; wins vacated; show-cause order for assistant men's basketball coach.

Texas Southern University
Conference: Southwestern Athletic Conference
Penalty year: 1996

Findings: Seven men's and women's track student-athletes received fraudulent academic credit that they needed to be eligible for NCAA competition. The student-athletes did not perform the work for these courses.

Penalties: Five years of probation; prohibition against postseason competition by the men's and women's track and field teams and by the cross
country teams for one year; prohibition against awarding any new
scholarships in men's and women's track and field and cross country
for two academic years; prohibition against participation in any invi-
tational meets for the institution's men's and women's track and field
teams for 1996–97 and for the men's and women's cross country teams
for 1997–98.

Baylor University

Conference: Southwest Conference

Penalty year: 1995

Findings: Coaches committed academic fraud in prospects' correspondence
courses by providing them with answers to examinations and materials for course papers to ensure passing grades.

Penalties: Reduction from 13 to 11 grants for 1994–95 and from 13 to 10
for 1995–96; reduction from 12 to 9 official visits for 1994–95; reduction
by one in the number of assistant coaches for 1994–95; recertification.

Alcorn State University

Conference: Southwestern Athletic Conference

Penalty year: 1994

Findings: Head football coach was aware that prospect did not take standardized test.

Penalties: Public reprimand; reduction of three days from football practice;
probation and one game suspension for head football coach during 1994
season; two-year postseason ban in men's basketball; reduction from 13
to 8 grants in men's basketball for 1995–96 and from 13 to 11 for 1996–
97; reduction from 63 to 60 equivalency grants in football for 1995–96
and from 63 to 62 for 1996–97; reduction from 85 to 81 counters in football for 1995–96 and from 85 to 83 for 1996–97; reduction from 15 to 14
grants in women's basketball for 1995–96 and 1996–97; reduction from
12 to 10 official visits in men's basketball for 1994–95 and 1995–96;

reduction from 27 to 26 permissible men's basketball contests for 1995–96; public reprimand of director of athletics; annual reports; recertification.

Texas State University
Conference: Southland Conference
Penalty year: 1994
Findings: Head coach gave fraudulent academic credit to baseball student-athletes.
Penalties: Public reprimand; annual reports; recertification.

Coastal Carolina University
Conference: Big South Conference
Penalty year: 1994
Findings: Head men's basketball coach and the former part-time assistant coach arranged for a prospective student-athlete to receive fraudulent academic credit and provided an improper benefit by paying his summer school tuition.
Penalties: Public reprimand; withdrawal from 1994 conference tournament; reduction from 15 to 10 official visits for 1993–94; forfeiture of all contests during 1992–93 and 1993–94 in which ineligible student-athlete participated; annual reports; reduction from 13 to 11 grants for 1995–96 and from 13 to 12 for 1996–97; reduction from 12 to 10 official visits for 1994–95; recertification.

Miami University of Ohio
Conference: Mid-American Conference
Penalty year: 1991
Findings: Head men's basketball coach fraudulently awarded a student-athlete a grade of A to retain eligibility.
Penalties: Public reprimand; annual reports; individual and team records stricken and all contests in which the ineligible student-athlete participated forfeited; recertification.

Drake University
Conference: Missouri Valley Conference
Penalty year: 1990
Findings: Academic fraud by an assistant men's basketball coach regarding the class assignments of at least three student-athletes.
Penalties: Show-cause order.

Northwestern State University
Conference: Southland Conference
Penalty year: 1990
Findings: Fraudulent entrance exam scores arranged by men's basketball coaches.
Penalties: Public reprimand; annual reports; recertification; maximum of 13 grants for 1990–91; maximum of two initial grants for 1991–92 and three for 1992–93; maximum of eight official visits for 1990–91 and 12 for 1991–92; reduction of one coach.

Notes

Preface

1. The Drake Group was founded in 1999 when Jon Ericson, a former professor and provost at Drake University, invited a distinguished group of college faculty, authors, and activists to a twenty-four-hour brainstorming session on how to end academic corruption in college sports. The conference participants included members of faculty senates, journalists, athletics directors, and members of organizations such as the NCAA and the Knight Commission on Intercollegiate Athletics.

2. These position statements are all available online (www.thedrakegroup.org).

Chapter 1

1. Ronald A. Smith, *Pay for Play: A History of Big-Time College Athletic Reform* (University of Illinois Press, 2011), p. 52.

2. Rodney K. Smith, "A Brief History of the National Collegiate Athletic Association's Role in Regulating Intercollegiate Athletics," *Marquette Sports Law Review* 11, no. 9 (2000) (http://scholarship.law.marquette.edu/sportslaw/vol11/iss1/5).

3. Quoted in R. A. Smith, *Pay for Play*, p. 37.

4. Randy R. Grant, John Leadley, and Zenon Zygmont, *The Economics of Intercollegiate Sport* (Hackensack, N.J.: World Scientific Publishing Co., 2008), p. 10.

5. Allen L. Sack and Ellen J. Staurowsky, *College Athletes for Hire* (Westport, Conn.: Greenwood Press, 1998), p. 20. In *Unsportsmanlike Conduct: The NCAA and the Business of College Football* (New York: Praeger, 1987), p. 6, Paul Lawrence writes: "A successful team saw its exploits printed in all the major newspapers and magazines (and later broadcast on the radio). While a superior academic department received little notice beyond educational circles, the nation's top college football teams had begun to receive national publicity." In 1909 Chancellor James Day of Syracuse University observed: "There are institutions that will not play or row with some other colleges whom they fear, because if beaten it would hurt their prestige and decrease the advertising value of their team or crew." Cited in Lawrence, *Unsportsmanlike Conduct*, p. 7.

6. Andrew Zimbalist, *Unpaid Professionals: Commercialism and Conflict in Big-Time College Sports* (Princeton University Press, 2001), p. 7.

7. W. J. Rorabaugh, *Berkeley at War: The 1960s* (Oxford University Press, 1989), p. 12 (http://content.cdlib.org/view?docId=kt687004sg&chunk.id=d0e21648&brand=calisphere&doc.view=entire_text).

8. Sack and Staurowsky, *College Athletes for Hire*, p. 21.

9. Cited in R. A. Smith, *Pay for Play*, p. 50.

10. Cited in ibid., p. 43.

11. William T. Foster, "An Indictment of Intercollegiate Athletics," *Atlantic Monthly* 116, no. 5 (November 1915).

12. R. A. Smith, *Pay for Play*, p. 63.

13. Ibid., p. 65.

14. Ibid., p. 15.

15. Arguably, there is one exception to this pattern—the reform movement led by Derek Bok and the American Council on Education (ACE) during the mid-1980s. We discuss this movement below, as does Joseph Crowley in his history of the NCAA, commissioned by the association: *In the Arena: The NCAA's First Century* (Indianapolis: NCAA, 2006).

16. NCAA, *FAR Study Report: Roles, Responsibilities and Perspectives of NCAA Faculty Athletics Representatives,* February 2013 (www.ncaa.org/sites/default/files/FAR_STUDY_Report_final_compressed.pdf).

17. R. A. Smith, *Pay for Play*, p. 52.

18. Ibid.

19. Ibid.

20. Grant and others, *The Economics of Intercollegiate Sport*, p. 23.

21. Intercollegiate Athletic Association of the United States (IAAUS), NCAA, *Proceedings of the First Annual Convention*, December 29, 1906, p. 33.

22. IAAUS, NCAA, *Proceedings of the Eleventh Annual Convention*, December 28, 1916, p. 118.

23. IAAUS, NCAA, *Proceedings of the Seventeenth Annual Convention*, December 29, 1922, p. 118.

24. *Bulletin 23 of the Carnegie Foundation for the Advancement of Higher Education* (New York, 1929).

25. Jack Falla, *NCAA: The Voice of College Sports* (Mission, Kan.: NCAA, 1981), pp. 9–17. In 1935 a total of eleven of thirteen colleges in the Southeast Conference voted to recognize athletic ability in determining financial aid assistance for football players, thus ignoring the NCAA amateur code on recruiting and subsidizing athletes. See "Sheepskin or Pig Skin?," *Washington Post*, December 18, 1935, clipping found in President Newcomb Papers, II, box 4, folder "Athletics," University of Virginia Archives.

26. Murray Sperber, *Onward to Victory* (New York: Henry Holt, 1998), p. 42.

27. Quoted in ibid., p. 168.

28. Arguably, this effort began at the 1939 NCAA Convention when they passed a rule enabling athletes to receive financial aid based on need, but the aid could not be conditioned on athletic participation. Hence, in principle, it was not a form of athletic aid; rather, it was need-based aid that could be allocated to all students, including athletes.

29. NCAA, *1947–48 Yearbook*, pp. 212–13. To counter the argument that financial awards specifically earmarked for athletes constituted "paid" for services rendered, the Sanity Code retained a clause stating that "No athlete will be deprived of financial aid . . . for failure to participate in intercollegiate athletics," pp. 77–79.

30. NCAA, *1956–57 Yearbook*, pp. 4–5.

31. Cost of attendance stipends have been allowed in Division I since January 2015. Their magnitude differs from school to school (and even from student to student in special cases). Their range in 2015 was roughly $1,500 to $5,500.

32. Walter Byers, the executive director of the NCAA from 1951 to 1987, has characterized the awarding of athletic scholarships as the beginning of a nationwide money laundering scheme whereby boosters who formerly gave money directly to athletes could now funnel it to athletes through legitimate university channels. See Walter Byers, *Unsportsmanlike Conduct: Exploiting College Athletes* (University of Michigan Press, 1995), p. 73.

33. Ibid., pp. 69, 75.

34. Clyde B. Smith, letter to Walter Byers, July 6, 1964, Walter Byers Papers, Long Range Planning folder, NCAA Headquarters, Overland Park, Kan.

35. Byers, *Unsportsmanlike Conduct*, p. 164.

36. Robert McCormick and Amy McCormack, "The Myth of the Student Athlete: The College Athlete as Employee," *Washington Law Review*, Vol. 81:71, 2006, p. 71. Further control was afforded by the long-standing rule that required any athlete changing schools would have to sit out a year of competition once enrolled at the new school. This rule, dating back to the NCAA's original constitution in 1906, was intended to deter the use of tramp athletes, that is, athletes who were not matriculated students and were paid under the table to play for school teams. The rule is still in place in 2016 and enforces an asymmetry wherein coaches can jump from school to school without a year of ineligibility but athletes cannot. Athletes who do not like playing for a coach or who are not playing as regularly as they would like face the penalty of a year's ineligibility if they choose to transfer to a new school. Of course, on some occasions the athlete may want to transfer

because of an issue with the academic program and would face a similar disincentive.

37. David Broughton, "Higher Limits Bring Gift Package Upgrades," *Sports Business Journal*, March 5–11, 2012. In 2012 the NCAA allowed each bowl to award up to $550 worth of gifts to 125 participants per school. In addition, participants were allowed to receive awards worth up to $400 from the school and up to $400 from the conference for postseason play, covering both conference title games and any bowl game. David Broughton, "Players Share the Wealth with Bowl Gifts," *Sports Business Journal*, December 3–9, 2012.

38. S. Rosner and K. Shropshire, eds., *The Business of Sports* (Sudbury, Mass.: Jones & Bartlett Learning, 2004); Lisa P. Masteralexis, Carol A. Barr, and Mary Hums, *Principles and Practices of Sport Management*, 5th ed. (Sudbury, Mass.: Jones & Bartlett Learning, 2014), p. 431.

39. Quoted in Anthony G. Weaver, "New Policies, New Structure, New Problems? Reviewing the NCAA's Autonomy Model," *Elon Law Review* 7, no 55 (2015), pp. 551–70 (https://elon.edu/docs/e-web/law/law_review/Issues/Elon_Law_Review _V7_No2_Weaver.pdf).

40. Ibid.

41. NCAA, "Divisional Differences and the History of Multidivision Classification" NCAA.org (http://www.ncaa.org/about/who-we-are/membership /divisional-differences-and-history-multidivision-classification).

42. Ibid.

43. NCAA, *Division I Steering Committee on Governance: Recommended Governance Model* (Indianapolis: NCAA, 2014).

44. Michelle Brutlag Hosick, "Board Adopts New Division I Structure," NCAA .org, August 7, 2014.

45. J. New, "Autonomy Gained," InsideHigherEd.com, August 8, 2014 ; Knight Commission on Intercollegiate Athletics, *Athletic & Academic Spending Database for NCAA Division I* (https://www.insidehighered.com/news/2014/08/08/ncaa -adopts-structure-giving-autonomy-richest-division-i-leagues-votes-college).

46. Bob Kustra, "An NCAA Power Grab," InsideHigherEd.com, August 5, 2014.

47. J. New, "Left Behind," InsideHigherEd.com, August 14, 2014.

48. Drake Group Position Statement: NCAA Division I Governance Proposal (Big 5 Conference Autonomy) (https://drakegroupblog.files.wordpress.com/2015 /02/combined-press-release-and-statement.pdf).

49. See NCAA, *2015–16 NCAA Division I Manual* (Indianapolis: NCAA, 2015), Bylaw 4.02.2, p. 18 (http://www.ncaapublications.com/productdownloads/D116 .pdf). On campuses, the NCAA's faculty athletics representative (FAR) is required at all member institutions. According to NCAA Bylaw 4.02.2, an institutional faculty athletics representative is recognized as the representative of the institution and its faculty in the relationship between the NCAA and the local campus.

50. NCAA, "Composition and Sport Sponsorship of the NCAA Membership: 2012–2013 Composition," NCAA.org (http://www.ncaa.org/about/who-we-are

/membership/composition-and-sport-sponsorship-membership) (hereafter "Composition of Membership").

51. Ibid.

52. Ibid.

53. See Gary T. Brown, "Division I Self-Sufficiency Expected—But Most Often Not Realized," *NCAA News,* August 29, 2005 (http://fs.ncaa.org/Docs/NCAANews Archive/2005/Division+I/division%2Bi%2Bself-sufficiency%2Bexpected%2B--% 2Bbut%2Bmost%2Boften%2Bnot%2Brealized%2B-%2B8-29-05%2Bncaa %2Bnews.html).

54. See NCAA, *2014–15 NCAA Division I Manual* (Indianapolis: NCAA, July 2014), art. 20.0.2(c), p. 347 (http://www.ncaapublications.com/productdownloads /D115.pdf) (hereafter *D-I Manual*).

55. "Composition of Membership," note 2.

56. Ibid. From the inception of the NCAA in 1906 through 1955, there were no separate membership divisions representing different levels of competition. From 1956 to 1972 there were two divisions: college (smaller schools) and university. In 1973 the NCAA adopted the current three-division structure, and in 1978 it split Division I into the current FBS, FCS, and nonfootball subdivisions. Brian D. Shannon and Jo Potuto, "NCAA Governance: Now & in the Future," PowerPoint presentation, Division I-A Faculty Representative Annual Meeting on NCAA Governance, September 22, 2013) (http://www.cbssports.com/images/collegefootball /NCAA-Governance-FAR.pdf).

57. *D-I Manual,* art. 20.9.2(e), p. 347.

58. "Composition of Membership." See also *D-1 Manual,* art. 20.9.2(e), p. 347 ("A member of Division I . . . [s]ponsors at the highest feasible level of intercollegiate competition one or both of the traditional *spectator-oriented, income-producing* sports of football and basketball" [emphasis added]).

59. *D-I Manual,* art. 20.9.9, pp. 353–54.

60. NCAA, *2004–13 Revenues & Expenses: NCAA Division I Intercollegiate Athletics Programs Report* Indianapolis: NCAA, 2014) (http://www.ncaapublications .com/productdownloads/D1REVEXP2013.pdf).

61. NCAA, *2004–14 Revenues & Expenses: NCAA Division I Intercollegiate Athletics Programs Report* (Indianapolis: NCAA, 2015) (https://www.ncaa.org /sites/default/files/2015%20Division%20I%20RE%20report.pdf), p. 24. Revenues for this calculation exclude institutional subsidies (such as transfers from the institution's general fund and mandated student fees allocated to support athletics), capital costs, and debt service expenditures.

62. Ibid., p 28.

63. Ibid., p. 28.

64. *D-I Manual,* arts. 15.5.6.2, 20.9.7.1, 20.9.8.1, 20.9.10, pp. 202, 352, 355.

65. NCAA, "Eleven-Year Trends in Division I Athletics Finances," PowerPoint presentation (Indianapolis: NCAA, September 2015), p. 6 (http://www.ncaa.org /sites/default/files/DivisionI_ElevenYearFinances-20150917.pdf).

66. Ibid., p. 14.

67. Ibid., p. 8.

68. Ibid., p. 13.

69. Ibid., p. 72.

70. *D-1 Manual*, arts. 20.9.3, .6–8, pp. 348–49, 352.

71. NCAA, "Eleven-Year Trends in Division I Athletics Finances," p. 6.

72. Ibid., p. 14.

73. Ibid., p. 8.

74. Ibid., p. 96.

75. The Power Five conferences include the Atlantic Coast Conference (ACC), the Southeastern Conference (SEC), the Big Twelve Conference, the Big Ten Conference, and the Pacific-12 Conference (Pac-12). See Kent Babb, "NCAA Board of Directors Approves Autonomy for 'Power Five' Conference Schools," *Washington Post*, August 7, 2014 (http://www.washingtonpost.com/sports/colleges/ncaa-board-of-directors-approves-autonomy-for-big-5-conference-schools/2014/08/07/807882b4-1e58-11e4-ab7b-696c295ddfd1_story.html).

76. NCAA, "Division II Strategic Positioning Platform," NCAA.org (http://www.ncaa.org/governance/committees/division-ii-strategic-positioning-platform).

77. NCAA, *2014–15 NCAA Division II Manual* (Indianapolis: NCAA, 2014), arts. Sec. 20.10.2, pp. 305–06 (http://www.ncaapublications.com/productdownloads/D215.pdf).

78. NCAA, *2004–14, Revenues & Expenses*, p. 6. See also NCAA, *Revenues & Expenses 2004–2013*, p. 42.

79. NCAA, *2004–14 Revenues & Expenses*, p. 6.

80. Ibid., p. 6. Institutional allocations fund 88 percent of athletic programs with football and 93 percent of those without football. *Id.*

81. Ibid., p. 6.

82. Ibid., p. 6.

83. NCAA, "Eleven-Year Trends in Division I Athletics Finances," p. 6; NCAA, *2014–15 NCAA Division III Manual* (Indianapolis: NCAA, 2014), art. 20.11, p. 187 (http://www.ncaapublications.com/p-4357-2014-2015-ncaa-division-iii-manual-august-version.aspx?CategoryID=0&SectionID=0&ManufacturerID=0&DistributorID=0&GenreID=0&VectorID=0&).

84. Ibid.

85. Ibid., p. 188.

86. Ibid., p. 6.

87. Ibid., p. 6.

Chapter 2

1. See National Collegiate Athletic Association (NCAA), "Finances," NCAA.org (www.ncaa.org/about/resources/finances).

2. Open championships include women's bowling, men's and women's fencing, men's and women's gymnastics, women's ice hockey, men's and women's rifle, men's and women's skiing, men's volleyball, and men's and women's water polo. See NCAA, *2014–15 NCAA Division I Manual* (Indianapolis: NCAA, July 2014), art. 20.8.1, p. 346 (http://www.ncaapublications.com/productdownloads/D115 .pdf) (hereafter *D-I Manual*).

3. See Mark Alesia, "NCAA Approaching $1 Billion per Year amid Challenges by Players," *IndyStar*, March 27, 2014 (www.indystar.com/story/news/2014/03/27 /ncaa-approaching-billion-per-year-amid-challenges-players/6973767/).

4. Ibid.

5. Ibid. See also *NCAA and Subsidiaries, Independent Auditors' Report & Consolidated Financial Statements* (Indianapolis: NCAA, 2013), p. 4 (www.ncaa.org /sites/default/files/NCAA_FS_2012-13_V1%20DOC1006715.pdf) (hereafter *NCAA Audit & Financial Statements*).

6. NCAA, "Finances."

7. NCAA, *2013–14 Division I Revenue Distribution Plan* (Indianapolis: NCAA, 2014 (http://www.ncaa.org/sites/default/files/2013-14%20Revenue%20Distribution%20Plan.pdf) (hereafter *D-I Revenue Distribution*).

8. Ibid., pp. 7, 8.

9. Ibid., p. 8.

10. Prior to 1991, NCAA Final Four revenues were distributed among only those teams that had participated in the Final Four. See NCAA, "Distributions," NCAA.org (http://www.ncaa.org/about/resources/finances/distributions). In 1991, broad-based distributions to all Division I institutions were initiated to help support academic, scholarship, and operating expenses. Ibid.

11. *D-I Revenue Distribution*, p. 10.

12. More precisely, as the value of a "unit" increases in each successive year, the payout will grow beyond $1.56 million annually. The growth rate in the value of a unit has been approximately 2 percent yearly.

13. See College Football Playoff, "Chronology," CollegeFootballPlayoff.com, 2015 (http://www.collegefootballplayoff.com/chronology).

14. See Richard Billingsley, "The Road to the BCS Has Been a Long One," ESPN, October 22, 2014 (http://assets.espn.go.com/ncf/s/historybcs.html).

15. See George Schroeder, "Power Five's College Football Playoff Revenues Will Double What BCS Paid," *USA Today,* July 16, 2014 (http://www.usatoday.com /story/sports/ncaaf/2014/07/16/college-football-playoff-financial-revenues-money -distribution-bill-hancock/127344897/).

16. See ibid.

17. College Football Playoff, "College Football Playoff Revenue-Distribution Policies," CollegeFootballPlayoff.com, 2015 (www.collegefootballplayoff.com /revenue-distribution).

18. See Jacob Pramuk, "Playoffs Are a Revenue Bonanza for College Football," *NBC News,* January 1, 2015 (www.nbcnews.com/business/business-news/playoffs -are-revenue-bonanza-college-football-n277641).

19. See Allie Grasgreen, *Division I Divisiveness,* InsideHigherEd.com, February 16, 2012 (www.insidehighered.com/news/2012/02/16/ncaa-governance-brink -reform).

20. *D-I Manual*, art. 4.6.4, p. 23.

21. See ibid., art. 4.6, pp. 23–24.

22. Ibid., arts. 4.1–4.2.2, pp. 20–21.

23. Ibid., arts. 4.01.2, 4.01.2.2.2.3, p. 17.

24. Ibid., art. 4.01.2.2.1, p. 17.

25. See "BCS Governance," ESPN, March 27, 2014 (http://www.bcsfootball.org /news/story?id–4809846). Following the adoption of this NCAA legislation in 1997, it was no accident that in 1998 the FBS conferences created the Bowl Championship Series (BCS) with five bowl games among the top ten teams. See Billingsley, "The Road to the BCS." In 2006 the FBS conferences added a number 1 versus number 2 national championship game the week after New Year's, effectively starting their own national championship. See ibid. The BCS was the predecessor to the four-team FBS College Football Playoff, which began in the fall of 2014. See College Football Playoff, "Chronology."

26. Prior to the 1997 Bowl Championship Series, first the Bowl Coalition (1992–94) and then the Bowl Alliance (1995–97), which consisted of all the conferences involved in the top three bowl games (Sugar, Orange, and Fiesta) plus Notre Dame, tried to line up the top football teams so there was a de facto national championship matchup at the end of the season. Because the Rose Bowl contract between the Pac-10 and the Big Ten precluded the participation of these top teams, the possibility of a true national championship didn't exist until the Rose Bowl was brought into the Bowl Championship Series in 1998.

27. *D-I Manual,* art. 4.01.2.2, p. 17.

28. Ibid., art. 4.01.2.1, p. 17.

29. NCAA, *2006 NCAA Membership Report* (Indianapolis: NCAA, 2006), p. 19 (https://www.ncaapublications.com/searchadv.aspx?IsSubmit=true&SearchTerm =membership+report).

30. *NCAA Audit & Financial Statements,* p. 4. The remaining funds are for association-wide programs and management expenses not broken down by division. Ibid., p. 4; see also NCAA, "Composition of Membership."

31. *NCAA Audit & Financial Statements*, p. 4.

32. Ibid.

33. See Brian Bennett, "NCAA Board Votes to Allow Autonomy," ESPN, August 8, 2014 (http://espn.go.com/college-sports/story/_/id/11321551/ncaa-board -votes-allow-autonomy-five-power-conferences).

34. See ibid. Not all college athletes are on "full" scholarships; however, the highest percentages of athletes on full scholarships are in Division I basketball and football.

35. See ibid.

36. See Tim Tucker, "Slive Threatens Move to 'Division 4' If Autonomy Isn't Approved," *Atlanta Journal Constitution*, May 30, 2014 (www.ajc.com/news/sports

/college/slive-threatens-move-to-division-4-if-autonomy-isn/nf9xH/#__federated
=1). Choosing to leave the NCAA or becoming a member of Division IV result in
the same outcome because of the regulations implemented in 1997 that allow new
subdivisions to keep their revenues. The practical effect of leaving the NCAA and
becoming Division IV would be to undermine the NCAA Final Four basketball
championship revenue distribution and all Division I institutions.

37. See, for example, O'Bannon v. NCAA, 7 F. Supp. 3d 955 (N.D. Cal. 2014); *In
re* NCAA Athletic Grant-in-Aid Cap Antitrust Litig., MDL No. 2541, 2014 WL
2547809 (J.P.M.L. June 4, 2014) (consolidating Alston v. NCAA, No. 4:14-01011,
N.D. Cal. June 6, 2014), and Jenkins v. NCAA, No. 3:14-01678 (D.N.J. June 18,
2014).

38. Nw. Univ., No. 13-RC-121359, 2014 WL 1922054, at *22–24 (N.L.R.B.
Mar. 26, 2014).

39. See, for example, Banks v. NCAA, 977 F.2d 1081 (7th Cir. 1992); McCormack v. NCAA, 845 F.2d 1338 (5th Cir. 1988); Hennessy v. NCAA, 564 F.2d 1136
(5th Cir. 1977); Justice v. NCAA, 577 F. Supp. 356 (D. Ariz. 1983).

40. See O'Bannon, 7 F. Supp. 3d at 1008, and O'Bannon v. NCAA, Fed. R. App
9th Cir.

41. See Bob Kustra, "NCAA Reforms a Subterfuge for Fueling the Arms Race
in Intercollegiate Athletic Spending," *CBS Sports* (www.cbssports.com/images
/collegefootball/Bob-Kustra-Boise-State-Division-I-NCAA-Reform.pdf).

42. *D-I Manual*, p. 4.

43. K. Trahan, "Athletes Are Getting Degrees, but Does That Actually Mean
Anything?," *SB Nation,* July 9, 2014 (http://www.sbnation.com/college-football
/2014/7/9/5885433/ncaa-trial-student-athletes-education).

44. William T. Foster, "An Indictment of Intercollegiate Athletics," *Atlantic
Monthly*, 116, no. 5 (November 1915).

45. Ronald A. Smith, *Pay for Play: A History of Big-Time College Athletic Reform* (University of Illinois Press, 2011), p. 29.

46. Ibid.

47. Walter Byers, quoted in ibid., p. 131.

48. M. Yost, *Varsity Green: A Behind the Scenes Look at Culture and Corruption in College Athletics* (Stanford University Press, 2009).

49. NCAA, "Appeals Court Rules for NCAA in Major Initial Eligibility Case,"
NCAA News, January 3, 2003.

50. Myles Brand, quoted in G. Gurney and R. Southall, "NCAA Reform Gone
Wrong," InsideHigherEd.com, February 14, 2013 (https://www.insidehighered
.com/views/2013/02/14/ncaa-academic-reform-has-hurt-higher-eds-integrity
-essay).

51. Allie Grasgreen, "Tough Choices for Athletes' Advisors," InsideHigherEd
.com, May 9, 2012 (https://www.insidehighered.com/news/2012/05/09/ncaa
-academic-rules-frustrate-advisers-athletes).

52. P. Thamel and D. Wilson, "Poor Grades Aside, Athletes Get into College
on a $399 Diploma," *New York Times*, November 27, 2005.

53. D. Wilson, "School That Gave Easy Grades to Athletes Is Closing," *New York Times*, December 24, 2005.

54. J. Munz, "Tyndall Hit Hard, USM on Probation from NCAA Case," *Clarion Ledger*, April 8, 2016 (http://www.clarionledger.com/story/sports/college /southern-miss/2016/04/08/report-tyndall-hit-hard-usms-case-ncaa/82789868/).

55. L. Johnson, "Exam Fraud, Recruit Payments among NCAA Accusations against UL-Lafayette, Ex-Assistant Coach David Saunders," *The Advocate,* October 11, 2015 (http://theadvocate.com/sports/ullafayette/13682425-128/ncaa-accuses -louisiana-lafayette-former-football).

56. J. O'Brien, "Summary: What Did Syracuse Do Wrong? NCAA Cites Academic Fraud, Extra Benefits, Drug Policy," Syracuse.com, March 6, 2015 (http:// www.syracuse.com/orangesports/index.ssf/2015/03/ncaa_finds_syracuse _violated_drug_policy_committed_academic_fraud_gave_extra_ben.html).

57. K. L. Wainstein, A. J. Jay III, and C. D. Dukowski, "Investigation of Irregular Classes in the Department of African and Afro-American Studies at the University of North Carolina at Chapel Hill," UNC.edu, October 16, 2014 (http:// carolinacommitment.unc.edu/reports-resources/investigation-of-irregular -classes-in-the-department-of-african-and-afro-american-studies-at-the -university-of-north-carolina-at-chapel-hill-2/).

58. D. Kane and J. Stancill, "Review Agency Hits UNC-Chapel Hill with Probation," *The News & Observer*, June 11, 2015 (http://www.newsobserver.com/news /local/education/unc-scandal/article23751628.html).

59. Gurney and Southall, "NCAA Reform Gone Wrong."

60. Brad Wolverton, "Confessions of a Fixer," *Chronicle of Higher Education.* December 30, 2014 (www.chronicle.com).

61. Brad Wolverton, "How Athletics and Academics Collided at One University," *Chronicle of Higher Education.* June 10, 2015 (www.chronicle.com).

62. The Civil Rights Restoration Act of 1978 made it clear that even if just one program in an educational institution received federal funds, all programs at the institution were prohibited from discriminating on the basis of gender, race/ ethnicity, and disability. Even private colleges and universities accept federal funds from students who qualify for Pell grants (Basic Educational Opportunity Grants).

63. Public Law 88–352 (78 Stat. 241).

64. Title 20 U.S.C. Sections 1681.

65. Public Law 93–112; Public Law 101–336.

66. According to the *Business Dictionary,* governance is defined as the "establishment of policies, and continuous monitoring of their proper implementation, by the members of the governing body of an organization. It includes the mechanisms required to balance the powers of the members (with the associated accountability), and their primary duty of enhancing the prosperity and viability of the organization." *Business Dictionary,* "Governance" (http://www.business-dictionary.com/definition/governance.html#ixzz40H0Y5Pdc).

67. TitleIX.info, "The Living Law" (http://www.titleix.info/history/the-living
-law.aspx). Co-author D. Lopiano was the director of women's athletics at the University of Texas at Austin in 1975–1992 and had numerous discussions with J.
Niels Thompson, the institution's NCAA faculty representative and former NCAA
president, who took credit for persuading Texas U.S. senator John Tower to sponsor the Tower Amendment, which would have exempted college men's basketball
and football from Title IX, and the NCAA's role in putting pressure on Congress
to defeat the 1975 Title IX athletics regulations (34 CFR 106.41; 34 CFR 106.37(c)),
which were finally approved by Congress on July 21, 1975.

68. Amy Wilson, *The Status of Women in Intercollegiate Athletics as Title IX
Turns 40* (Indianapolis: NCAA, 2012), p. 2 (https://www.ncaapublications.com/p
-4289-the-status-of-women-in-intercollegiate-athletics-as-title-ix-turns-40-june
-2012.aspx).

69. NCAA, *2015–16 NCAA Division I Manual* (Indianapolis: NCAA, 2015),
pp. 3–4 (http://www.ncaapublications.com/productdownloads/D116.pdf). For example, the NCAA's 2.2.2 Cultural Diversity and Gender Equity principle, "It is
the responsibility of each member institution to establish and maintain an environment that values cultural diversity and gender equity among its student-
athletes and intercollegiate athletics department staff," was not adopted until
1995, and no legislative provisions are related to the implementation of this principle. Rather, the principle transfers responsibility from the national governance
organization to the member institution, with no NCAA responsibility for oversight. The NCAA's 2.3 Principle of Gender Equity, which includes 2.3.1, "Compliance With Federal and State Legislation. It is the responsibility of each member
institution to comply with federal and state laws regarding gender equity," not
adopted until 1994, is a similar transfer of responsibility to the member with no
national governance mechanism for accountability. The NCAA's 2.6 Principle of
Nondiscrimination: "The Association shall promote an atmosphere of respect for
and sensitivity to the dignity of every person. It is the policy of the Association to
refrain from discrimination with respect to its governance policies, educational
programs, activities and employment policies, including on the basis of age, color,
disability, gender, national origin, race, religion, creed or sexual orientation. It is
the responsibility of each member institution to determine independently its own
policy regarding nondiscrimination," was not adopted until 1993 and again shifts
responsibility from the national governance association to the member institution.
Even the NCAA's 2.7 Principle of Diversity Within Governance Structures, directly applicable to the responsibility of the national governance organization—
"The Association shall promote diversity of representation within its various divisional governance structures and substructures. Each divisional governing body
must assure gender and ethnic diversity among the membership of the bodies in
the division's administrative structure"—adopted in 1996, has been disregarded.
The NCAA does not publish the gender and racial composition of its governance
structures and substructures. Even its own committees must request such

information rather than have it be regularly reported as a mechanism for implementing a governance principle. These are concrete examples demonstrating that the NCAA principles for the conduct of athletics are more window dressing than substantive.

70. U.S. Department of Education Office for Civil Rights, letter, "Dear Colleague: Students with Disabilities in Extracurricular Athletics," January 23, 2013 (http://www.ed.gov/ocr/letters/colleague-201301-504.pdf).

71. NCAA, Sports Sponsorship, Participation and Demographic Search, database (http://web1.ncaa.org/rgdSearch/exec/main). While one year (1999–2000) of data prior to 2007–08 is available, such data were provided on a voluntary basis by member institutions, with not all members reporting.

72. NCAA, "Minority Opportunities and Interests Committee," NCAA.org (http://www.ncaa.org/governance/committees/minority-opportunities-and -interests-committee).

73. NCAA, "NCAA Inclusion," NCAA.org (http://www.ncaa.org/about /resources/inclusion).

74. NCAA, "NCAA Committee on Women's Athletics," NCAA.org (http:// www.ncaa.org/governance/committees/committee-womens-athletics).

75. For example, in 2013–14, every Ivy League institution had a women's rugby club sport program, and none of the league's member institutions, according to those institutions' Equity in Athletics Disclosure Act reports (see http://ope.ed.gov/athletics/), met the Title IX Prong One participation requirement, that the proportion of females in the athletic program match the proportion of females in the undergraduate student body. While some of the Ivy League institutions have elevated these club programs to varsity in the last two years, this could have happened earlier if there had been an NCAA legislative mandate.

76. Chicago State University, "NCAA Division I Athletics Certification Program History," CSU.edu (http://www.csu.edu/NCAA/aboutcertification.htm). The program was approved at the 1993 NCAA Convention after a two-year, thirty-four-institution pilot program, as part of a reform agenda supported by the former NCAA Presidents' Commission, the former NCAA Council, and the Knight Commission on Intercollegiate Athletics.

77. NCAA, "NCAA Announces Latest Division I Certification Decisions," press release, August 18, 2011 (http://fs.ncaa.org/Docs/PressArchive/2011/2011 0818+athletic+cert+rls.htm).

78. Women's Sports Foundation, "NCAA Certification Process and Gender Equity," letter to NCAA President Mark Emmert from twenty-one organizational leader signatories, August 5, 2011 (https://www.womenssportsfoundation.org /home/advocate/title-ix-and-issues/history-of-title-ix/~/media/PDFs/Misc /NCAA%20Certification%20Gender%20Equity%2072011%20FINAL.pdf).

79. NCAA, "Division I Committee on Institutional Performance," NCAA.org (http://www.ncaa.org/governance/committees/division-i-committee

-institutional-performance). The IPP had not yet been implemented at the time of this writing.

80. NCAA, *2015–16 NCAA Division I Manual*, pp. 1–5.

81. The Independent Sector consists of hundreds of charities, foundations, corporate philanthropy units and businesses that sponsor research, advance public policies that support a dynamic, independent sector, and share governance and other resources so that staff, boards, and volunteers can improve their not-for-profit organizations and better serve their communities. (www.independentsector.org).

82. Panel on the Nonprofit Sector, "Principles for Good Governance and Ethical Practice: A Guide for Charities and Foundations," Independent Sector, October 2007 (www.independentsector.org/principles).

83. Ibid., p. 8.

84. Ibid., p. 12.

85. Ibid., p. 15.

86. For a more detailed discussion of the tax preferences that benefit intercollegiate athletics, see Andrew Zimbalist, "Taxation of College Sports: Policies and Controversies," in *Introduction to Intercollegiate Athletics*, edited by Eddie Comeaux (Johns Hopkins University Press, 2015).

Chapter 3

1. National Collegiate Athletic Association (NCAA), "Infractions Panel Penalizes Georgia Southern," *NCAA News Archive*, January 20, 2010 (http://fs.ncaa.org /Docs/NCAANewsArchive/2010/d1/infractions_panel_penalizes_georgia _southern.html).

2. Emily James, "Former Georgia Southern Staff Members Provided Impermissible Academic Assistance," NCAA.com, July 7, 2016 (http://www.ncaa.com /news/ncaa/article/2016-07-07/former-georgia-southern-staff-members-provided -impermissible-academic).

3. The first year for which the NCAA provides data is 1999.

4. NCAA, "Infractions Panel Penalizes Georgia Southern." Of course, another factor possibly affecting these numbers is that the percentage point increase may occur more readily when the starting level is lower.

5. Ibid.

6. NCAA, *2015–16 NCAA Division I Manual* (Indianapolis: NCAA, 2015), pp. 155–61 (http://www.ncaapublications.com/productdownloads/D116.pdf).

7. Gerald Gurney, Donna Lopiano, Eric Snyder, Mary Willingham, Jayma Meyer, Brian Porto, David Ridpath, Allen Sack, and Andrew Zimbalist, "The Drake Group Position Statement: Why the NCAA Academic Progress Rate (APR) and Graduation Success Rate (GSR) Should Be Abandoned and Replaced with More Effective Academic Metrics," Drake Group, 2015.

8. The Jeanne Clery Disclosure of Campus Security Policy and Campus Crime Statistics Act. 20 U.S.C. § 1092; 34 C.F.R. §§ 668.41; 668.45.

9. The Jeanne Clery Disclosure of Campus Security Policy and Campus Crime Statistics Act. 20 U.S.C. § 1092 (e) and 34 § CFR 668.48.

10. Michelle Brutlag Hosick, "Graduation Rates Continue to Climb: More Student-Athletes than Ever Are Earning Degrees," NCAA.org (November 4, 2015) (http://www.ncaa.org/about/resources/media-center/news/graduation-success-rate-continues-climb); NCAA, "Division: Overall Division I Graduation Rates," NCAA.org, 2015 (http://www.ncaa.org/about/resources/media-center/news/graduation-success-rate-continues-climb).

11. Michelle Brutlag Hosick, "Student-Athletes Earn Diplomas at Record Rate," NCAA.org (October 28, 2014) (http://www.ncaa.org/about/resources/media-center/news/student-athletes-earn-diplomas-record-rate).

12. Albert Bimper, "Is There an Elephant on the Roster? Race, Racism, and High Profile Intercollegiate Sport," *The Journal of Blacks in Higher Education.* paper filed online in *Research and Studies*, May 2, 2013. (https://www.jbhe.com/2013/05/kansas-state-scholar-examines-the-classroom-experiences-of-black-student-athletes/); Robert B. Slater, "Kansas State Scholar Examines the Classroom Experiences of Black Student Athletes," *Journal of Blacks in Higher Education*, May 2, 2013 (www.jbhe.com/2013/05/kansas-state-scholar-examines-the-classroom-experiences-of-black-student-athletes/).

13. NCAA, "Frequently Asked Questions about Academic Progress Rate," NCAA.org, 2015 (http://www.ncaa.org/about/resources/research/frequently-asked-questions-about-academic-progress-rate-apr).

14. It should be noted that an institution can appeal this penalty on the basis of unusual circumstances.

15. Gerald S. Gurney and Richard M. Southall, "College Sports' Bait and Switch," ESPN, August 9, 2012 (http://espn.go.com/college-sports/story/_/id/8248046/college-sports-programs-find-multitude-ways-game-ncaa-apr).

16. Ibid.

17. C. McDonald, "Back in the Game: Cal Program Helps Former Student-Athletes Graduate," *California Magazine,* Spring 2015 (http://alumni.berkeley.edu/california-magazine/spring-2015-dropouts-and-drop-ins/back-game-cal-program-helps-former-student).

18. Ibid.

19. E. Ekerd, "NCAA Graduation Rates: Less Than Meets the Eye," *Journal of Sport Management* 24 (2010), pp. 145–59 (http://journals.humankinetics.com/AcuCustom/Sitename/Documents/DocumentItem/17759.pdf).

20. College Sports Research Institute, "2016 Adjusted Graduation Gap Report: NCAA Division-I Basketball," April 6, 2016 (http://csri-sc.org/wp-content/uploads/2013/09/2016-Basketball-AGG-Report_Final.pdf).

21. Michelle Brutlag Hosick, "NCAA Releases Academic Progress Rates for Coaches," NCAA.com, August 5, 2010 (updated December 15, 2010) (http://www

.ncaa.com/news/basketball-women/article/2010-08-05/ncaa-releases-academic
-progress-rates-coaches).

22. Gerald Gurney, Donna Lopiano, Eric Snyder, et. al. "The Drake Group Position Statement: Why the NCAA Academic Progress Rate (APR) and Graduation Success Rate (GSR) Should Be Abandoned and Replaced with More Effective Academic Metrics, Drake Group," October 2015 (https://thedrakegroup.org/2015/06/07/drake-group-questions-ncaa-academic-metrics/). See also F. Splitt, *The Faculty-Driven Movement to Reform Big-Time College Sports* (Northwestern University Press, 2004).

23. M. Knobler, "College Athletes: Academic Performance: Behind the Line on Grades," *Atlantic Journal Constitution*, December 28, 2008 (http://www.ajc.com/services/content/printedition/2008/12/28/acadmain.html).

24. NCAA, *Division I Results from the NCAA GOALS Study on the Student-Athlete Experience* (www.ncaa.org/sites/default/files/DI_GOALS_FARA_final_1.pdf, NCAA, 2011).

25. Penn Schoen Berland, "Student-Athlete Time Demands," April 2015 (http://www.cbssports.com/images/Pac-12-Student-Athlete-Time-Demands-Obtained-by-CBS-Sports.pdf).

26. National Labor Relations Board, "NLRB Director for Region 13 Issues Decision in Northwestern University Athletes Case," press release, March 26, 2014 (www.nlrb.gov/news-outreach/news-story/nlrb-director-region-13-issues-decision-northwestern-university-athletes).

27. Ibid.

28. "Student Athletes and Literacy: The Kevin Ross Story," blog post (http://studentathletesandliteracy.weebly.com/the-kevin-ross-story.html); E. J. Sherman, "Good Sports, Bad Sports: The District Court Abandons College Athletes in Ross v. Creighton University," *Loyola of Los Angeles Entertainment Law Review* 11, no. 2 (March 1, 1991), no. 657 (http://digitalcommons.lmu.edu/elr/vol11/iss2/12).

29. S. Kogod, "Cocaine, Illiteracy and Football Could Not Stop Dexter Manley," SBNation.com, June 23, 2015.

30. C. Winters and G. Gurney, "Academic Preparation of Specially Admitted Student-Athletes: A Question of Basic Skills," *College and University Journal* 88, no. 2 (Fall 2012) (https://aacrao-web.s3.amazonaws.com/files/Q63EQfrQpiJmA21pS52b_CUJ8802_WEB.pdf); B. Wolverton, "NCAA's Eligibility Standards Miss the Mark, Researcher Says," *Chronicle of Higher Education,* January 9, 2012 (http://chronicle.com/blogs/players/ncaas-eligibility-standards-miss-mark-researcher-says/29369).

31. S. Shenauda, "Schlissel Talks Athletic Culture and Academic Performance Issues," *Michigan Daily,* November 10, 2014 (https://www.michigandaily.com/article/schlissel-talks-athletics-and-administration-sacua).

32. D. Murphy, "Michigan President Apologizes," ESPN, November 12, 2014 (http://espn.go.com/college-football/story/_/id/11863811/michigan-president-mark-schlissel-apologizes-brady-hoke-comments-academics).

33. Billy Hawkins, *The New Plantation: Black Athletes, College Sports, and Predominantly White NCAA Institutions* (New York: Palgrave Macmillan, 2010); Taylor Branch, "The Shame of College Sports," *The Atlantic*, October 2011 (http://www.theatlantic.com/magazine/archive/2011/10/the-shame-of-college-sports/308643/).

34. B. Wolverton, "The Education of Dasmine Cathey." *Chronicle of Higher Education*, June 2, 2012; B. Wolverton, "Dasmine Cathey Stars in HBO Report on Academic Reform in College Sports," *Chronicle of Higher Education*, March 25, 2014.

35. J. Newman, "At Top Athletics Programs, Students Often Major in Eligibility," *Chronicle of Higher Education*. December 18, 2014.

36. J. Solomon, "Mark Emmert's Pay, NCAA Legal Fees Increase," *CBS Sports*, June 30, 2015.

37. B. Wolverton, "I Was an Athlete Masquerading as a Student," *Chronicle of Higher Education*, June 10, 2014.

38. S. Berkowitz, "NCAA Drastically Increases Its Spending on Lobbying." *USA Today*, January 20, 2015.

39. D. Rovell, "NCAA Prez: We Won't Pay Student Athletes, Give Jersey Royalties," CNBC, December 8, 2010.

40. Associated Press, "New NCAA Legislation in the Works," ESPN, March 3, 2015 (http://espn.go.com/college-sports/story/_/id/12413981/new-ncaa-legislation-academic-misconduct-works).

41. Ibid.

42. Associated Press, "K-State President Defends NCAA Involvement in Academics," *Fox Sports,* April 2, 2015 (http://www.foxsports.com/college-basketball/story/k-state-president-defends-ncaa-involvement-in-academics-040215).

43. G. Leef, "Phi Beta Cons," *National Review,* March 2, 2015 (http://www.nationalreview.com/phi-beta-cons/414674/cheated-jay-smith-and-mary-willingham-reviewed-george-leef).

44. Pac-12 Conference, "McCants vs. NCAA, UNC in Academic Fraud Lawsuit," Pac-12.com, February 2, 2015 (http://compliance.pac-12.org/hot-topics/mccants-vs-ncaa-unc-in-academic-fraud-lawsuit/).

45. M. Strachan, "The NCAA on Academic Fraud at NCAA Schools: Not Our Responsibility!," *Huffington Post*, March 3, 2015.

46. NCAA, *2014–15 NCAA Division I Manual* (Indianapolis: NCAA, July 2014), art. 2.5, p. 4. (http://www.ncaapublications.com/productdownloads/D115.pdf).

47. Ibid.

48. Ibid., pp. 147–81.

49. Ibid., pp. 313–39.

Chapter 4

1. William T. Foster, "An Indictment of Intercollegiate Athletics," *Atlantic Monthly* 116, no. 5 (November 2015).

2. Ben Cohen, "Ohio State's New President Tackles Football," *Wall Street Journal*, November 18, 2015 (http://www.wsj.com/articles/ohio-states-new-president -tackles-football-1447893940).

3. "Flutie Effect," *The Economist*, blog post, January 3, 2007 (http://www .economist.com/blogs/freeexchange/2007/01/flutie_effect); Robert E. Litan, Jonathan M Orszag, and Peter R. Orszag, *The Empirical Effects of Collegiate Athletics: An Interim Report.* Sebago Associates, NCAA (August 2003) (http://www.rfp .research.sc.edu/faculty/PDF/baseline.pdf).

4. Ibid.

5. Allie Grasgreen, "Seeking Answers in College Sports," InsideHigherEd.com (April 22, 2013) (https://www.insidehighered.com/news/2013/04/22/u-north -carolina-panel-weighs-future-college-sports).

6. Kitty Pittman, "Cross, George Lynn," in *Encyclopedia of Oklahoma History and Culture* (Oklahoma City: Oklahoma Historical Society, 2009) (http://www.okhistory .org/publications/enc/entry.php?entryname=GEORGE%20LYNN%20CROSS).

7. Joseph N. Crowley, *In the Arena: The NCAA's First Century,* digital edition (Indianapolis: NCAA, 2006), p. 68.

8. Ibid.

9. Ronald A. Smith, *Pay for Play: A History of Big-Time College Athletic Reform* (University of Illinois Press, 2011).

10. Ibid., p. 75.

11. Ibid., p. 76.

12. Ibid.

13. NCAA, "Division I Athletics Certification Self-Study Instrument: 2009–10 Cycle 3, Class 3" (Indianapolis: NCAA, 2010).

14. Ibid.

15. The first two cycles of the certification program were conducted every five years before the cycle was changed to ten years. When the program was suspended in 2011, institutions were in the middle of their third cycle.

16. Crowley, *In the Arena,* p. 82.

17. NCAA, *Division I Steering Committee on Governance: Recommended Governance Model* (Indianapolis: NCAA, 2014) (https://www.ncaa.org/sites/default /files/DI%20Steering%20Commitee%20on%20Gov%20Proposed%20Model%20 07%2018%2014%204.pdf).

18. Ibid.

19. NCAA, *2015–16 NCAA Division I Manual* (Indianapolis: NCAA, 2015) (http://www.ncaapublications.com/productdownloads/D116.pdf).

20. Michelle Brutlag Hosick, "Changes Likely for Athletic Certification Program," NCAA.org, November 1, 2011 (http://sidearm.sites.s3.amazonaws.com

/nicholls.sidearmsports.com/documents/2012/7/9/Southland_Conference
_Compliance_Corner_December_2011.pdf?id=422).

21. Art and Science Group, *Quantitative and Qualitative Research with Football Bowl Subdivision University Presidents on the Costs and Financing of Intercollegiate Athletics* (Knight Commission on Intercollegiate Athletics, 2009) (knightcommissionmedia.org/images/President_Survey_FINAL.pdf).

22. NCAA, *2015–16 NCAA Division I Manual,* p. 3.

23. Kellie Woodhouse, "Higher Ed's Incurable Sports Problem," InsideHigher Ed.com, July 14, 2015.

24. Charles Clotfelter, *Big Time Sports in American Universities* (Cambridge University Press, 2011), p. 47.

25. Alex Scarborough, "UAB to Reinstate Football for 2017 Season," ESPN, July 15, 2015.

26. NCAA, *2014–15 NCAA Division I Manual* (Indianapolis: NCAA, 2014) (http://www.ncaapublications.com/productdownloads/D115.pdf).

27. Jake New, "Autonomy Gained," InsideHigherEd.com, August 8, 2014; Knight Commission on Intercollegiate Athletics, *Athletic & Academic Spending Database for NCAA Division I* (http://spendingdatabase.knightcommission.org)

28. Bob Kustra, "An NCAA Power Grab," InsideHigherEd.com, August 5, 2014.

29. Jake New, "Left Behind," InsideHigherEd.com, August 5, 2014.

30. Brian Porto, Gerald Gurney, Donna Lopiano, David Ridpath, Allen Sack, Mary Willingham, and Andrew Zimbalist, "The Drake Group Position Statement: Fixing the Dysfunctional NCAA Enforcement System," Drake Group, April 7, 2015 (https://thedrakegroup.org/2015/06/03/drake-group-addresses-dysfunctional-ncaa-enforcement-system/).

31. Crowley, *In the Arena*, p. 36.

32. Porto and others, "The Drake Group Position Statement," pp. 3–4.

33. Ibid.

34. Nicole Auerbach, "NCAA Athletes Demand Greater Influence, Inclusion," *USA Today,* June 17, 2014 (http://www.usatoday.com/story/sports/college/2014/01/17/ncaa-convention-saac-student-athlete-vote-representation/4592935/).

35. Ted Stevens Olympic and Amateur Sports Act. U.S.C. §220501; §222504.2(b) (https://www.adreducation.org/media/12832/1998%20ted%20stevens%20olympic%20and%20amateur%20sports%20act.pdf).

36. NCAA, *2015–16 NCAA Division I Manual*, p. 18 (Section 4.01.2).

37. NCAA, *1998 NCAA Faculty Athletics Representative Handbook* (Indianapolis: NCAA, 1998) (https://www.nmu.edu/sites/DrupalSportsAthletics/files/UserFiles/Files/Pre-Drupal/SiteSections/Otherlinks/Documents/far_handbook.pdf).

38. NCAA, *FAR Study Report: Roles, Responsibilities and Perspectives of Faculty Athletics Representatives* (Indianapolis: NCAA, 2013) (http://www.ncaa.org/sites/default/files/FAR_STUDY_Report_final.pdf).

39. See the website of the Coalition on Intercollegiate Athletics (http://sites.comm.psu.edu/thecoia/).

Chapter 5

1. Gerald Gurney, Donna Lopiano, Eric Snyder, Mary Willingham, Jayma Meyer, Brian Porto, David Ridpath, Allen Sack, and Andrew Zimbalist, "The Drake Group Position Statement: Why the NCAA Academic Progress Rate (APR) and Graduation Success Rate (GSR) Should Be Abandoned and Replaced with More Effective Academic Metrics," Drake Group, October 2015 (http://thedra kegroup.org/2015/10/05/drake-group-questions-ncaa-academic-metrics/).

2. Ohio State University, Office of Student Life, "Student Athletes: A Profile of Ohio State Student Athletes," March 2013 (http://cssl.osu.edu/posts/documents /athlete-brief-final-w-executive-summary.pdf). See also Michael T. Maloney and Robert E. McCormick, "An Examination of the Role That Intercollegiate Athletic Participation Plays in Academic Achievement: Athletes' Feats in the Classroom," *Journal of Human Resources* 28, no. 3 (Summer 1993), pp. 555–70.

3. Peter Adler and Patricia A. Adler, "From Idealism to Pragmatic Detachment: The Academic Performance of College Athletes," *Sociology of Education* 58, no. 241 (October 1985), pp. 241–58.

4. National Labor Relations Board, Region 13, Northwestern University, Employers and College Athletes Players Association (CAPA), Petitioner, Case 13-RC-121359, decision of August 17, 2015 (https://www.nlrb.gov/case/13-RC-121359).

5. Penn Schoen Berland, "Student-Athlete Time Demands," April 2015 (http://www.cbssports.com/images/Pac-12-Student-Athlete-Time-Demands-Obtained -by-CBS-Sports.pdf).

6. Kevin Scarbinsky, "College Athletes' Rights: National Letter of Intent Plus NCAA Transfer Rules Tie Student-Athletes to Schools," Al.com, November 27, 2011 (http://www.al.com/sports/index.ssf/2011/11/college_athletes_rights_nation .html).

7. Josh Levin, "The NCAA Has Truly Lost Its Mind," Slate.com, July 2, 2013 (http://www.slate.com/articles/sports/sports_nut/2013/07/ncaa_transfer_rule _college_coaches_can_block_their_former_players_from_getting.html).

8. U.S. Department of Education, *Six-Year Attainment, Persistence, Transfer, Retention, and Withdrawal Rates of Students Who Began Postsecondary Education in 2003–04*, NCES 2011-152, July 2011 (http://nces.ed.gov/pubs2011/2011152.pdf).

9. Donna Lopiano, Gerald Gurney, Mary Willingham, Jayma Meyer, Brian Porto, David Ridpath, Allen Sack, and Andrew Zimbalist, "The Drake Group Position Statement: Rights of College Athletes," Drake Group, June 4, 2015 (https:// thedrakegroup.org/2015/06/05/rights-of-college-athletes/).

10. Chelsea L. Dixon, "When Student-Athletes Get Injured, Who Pays?" Noodle.com, October 7, 2015 (https://www.noodle.com/articles/when-student -athletes-get-injured-who-pays134).

11. NCAA, *2015–16 NCAA Division I Manual* (Indianapolis: NCAA, 2015) (http://www.ncaapublications.com/productdownloads/D116.pdf). See section 3.2.4.8, which also appears in NCAA Division II and Division III manuals.

12. Yale University Athletics, "Yale Athletics Training Insurance Information," YaleBulldogs.com, 2010 (http://www.yalebulldogs.com/information/athlete _services/training/insurance).

13. Kristina Peterson, "Athletes Stuck with the Bill after Injuries," *New York Times,* July 15, 2009 (http://www.nytimes.com/2009/07/16/sports/16athletes.html ?pagewanted=all&_r=1).

14. See NCAA Division I, II, and III manuals, available at: http://www .ncaapublications.com/s-13-Manuals.aspx.

15. See http://grfx.cstv.com/photos/schools/csfu/genrel/auto_pdf/2011-12/misc _non_event/NCAA-medical-expense-info.pdf. Prior to 2013, when the NCAA adopted its current permissive statement allowing institutions to pay for any medical expense, these were the conditions listed in the 2012–13 NCAA Division I Manuals (p. 227), which identified what an institution was allowed to pay for— but not required to do so.

16. NCAA, "Student-Athlete Insurance Programs / Exceptional Student-Athlete Disability Insurance Program," NCAA.org (http://www.ncaa.org/about /resources/insurance/student-athlete-insurance-programs).

17. Richard Giller, "NCAA Insurance News: A Step in the Right Direction," Law360.com, October 20, 2014 (http://www.law360.com/articles/588210/ncaa -insurance-news-a-step-in-the-right-direction).

18. Experts estimate that an NCAA umbrella athletics injury insurance policy covering 430,000 athletes with a deductible of between $500 and $1,500 for institutions without football programs, and higher for institutions with football programs, would cost $120–$180 million annually. Generally, the larger the risk pool, the lower the insurance costs. An additional $50–$80 million should fund "gap" costs, the difference between (1) institutional costs for uncovered medical expenses and NCAA insurance deductibles and copays (with the NCAA paying insurance policy costs) and (2) what NCAA member institutions are currently paying for both athletics injury insurance policies and uncovered medical costs, deductibles, and copays—if any. It is reasonable to ask whether these cost estimates are reliable. Information related to medical expenses and premiums is collected as part of an institution's Equity in Athletics Disclosure Act report and is included in the NCAA Financial Reporting System. For the 2011–12 academic year, Division I members spent $135.2 million, Division II members spent $25.6 million, and Division III spent a reported $10.8 million (only 60 percent of Division III members responded with data). By estimating the average institutional cost of 60 percent of Division III members, a 100 percent figure of $18 million was extrapolated. Thus, the total insurance and medical cost for NCAA institutions was $178.8 million. Thus, an NCAA insurance budget of $260 million ($180 million for the policy and another $80 million for gap costs from national championship media revenues) in addition to these institutional costs, which would be used to cover deductibles, copays, and uncovered costs, seems more than adequate to provide the proposed benefits at no additional cost to member institutions.

19. NCAA, *2014–15 NCAA Sports Medicine Handbook* (Indianapolis: NCAA, 2014) (https://www.ncaapublications.com/searchadv.aspx?IsSubmit=true&Search Term=MEDICINE).

20. Ibid., p. 2.

21. Ibid.

22. Z. Y. Kerr, T. P. Dompier, E. M. Snook, S. W. Marshall, D. Klossner, B. Hainline, and J. Corlette, "National Collegiate Athletic Association Injury Surveillance System: Review of Methods for 2004–2005 through 2013–2014 Data Collection," *Journal of Athletic Training* 49, no. 4 (July–August 2014), pp. 552–60.

23. See, for example, Jennifer Hootman, Randall Dick, and Julie Agel, "Epidemiology of Collegiate Injuries for 15 Sports: Summary and Recommendations for Injury Prevention Initiatives," *Journal of Athletic Training* 42, no. 2 (April–June 2017), pp. 311–19. Any issue of the *Journal of Athletic Training* may be examined for similar studies conducted using the NCAA's ISS data.

24. S. L. Zuckerman, A. Yengo-Kahn, E. Wasserman, T. Covasin, and G. S. Solomon, "Epidemiology of Sports-Related Concussion in NCAA Athletes from 2009–10 to 2013–14: Incidence, Recurrence, and Mechanisms," *American Journal of Sports Medicine* 43, no. 11 (September 2015).

25. K. G. Harmon, I. M. Asif, J. J. Maleszewski, D. S. Owens, J. M. Prutkin, J. C. Salerno, M. L. Zigman, R. Ellenbogen, A. L. Rao, M. J. Ackerman, and J. A. Drezner, "Incidence, Cause, and Comparative Frequency of Sudden Cardiac Death in National Collegiate Athletic Association Athletes: A Decade in Review," *Circulation* 132, no. 1 (July 2015), pp. 10–19.

26. U.S. District Court for the Northern District of Illinois, Eastern Division, National Collegiate Athletic Association Student-Athlete Concussion Injury Litigation, case number 1:13-cv-09116, January 26, 2016, decision of Judge John Z. Lee on the Joint Motion for Preliminary Approval of Amended Class Settlement and Certification of Settlement Class, p. 154. This ruling covered thirteen lawsuits consolidated before this court.

27. J. Solomon, "Judge Approves Settlement in NCAA Concussion Case with Conditions," *CBS Sports*, January 26, 2016 (www.cbssports.com/collegefootball /writer/jon-solomon/25463412/judge-approves-settlement-in-ncaa-concussion -case).

28. A. Wolfe, "Is the Era of Abusive College Coaches Finally Coming to an End?," *Sports Illustrated*, September 28, 2015 (http://www.si.com/college-basket ball/2015/09/29/end-abusive-coaches-college-football-basketball).

29. E. Adelson, "Why Do Athletes Tolerate Abusive Coaches?," *Yahoo Sports*, April 4, 2013 (http://sports.yahoo.com/news/ncaab--why-don-t-college-athletes -call-out-abusive-coaches--222535612.html).

30. Associated Press, "Lawsuit Alleges Abuse by Mike Rice," December 10, 2013 (http://espn.go.com/new-york/ncb/story/_/id/10114698/former-rutgers-scarlet -knights-player-sues-coach-mike-rice-behavior).

31. E. Frere, "Santa Ana Boxing Club Coach Accused of Sexual Abuse," KABC-TV/DT, Santa Ana, Calif., July 16, 2012 (http://abclocal.go.com/kabc /story?section=news/local/orange_county&id=8738059); Kendra Kozen, "More Coaches Accused of Sexual Abuse," *Aquatics International,* July 2012 (http:// www.aquaticsintl.com/2012/sep/1209n_abuse.html#.UAqTNaNRC1g); Kathryn Marchocki, "Sex Abuse Investigation into Former York Youth Baseball Coach Broadens," *New Hampshire Union Leader,* July 19, 2012 (http://bangordailynews .com/2012/07/19/news/portland/sex-abuse-investigation-into-former-york-youth -baseball-coach-broadens/); B. Mikelway, "Accusers Confront Cheerleading Coach in Henrico Sex-Abuse Case," *Richmond Times-Dispatch,* June 27, 2012 (http://www2.timesdispatch.com/news/2012/jun/27/tdmet01-accusers-confront -cheerleading-coach-in-he-ar-2016009/); J. O'Donnell, "Agreement Reached in Sandburg Coach's Sexual Abuse Case, Sentence to Come," *Orlando Park Patch,* July 9, 2012 (http://orlandpark.patch.com/articles/agreement-reached-in -sandburg-coachs-sexual-abuse-case-sentence-to-come); Shavonne Potts, "Soccer Group Puts Ex-Coach on Indefinite Suspension after Sex Abuse Charges," *Salisbury Post,* July 20, 2012 (http://www.salisburypost.com/News/072012-crime -Ralph-Wager-charged-sex-offense-suspended-soccer-association-qcd).

32. Christine Willmsen and Maureen O'Hagan, "Coaches Who Prey: The Abuse of Girls and the System that Follows It," *Seattle Times,* December 14, 2003 (http://community.seattletimes.nwsource.com/archive/?date=20031214&slug =coaches14m).

33. USA Swimming, "Individuals Suspended or Ineligible—Permanently" (Updated 6/7/2016) (http://www.usaswimming.org/ViewMiscArticle.aspx?TabId =1963&mid=10011&ItemId=5107).

34. USA Gymnastics, "Permanently Ineligible Members," 2013 (http://usagym .org/pages/aboutus/pages/permanently_ineligible_members.html).

35. See the Safe Sport page on the U.S. Olympic Committee website for a full description of the program (http://safesport.org/what-is-safesport/the-usoc -program/).

36. U.S. Internal Revenue Service, *Scholarships, Fellowship Grants, Grants, and Tuition Reductions,* publication 970 (https://www.irs.gov/publications/p970/ch01 .html). Note that the room and board portions of academic or athletic scholarships are taxable. Only that portion of the scholarship that covers tuition and course-related expenses is tax-free.

37. National Labor Relations Board, Region 13, Northwestern University, Employers and College Athletes Players Association (CAPA), p. 13.

38. Ibid., p. 16. While an appeal of this decision was not upheld, the full Labor Relations Board declined to rule on the merits of the case, asking Congress to make its wishes known on the issue of college athletes as employees.

39. Dan Wolken and Steve Berkowitz, "NCAA Removes Name-Likeness Release from Athlete Forms," *USA Today,* July 18, 2014 (http://www.usatoday.com /story/sports/college/2014/07/18/ncaa-name-and-likeness-release-student-athlete -statement-form/12840997/).

40. J. Kellman and J. S. Hopkins, "College Athletes Routinely Sign Away Rights to Be Paid for Names, Images," *Chicago Tribune,* March 26, 2015 (http://www .chicagotribune.com/sports/college/ct-ncaa-waivers-met-20150326-story.html).

41. NCAA, *2015–16 NCAA Division I Manual*, section 12.5.

42. Ibid., p. 70; see section 12.4.4.

43. Ibid.; see section 12.4.2 (f).

44. Ibid., p. 72; see section 12.5.1.3.

45. Ibid., p. 73; see section 12.5.2.

46. Tony Manfred, "Oregon's New $68 Million Football Facility Is like Nothing We've Ever Seen in College Sports," *Business Insider,* July 31, 2013 (http://www .businessinsider.com/new-oregon-football-building-photos-2013-7).

47. Ibid. See also Dan Greenspan, "Oregon Unveils Eye-Popping New Football Performance Center," NFL.com, July 31, 2013 (http://www.nfl.com/news/story /0ap1000000224020/article/oregon-unveils-eyepopping-new-football-performance -center).

48. Steven Davis, "University of Oregon Athletics Unveils Latest Technology in Facility Makeover," Sport Techie, July 26, 2012 (http://www.sporttechie.com /2012/07/26/university-of-oregon-170/).

49. Ibid. See also Go Ducks, "Casanova Center," GoDucks.com, June 21, 2011 (http://www.goducks.com/ViewArticle.dbml?ATCLID=205174793).

50. West Virginia Mountaineers, "Basketball Practice Facility" (http://www .wvusports.com/page.cfm?section=18089).

51. Ibid.

52. Texas A&M University Athletics, "Bright Football Complex Tour," July 31, 2014 (http://sports.yahoo.com/blogs/ncaaf-dr-saturday/texas-a-m-s-renovated -football-complex-is-extremely-impressive--video-photos-214736505.html).

53. Ibid.

54. Ibid.

55. Ibid.

56. Ibid.

57. Will Hobson and Steven Rich, "The Latest Extravagances in College Sports Arms Race? Laser Tag and Mini Golf," *Washington Post*, December 15, 2015.

58. Lisa Horne, "Oklahoma's New $75 Million Headington Hall Will Lure Football Recruits," *Bleacher Report,* July 31, 2013 (http://bleacherreport.com /articles/1723178-oklahomas-new-75-million-headington-hall-will-lure-football -recruits).

59. NCAA, *2015–16 NCAA Division I Manual,* p. 195.

60. Ibid., p. 197.

61. Aimee Vergon Gibbs, "Disciplinary Sanctions and Due Process Rights," Law and Higher Education (http://lawhigheredu.com/43-disciplinary-sanctions -and-due-process-rights.html).

62. "United States Olympic Committee Due Process Checklist" (https://www .google.com/#q=USOC+Due+process+checklist).

63. NCAA, *2015–16 NCAA Division I Manual,* pp. 329–30.

64. Ibid., p. 312; see section 19.2.3.1.

65. Ibid., p. 315; see section 19.2.3.2.

66. Ibid., p. 217; see section 19.5.1.

Chapter 6

1. Wall Street Journal/NBC News Poll (2000) (http://www.wsj.com/articles /SB119188060199152666); Elizabeth Crowley, "Title IX Levels the Playing Field for Women's Sports. *Wall Street Journal*, June 22, 2000 (http://www.wsj.com /articles/SB961615734821443407); The Wall Street Journal/NBC News poll (2000) found that the public understands the importance of women's health and wellness issues as represented by Title IX, fully supports Title IX, and opposes unnecessary efforts to protect men's sports. Results included the following: 79 percent of respondents approved of Title IX and 76 percent approved even if it meant cutting men's sports, with responses consistent between men and women and between Republicans and Democrats. See also Heather Mason Kiefer, "What Do Americans See in Title IX's Future?," Gallup.com, January 28, 2003 (www.gallup .com/poll/7663/what-americans-see-title-ixs-future.aspx); National Women's Law Center, "Public Supports Title IX, but Discrimination against Girls and Women Remains Widespread," June 19, 2007 (http://nwlc.org/press-releases/public -supports-title-ix-discrimination-against-girls-and-women-remains -widespread-june-19-2007/).

2. NCAA, Sport Sponsorship, Participation and Demographics Search database, NCAA.org, 2016 (http://web1.ncaa.org/rgdSearch/exec/main). Data are available by sport, by conference, and by division.

3. This figure assumes that current male participation opportunities remain constant and that the number represents the percentage of male undergraduates in college as 43 percent.

4. Amy Wilson, *The Status of Women in Intercollegiate Athletics as Title IX Turns* 40 (Indianapolis: NCAA, June 2012) (www.ncaapublications.com/p-4289 -the-status-of-women-in-intercollegiate-athletics-as-title-ix-turns-40-june-2012 .aspx).

5. Ibid., pp. 5–18.

6. NCAA, Sport Sponsorship, Participation and Demographics Search database.

7. U.S. Department of Education (DOE), Laws and Guidance / Civil Rights, "Dear Colleague Letter: Title IX Coordinators," April 24, 2015 (http://www2.ed .gov/about/offices/list/ocr/letters/colleague-201504-title-ix-coordinators.pdf).

8. U.S. DOE, Laws and Guidance / Civil Rights, "Title IX of the Education Amendments of 1972: A Policy Interpretation; Title IX and Intercollegiate Athletics," *Federal Register* 44, no. 239 (December 11, 1979).

9. Ibid., p. 71418.

10. U.S. DOE, Laws and Guidance / Civil Rights, "Clarification of Intercollegiate Athletics Policy Guidance: The Three-Part Test," January 16, 1996, p. 9 (http://www2.ed.gov/about/offices/list/ocr/docs/clarific.html).

11. National Federation of State High School Associations, "Participation Statistics," NHFS.org, 2015 (http://www.nfhs.org/ParticipationStatics/Participation Statics.aspx/).

12. NCAA, *Student-Athlete Participation: 1981–82 to 2014–15* (Indianapolis: NCAA, 2015), p. 77.

13. Ibid., pp. 11–12.

14. Ibid., p. 12.

15. NCAA, *NCAA Sports Sponsorship and Participation Report 1981–82 to 2014–15* (Indianapolis: NCAA, 2015), p. 259.

16. NCAA, *Student-Athlete Participation: 1981–82 to 2014–15*, p. 77.

17. Valerie M. Bonnett and Lamar Daniel, *Title IX Athletics Investigators' Manual* (Washington, DC: U.S. Department of Education, Office for Civil Rights, 1990), p. 17 (http://eric.ed.gov/?id=ED400763).

18. Janet Judge and Timothy O'Brien, *Gender Equity in Intercollegiate Athletics: A Practical Guide for Colleges and Universities—2010* (Indianapolis: NCAA, 2011), p. 31 (https://www.ncaapublications.com/p-4206-gender-equity-online -manual.aspx).

19. U.S. DOE, Office of Postsecondary Education, The Equity in Athletics Disclosure Act database (http://ope.ed.gov/athletics/).

20. U.S. DOE, Laws and Guidance / Civil Rights, "Title IX of the Education Amendments of 1972: A Policy Interpretation; Title IX and Intercollegiate Athletics," p. 71415.

21. NCAA, Sport Sponsorship, Participation and Demographics Search database.

22. Ibid.

23. Ibid.

24. Nicole M. LaVoi, *Women in Sports Coaching* (New York: Routledge, 2016), Kindle edition, table 1-1 (at location 563).

25. Don Sabo, Phillip Veliz, and Ellen J. Staurowsky, *Beyond X's & O's: Gender Bias and Coaches of Women's College Sports* (East Meadow, N.Y.: Women's Sports Foundation, 2016).

26. NCAA, *2015–16 NCAA Division I Manual* (Indianapolis: NCAA, 2015), p. 18 (http://www.ncaapublications.com/productdownloads/D116.pdf).

27. Ibid.

28. Nicole M. LaVoi, "Occupational Sex Segregation in a Youth Soccer Organization: Females in Positions of Power," *Women in Sport & Physical Activity Journal* 18, no. 2 (2009); Nicole M. LaVoi and Julia K. Dutove, "Barriers and Supports for Female Coaches: An Ecological Model," *Sports Coaching Review* 1, no. 1 (2012); Jacqueline McDowell, George B. Cunningham, and John N. Singer, "The Supply and Demand Side of Occupational Segregation: The Case of an Intercollegiate

Athletic Department," *Journal of African American Studies* 13, no. 4 (2009); Warren A. Whisenant and Susan P. Mullane (2007) "Sports Information Directors and Homologous Reproduction," *International Journal of Sport Management and Marketing* 2, no. 3 (2007); Michael Sagas, George B. Cunningham, and Ken Teed, "An Examination of Homologous Reproduction in the Representation of Assistant Coaches of Women's Teams," *Sex Roles* 56, no. 7 (2006).

29. Ibid.; LaVoi, *Women in Sports Coaching.*

30. NCAA, Sport Sponsorship, Participation and Demographics Search database.

31. Shaun R. Harper, "Black Male Student-Athletes and Racial Inequities in NCAA Division I College Sports" (University of Pennsylvania Graduate School of Education Center for the Study of Race and Equity in Education, 2016), p. 6 (http://www.gse.upenn.edu/equity/sports2016).

32. Ibid., p. 1.

33. Interviews and documents obtained by the *Baltimore Sun* through more than a dozen public records requests offer a rare profile of hundreds of these athletes and show that the "special admits" typically have not performed as well as other players in the classroom and pose unique and expensive academic challenges at the University of Maryland, North Carolina State, Georgia Tech, and other schools. Jeff Barker, "'Special Admissions' Bring Colleges Top Athletes, Educational Challenges," *Baltimore Sun,* December 22, 2012 (http://articles.baltimoresun.com/2012-12-22/sports/bs-sp-acc-sports-special-admits-20121222_1_athletes-graduation-success-rate-college-courses). See also Associated Press, "Report: Exemptions Benefit Athletes," ESPN, December 30, 2009 (http://sports.espn.go.com/ncf/news/story?id=4781264).

34. A double-digit FBS football graduation gap persists. See College Sport Research Institute, "2014 Adjusted Graduation Gap Report: NCAA FBS Football" (Columbia, S.C.: College Sport Research Institute, October 5, 2014).

35. B. Hawkins, *The New Plantation: Black Athletes, College Sports, and Predominantly White Institutions* (New York: Palgrave Macmillan, 2010), pp. 30–31.

36. See an extensive discussion of such research in Bruce Douglas, Chance W. Lewis, Adrian Douglas, Malcolm E. Scott, and Dorothy Garrison-Wade, "The Impact of White Teachers on the Academic Achievement of Black Students: An Exploratory Qualitative Analysis," *Educational Foundations,* Winter–Spring 2008, pp. 47–62.

37. See an extensive discussion of such research in George B. Cunningham, Kathi Miner, and Jennifer McDonald, "Being Different and Suffering the Consequences: The Influence of Head Coach-Player Racial Dissimilarity on Experienced Incivility," *International Review for the Sociology of Sport,* June 12, 2012, doi: 10.1177/1012690212446382. http://irs.sagepub.com/content/early/2012/06/07/1012690212446382

38. The Institute for Diversity and Ethics in Sport, University of Central Florida, *The 2014 Racial and Gender Report Card: College Sport,* Tidesport.org, 2015

(http://nebula.wsimg.com/308fbfef97c47edb705ff195306a2d50?AccessKeyId =DAC3A56D8FB782449D2A&disposition=0&alloworigin=1).

39. *Code of Federal Regulations,* Title 34, Part 104, "Nondiscrimination on the Basis of Handicap in Programs or Activities Receiving Federal Financial Assistance," 104.43(a).

40. U.S. DOE, Laws and Guidance / Civil Rights, "Dear Colleague: Students with Disabilities in Extracurricular Athletics," January 23, 2013 (http://www.ed .gov/ocr/letters/colleague-201301-504.pdf).

41. U.S. Government Accountability Office, *Students with Disabilities: More Information and Guidance Could Improve Opportunities in Physical Education and Athletics,* GAO-10-519 (GAO, June 2010), pp. 1, 31 (http://www.gao.gov/assets/310 /305770.pdf).

42. Ibid.; U.S. DOE, "Dear Colleague: Students with Disabilities in Extracurricular Athletics," p. 7.

43. John Infante, "NCAA Adapted Sports Are a Long Term Possibility," Athnet, May 20, 2014 (http://www.athleticscholarships.net/2014/05/20/ncaa-adapted -sports-are-a-long-term-possibility.htm).

44. National Wheelchair Basketball Association, "Find a Team," NWBA.org (http://www.nwba.org/page/show/2065393-find-a-team).

45. Eastern Collegiate Athletic Conference (ECAC), "ECAC Board of Directors Cast Historic Vote to Add Varsity Sports Opportunities for Student-Athletes with Disabilities in ECAC Leagues and Championships," press release, January 22, 2015 (http://www.ecacsports.com/news/2015/1/22/1_22_2015_201.aspx ?path=gen0).

46. Ted Fay, telephone interview, March 8, 2016. Fay is a sport management professor at SUNY Cortland, a Paralympic expert, and an ECAC senior adviser on inclusive sport. See also minutes of the ECAC Board of Directors meeting, September 30, 2014, "Motion: Providing Varsity Sport Opportunities for Student-Athletes with Disabilities in ECAC Competition, Leagues and Championships." Available from ECAC, 39 Old Ridgebury Road, Danbury, Connecticut 06810.

47. ECAC, "ECAC Board of Directors Cast Historic Vote."

48. Ibid; Fray, interview, March 8, 2016.

Chapter 7

1. To be clear, we are not advocating that all, or even most, schools be able to pursue athletic glory. The problem is that schools choose to do so even when it is infeasible, and in the process they undermine their own finances and educational mission.

2. NCAA, *2002–03 Revenues & Expenses: NCAA Division I Intercollegiate Athletics Programs Report* (Indianapolis: NCAA, 2005); NCAA, *2004–06 Revenues &*

Expenses (Indianapolis: NCAA, 2008); NCAA, *2004–10 Revenues & Expenses* (Indianapolis: NCAA, 2011, 2013, 2015) (reports for various years can be found at https://www.ncaapublications.com/searchadv.aspx?IsSubmit=true&SearchTerm =revenues+and+expenses).

3. NCAA, *2004–14 Revenues & Expenses: NCAA Division I Intercollegiate Athletics Programs Report*, (Indianapolis: NCAA, 2015) (https://www.ncaa.org/sites /default/files/2015%20Division%20I%20RE%20report.pdf).

4. Ibid.; Jonathan Orszag and Peter Orszag, "The Physical Capital Stock Used in Collegiate Athletics," Report to the NCAA, April 2005.

5. Will Hobson and Steven Rich, "Why Students Foot the Bill for College Sports and How Some Are Fighting Back," *Washington Post,* November 30, 2015.

6. Steve Berkowitz, "A Proposal for Better Balance Sheets among NCAA Members," *USA Today*, June 19, 2013 (www.usatoday.com/story/sports/college/2013/06 /18/ncaa-athletic-subsidies-accounting-changes/2435527/); Steve Berkowitz, J. Upton, M. McCarthy, and J. Gillum, "How Students Fees Boost College Sports amid Rising Budgets," *USA Today,* October 6, 2010 (http://www.usatoday.com /sports/college/2010-09-21-student-fees-boost-college-sports_N.htm#uslPageReturn); Steve Berkowitz, Jodi Upton, and Erik Brady, "Most NCAA Division I Athletic Departments Take Subsidies," *USA Today,* May 7, 2013 (http://www.usatoday .com/story/sports/college/2013/05/07/ncaa-finances-subsidies/2142443/).

7. "Costliest College Network in the Country Has Lost Millions," *Sports Business News*, December 30, 2015.

8. Although as we write, in October 2015, the NCAA data are not in for years subsequent to FY2014, it is clear from the arc of the regional television contracts of the Power Five conferences that the inequality will become appreciably more acute in the coming years. As an example, the SEC distributions to member schools in May 2014 were $20 million; they increased to $30 million in 2015, and will likely be $40 million in 2016.

9. The NCAA previously allowed the use of special opportunity funds to pay for disability insurance, and some conferences have offered extended medical coverage for injuries suffered during athletic competition. For instance, in October 2014 the Pac-12 introduced a plan to cover athletes' medical expenses for injuries incurred in competition for up to four years after they leave the institution. See Pac-12 Conference, "Pac-12 Universities Adopt Sweeping Reforms for Student-Athletes, Guaranteeing Scholarships, Improving Health Care, and More," October 27, 2014 (http://pac-12.com/article/2014/10/27/pac-12-universities-adopt -sweeping-reforms-student-athletes-guaranteeing).

10. These figures are based on a series of investigative reports by the *Washington Post*, which surveyed the schools in the Power Five conferences. There are fifty-three public schools in the five conferences. Five of them would not provide data for 2004 because state public record laws did not require them to do so. Hence the data come from forty-eight public schools in the Power Five conferences. See (www.washingtonpost.com/sf/sports/wp/2015/11/23/running-up-the-bills/; www

.washingtonpost.com/sports/as-college-sports-revenues-spike-coaches-arent
-only-ones-cashing-in/2015/12/29/bbdb924e-ae15-11e5-9ab0-884d1cc4b33e
_story.html); and (https://www.washingtonpost.com/sports/why-students-foot
-the-bill-for-college-sports-and-how-some-are-fighting-back/2015/11/30
/7ca47476-8d3e-11e5-ae1f-af46b7df8483_story.html). The increase in noncoaching
staff compensation resulted in part from a fast growth in the number of administrative personnel and in part from higher salaries. The administrative staff of the
University of Michigan's Athletics Department, for instance, grew from 102 full-
time employees to 179 between 2004 and 2014, while the number of those staffers
earning a salary of more than $100,000 increased from fifteen to thirty-four.
Meanwhile, the football noncoaching support staff payroll at Clemson University
bloated from $480,000 in 2004 to $2.5 million in 2014.

11. NCAA, *2004–14 Revenues & Expenses,* p. 29.

12. It might be objected that the true cost of educating an additional athlete
(marginal cost) is below the nominal tuition of the school. Since the nominal tuition is used in computing the value of scholarships and scholarships are attributed as expenses to the athletics department, the actual economic costs are lower
than the reported costs. While this observation is largely accurate, it is also true
that the necessary adjustment to account for the difference between the marginal
and accounting costs is on the order of a few million dollars, while the adjustment
for the inclusion of capital and indirect costs is on the order of tens of millions of
dollars.

13. With rising tuitions, federal student loans grew from $400 million in 2005
to more than $1 trillion in 2013. This situation is increasingly burdensome for low-
and middle-income students. The prospect of diminishing student loans in an era
of rising tuitions is daunting for prospective students and threatening to college
admissions.

Chapter 8

1. Curiously, Andrew Schwartz, perhaps the principal proponent among economists for a market-oriented reform, has estimated that the marginal revenue
product of star college athletes in football and men's basketball is only about
$100,000. If this were true, the top-paid college athletes would receive an after-tax
(federal income tax and FICA tax, but not any state income tax) income of around
$60,000. This is a lower value than the nominal value of a full-ride scholarship at
private universities. See http://nytschoolsfortomorrow.com/gallery/schools-for
-tomorrow-0/2015-videos.

2. Joe Nocera of the *New York Times* proposed a salary cap, along with other
market constraints, and asserted that those constraints could be legally negotiated
by the National College Players Association (NCPA). The NCPA, however, is an
association, not a bargaining unit, whose leader is not elected. The nonstatutory

exemption, which is the source of the various labor market constraints in professional sports, cannot apply to the NCPA. Many other problems encumber Nocera's nostrum for paying players. Joe Nocera, "A Way to Start Paying College Athletes," *New York Times*, January 8, 2016.

3. These and other figures, if not otherwise noted, come from the most recent NCAA, *2004–14 Revenues & Expenses: NCAA Division I Intercollegiate Athletics Programs Report* (Indianapolis: NCAA, 2015) (https://www.ncaa.org/sites/default /files/2015%20Division%20I%20RE%20report.pdf).

4. To be clear, our concern here is not the potential diminution of Olympic medals for the United States but rather the reduction in support for team sports: when conducted properly, team sports offer substantial physical, emotional, and developmental benefits to college students.

5. The NCAA has also appealed, seeking to have that part of the Wilken and Ninth Circuit rulings that concluded a scholarship that precluded a COA payment was unnecessarily restrictive and violative of antitrust law. In other words, these decisions said that NCAA labor market rules were ultimately subject to antitrust law. This contradicted the longstanding NCAA argument that the Supreme Court in *Board of Regents* had declared that college athletes could not be paid, even though this position was clearly dicta in *Board of Regents*.

6. In a sample of forty-five Division I public universities, the Duke University economist Charles Clotfelter found that between 1986 and 2007, the average compensation of full professors rose 30 percent, while that of university presidents grew 100 percent, that of head basketball coaches jumped 400 percent, and that of head football coaches increased 500 percent (Clotfelter, unpublished research. Clotfelter had full data on basketball salaries for twenty-two schools and on football salaries for forty-five).

7. One eye-popping severance clause appeared in the contract of Mike Sherman, Texas A&M University's football coach, who, if terminated, would have been paid $150,000 a month for the remainder of his contract, which would have amounted to a $7.8 million golden handshake.

8. In a forty-first state, New Hampshire, the head ice hockey coach earns more than the governor.

9. James Johnson, "The Suicide Season," *Shreveport Times*, September 4, 2008.

10. Allen Barra, *The Last Coach: A Life of Paul "Bear" Bryant* (New York: W. W. Norton, 2005).

11. The revenue estimates for NBA and NFL teams come from the 2015 *Forbes* annual reports. Those for college football and basketball teams come from the 2015 *NCAA Revenues and Expenses* bi-annual report.

12. College coaches have protested that college football teams cannot be properly compared to professional teams. The latter, they say, can always call up reserves when players get injured, but college teams must have players on their rosters to replace the injured. First, NFL teams have a maximum of sixteen players on reserve and practice squads to complement their forty-five-men active rosters.

Second, the NCAA Injury Surveillance System Summary reports that for the 2000–01 season, the serious-injury rate during games in football was 14.1 per 1,000 exposures, while the rate in football practices was 1.6 per 1,000. If we assume that sixty players enter a game and the team plays thirteen games during the year (that is, including a postseason game), then the average total number of serious injuries (requiring a player to be out seven or more days) from games is eleven per year. If on average each such player misses two games, then the average number of game-injured players is 1.69 per game. Performing a similar calculation for practice-injured players yields 1.48 per game, for a combined average of 3.17 injured players per game. This hardly constitutes a justification for carrying 85 scholarship players and 117 total players on an FBS team.

13. Teams are also allowed to carry up to eight additional players on their practice squads.

14. NCAA, *2005–06 NCAA Gender Equity Report* (Indianapolis: NCAA, 2005), p. 27 (https://www.ncaapublications.com/p-3849-2005-06-ncaa-gender-equity -report.aspx).

15. This number is based on twenty-five men's scholarships at $40,000 each, plus the possibility of realizing savings on women's scholarships and the probable reduction in costs for athletic support staff and equipment.

16. NCAA, *2004–08 Revenues & Expenses: NCAA Division I Intercollegiate Athletics Programs Report* (Indianapolis: NCAA, October 2009), p. 37 (https:// www.ncaapublications.com/p-4135-revenues-expenses-2004-08-ncaa-revenues -and-expenses-of-division-i-intercollegiate-athletics-programs-report.aspx).

17. This sliding scale eligibility was introduced after a two-decade struggle with the Black Coaches Association, which claimed that a hard cutoff on standardized tests was arbitrary and discriminatory toward minority athletes. It is interesting to note the growth in the participation of African American athletes in college sports actually was more rapid before 2003 than it was after. In 2016 the GPA threshold is at 3.55 for students with the lowest possible score on standardized tests.

18. The district court in *O'Bannon* ruled that the NCAA was responsible for this sum. As we write, the plaintiffs have challenged part of the Ninth Circuit Court of Appeals ruling and asked for review by the U.S. Supreme Court. Depending on whether the Supreme Court grants certiorari and, if so, whether it upholds the antitrust violation found in the district court, the payment of the lawyers' fees by the NCAA may be reversed. Note that some part of these litigation costs may be picked up by the NCAA's insurance underwriter.

Chapter 9

1. "College Extracurricular Activities—Impact on Students, Types of Extracurricular Activities," StateUniversity.com (http://education.stateuniversity.com /pages/1855/College-Extracurricular-Activities.html#ixzz3RYLjNs8c).

2. Donna Lopiano and Gerald Gurney, "Don't Reform the NCAA—Replace It," InsideHigherEd.com, September 11, 2014 (www.insidehighered.com/views/2014/09/11/ncaa-cant-be-reformed-congress-should-replace-it-essay).

3. Ibid., p. 10.

4. G. Gurney and others, "The Drake Group Position Statement: Why the NCAA Academic Progress Rate (APR) and Graduation Success Rate (GSR) Should Be Abandoned and Replaced with More Effective Academic Metrics," Drake Group, 2015.

Index

AAA (American Arbitration Association), 241
AAU (Amateur Athletic Union), 15, 215, 219, 225
Abuse of student-athletes, 116, 122–24, 128, 238
Academic clustering, 70, 71, 184, 187–88
Academic fraud, 75–83; for eligibility maintenance, 55–56; growth of, 75, 94; at high school level, 38, 56; institutional accountability for, 77–83; NCAA role in protecting athletes from, 75–77; scandals involving, 37–39, 53–54, 247–61; shared responsibility system in, 77–83; whistleblower protections concerning, 48, 79, 82
Academic integrity: and admission requirements, 55; and antitrust exemptions, 219; challenges to, 19, 55, 244–45; clashes with college sports, 33–34, 71; guidelines for, 233; promotion of, 57, 214;

responsibility for assurance of, 77, 81, 104–05; and transparency, 70
Academic Performance Program, 36
Academic Progress Rate (APR): for coaches, 69–70; establishment of, 37, 64; formula for calculation of, 37, 64; limitations of, 37, 65, 68, 69; manipulation of, 65–67; penalties resulting from, 37, 38, 64–65, 69
Academic redshirt policy, 56
Academic standards: for eligibility, 34–39, 54–59, 108, 229; failure to maintain, 6, 37, 244; governing principles on, 45; literacy considerations, 72–74, 108; for minority student-athletes, 35–36, 55; 1.6 Predictor Rule for, 34–35; Proposition 48 on, 35; reform movements on, 34–37, 90; transparency in, 70–71; 2.0 rule for, 35. *See also* Academic fraud; Academic Progress Rate; Graduation rates

Summary disposition process, 99
Support programs for student athletes, 37, 46, 56, 74, 78–79, 220
SWAs. *See* Senior woman administrators
Syracuse University, academic fraud at, 38, 39, 54, 248

Tarkanian v. NCAA (1984), 99
Teachers. *See* Faculty
Ted Stevens Olympic and Amateur Sports Act of 1978, 101, 103, 137
Television revenue, 198, 199, 203, 205
Tennis, amateurism in, 15–16
Texas A&M University, athlete-only facilities at, 132
Texas Christian University, academic fraud at, 252–53
Texas Southern University, academic fraud at, 258–59
Texas State University, academic fraud at, 260
Texas Tech University, academic fraud at, 258
Thamel, Pete, 37
Thomas, Sidney, 215
Thompson, John, 35–36
Thorp, Holden, 87–88
Tiering mechanisms, 167–69
Time demands on student-athletes, 71–72, 107, 111–13, 228, 237
Title VI (Civil Rights Act of 1964), 36
Title VII (Civil Rights Act of 1964), 40
Title IX (Education Amendments of 1972): athletics-related financial aid obligations under, 163–67; competition level requirements in, 161; fear of reporting violations, 150, 171; grant-in-aid policies consistent with, 228; ineffectiveness of, 143–44, 145; lack of mandates

for compliance with, 43, 147–51; lawsuits and complaints involving, 148, 150–51; participation standards in, 146, 151–52, 156; penalties for noncompliance with, 151; principles of, 40, 150; Prong One proportionality standard in, 151, 152, 154, 159; Prong Three exception to, 43, 153–54; resistance to, 40–41, 91, 143; on retaliation, 150–51; self-assessments regarding, 147, 148–49; sexual harassment provisions of, 149; on tiering mechanisms, 168
Track programs, roster inflation in, 156, 159, 162–63
Transfer rules, 113–15, 220
Transgender athletes and coaches, 171, 188
Transparency: in academic standards, 70–71; governing principles on, 48; guidelines for, 232; in nonprofit organizations, 48
Triple counting tactics, 156, 159, 162–63
Tucker, Irvin, 87
2.0 rule, 35
2014 Racial and Gender Report Card: College Sport (Institute for Diversity and Ethics in Sports), 188, 190–91

Unduplicated counts, 163–65, 166–67
Unionization of student-athletes, 32, 112, 205
United States Golf Association, 15, 215
United States Olympic Committee (USOC), 103, 123, 137–38, 225
Universities. *See* Educational institutions; *specific universities*
University of Alabama: adaptive sports programs at, 193; coaching salaries